# HOME-BASED CARE,
# THE ELDERLY,
# THE FAMILY,
# AND THE WELFARE STATE:
# AN INTERNATIONAL
# COMPARISON

# HOME-BASED CARE,
# THE ELDERLY,
# THE FAMILY,
# AND THE WELFARE STATE:
# AN INTERNATIONAL
# COMPARISON

Edited by
**FRÉDÉRIC LESEMANN**
Université de Montréal
**CLAUDE MARTIN**
École nationale de la santé publique,
Rennes

**University of Ottawa Press**

The publication of this book has been made possible thanks to generous grants from
Mission interministérielle recherche et expérimentation (MIRE),
Ministère des affaires sociales et de l'intégration, Paris, and
Health & Welfare Canada, National Welfare Grants (4577-14-12P).

© University of Ottawa Press, 1993
Printed and bound in Canada
ISBN 0-7766-0369-8

**Canadian Cataloguing in Publication Data**
Main entry under title:
Home-based care, the elderly, the family and
the welfare state: an international comparison

(Sciences sociales)
Includes bibliographical references and index.
ISBN 0-7766-0369-8

1. Aged—Home care. 2. Aged—Home care—
Government policy—Europe. 3. Aged—Home care—
Government policy—Canada. 4. Aged—Home care—
Government policy—United States. I. Lesemann,
Frédéric, 1942–. II. Martin, Claude, 1955–.
III. Series.

HV1451.H65 1993      362.6'3      C93-090390-0

# CONTENTS

# PREFACE

Examination of family support networks, mutual aid, and social, relational and community support currently represents an important aspect of discussions on the future of social care and the welfare state. Indeed, health and social insurance and assistance systems established in industrial societies after the second world war to protect certain groups against social "risks" are now in a crisis state, due to changes transforming these societies: rising unemployment, aging populations, problems in social integration of the young, etc. Concerned about spiralling increases in the costs of such systems, governments are redefining the parameters, conditions and methods of this type of protection, as well as, in many cases, planning budget restrictions.

Various strategies have been implemented to counter such inflation: reducing certain benefits, limiting access to certain services and decentralizing their management, privatization approaches, allocation of financial aid to individuals to enable them to purchase what they need in the service market, etc. There is also broader use of evaluation procedures to enhance and monitor professional and organizational efficiency, by comparing their objectives, methods and performance. Finally, we might point to attempts to highlight the contribution already being offered or that could potentially be supplied by front-line resources: families, friends and neighbourhoods, as well as peer self-help at the home or community level, which provide a form of primary care.

And therein lies the source for the interest in the actual and potential role of family and/or informal support, at least from the viewpoint of social policy and managerial rationalization. Policies are beginning to develop an instrumental relationship with what is now recognized as an additional or substitutive "resource" in the overall area of satisfying needs for care, custody, shelter, integration, rehabilitation and indeed socialization, which, governments now seem to be discovering, can often be more effectively and advantageously met by simple, flexible resources based on primary and private relationships.

Such a perspective, although interesting from a management viewpoint, needs to be examined and debated. In any case, it has led to the development of an intermediary area of reflection between the domain of social policy and that of the family. In order to investigate such issues, specialists from these two fields of research have had to step outside their usual concerns and to cross conceptual and academic barriers. Among other effects, such questioning has prompted a re-examination of certain issues or themes in the social sciences field of the family, such as kinship support networks. As Martine Segalen stated in her article "Les relations de parenté" in F. de Singly, *La famille. L'état des savoirs* (Paris: La Découverte, 1991, p. 233): "The renewal of sociological interest in kinship relationships has emerged from transformations in ideological positions and profound demographic and social changes affecting society as a whole, especially in terms of population aging. Due to the crisis in the welfare state, other types of support have been recognized, particularly intergenerational family support networks."

The purpose of this book is to present, based on overviews from seven industrial countries (the United States, United Kingdom, Canada, Netherlands, Sweden, France and Italy), the ways in which national social policy systems are attempting to respond to care needs among the dependent elderly. More specifically, the various contributions look at government interventions targeting this group and situate these in the framework of demographic change and a history of social services and social policy; they identify current challenges and highlight certain response strategies, which often represent experimental solutions. Particular attention is accorded to links, or the breakdown of ties, between formal and informal support initiatives, between public and family support systems. In this context, the *home* assumes a special role with regard to social policy. Under the influence of the general trend toward population aging, the home is in fact increasingly becoming the managerial arena for both problems associated with physical and mental frailty and solutions as well, whether deriving from public or private services, "intermediary" resources or care provided by the family network.

This book will hopefully contribute to the debate on the ongoing transformation in relationships between public and family support systems in several industrial countries where there has been considerable growth in government involvement in the social care sector over the past quarter century. The international perspective emphasized here will enable the reader to identify major trends which consistently seek to reduce the pressures placed on public care systems by calling upon "new" actors, now seen as partners in the search for support for dependent individuals and indeed for ways to enhance their quality of life, whether involving families, informal support networks or the use of private service markets. In short, there is a trend toward diversification and multiplication of care and assistance resources, now viewed as more effective solutions to needs more often understood as unique, since they derive from specific social situations. Due to a greater focus on individuals, increasingly seen in terms of their desire for personal autonomy and their primary responsibility in organizing their living conditions, there has been less emphasis on universal and uniform care systems. But the counterpart to this development obviously involves the significant possibility that equitable and universal guaranties of social and healthcare risk coverage will be reduced or even abandoned, as overall interest grows in the dynamics and strategies operating for those with the requisite cultural or material resources, whether financial or regarding access to support networks.

Again, the international perspective will illustrate that beyond major common trends, specific strategies have been developed in each national context to restructure relationships between public and informal support systems. These are marked by particular institutional histories, political situations and economic and fiscal constraints that have individually resulted in certain issues, actors and strategies being highlighted in any given country, so that each situation must be grasped from its unique perspective.

Thus, we have underscored an explicitly reduced commitment of public resources in the United Kingdom and the effect this has had at the community level. In other countries, such as Sweden, we will look at an extremely extensive system of government intervention with few apparent gaps in coverage and little competition from informal care resources. The United States, on the contrary, has experimented with a traditionally limited involvement in protection systems, while Canada, despite its acknowledged liberal tradition, has developed broad public home care support systems in most provinces. The Netherlands seem to be primarily concerned with establishing new care insurance schemes and to be heading, in the context of such schemes, toward greater diversification and multiplication of care resources. In France, there is a deeply rooted tradition of state social services, with a predominant institutional approach to care, a situation Italy is currently seeking to change by focusing on the "territory"—which we would tend to term the community—as opposed to the institution. In these different contexts, family and informal support systems are unfailingly in evidence as they seek, with varying degrees of success, to achieve recognition for their particular situations and unique contributions.

In our conclusion, we will outline the problems involved in comparing countries on a conceptual and cultural level, and try to synthesize, in an inevitably limited fashion, some of the "lessons" that can be drawn from the various national contributions and the literature that has inspired them, with respect to both family care practices and formal care services as well as interrelationships between the two areas.

* * * * *

This international survey could not have been realized without the support of the Mission Interministérielle Recherche et Expérimentation (MIRE) of the departments of social affairs and labour in France. For the past ten years, MIRE has helped to organize research in the areas of social policy, employment and health. Health & Welfare Canada also provided financial assistance for the translation and English-language publication of this work. We are grateful as well to our contributors for being able to meet our requirements and thus highlight, for both English- and French-speaking readers, the conditions involved in the issue of home care and the family's contribution to care for the dependent elderly. The chapters our contributors prepared in 1991 provide an overview of the situation up to that time; a number of changes may obviously have come about in the meantime.

*Frédéric Lesemann and Claude Martin*
Montréal and Rennes
Summer 1992.

# HOME-BASED CARE, THE ELDERLY, THE FAMILY, AND THE WELFARE STATE: AN INTERNATIONAL COMPARISON

# one

## Home Care Services for the Aged and Disabled in the United States of America

*Abraham Monk*
and
*Carole Cox*

Home care is a generic designation that covers a wide range of service supports for dependent and disabled individuals. Some of these services consist of unskilled personal care and homemaker tasks which require minimal training, while others include technologically sophisticated modalities of professional treatment. Home care may also differ in terms of the duration of the services: some are for short term rehabilitation, usually following a spell of hospitalization; others consist of indefinite or prolonged custodial and maintenance assistance, as required by chronically impaired patients.

Observers of the United States home care landscape are intrigued with the seemingly incoherent diversity of programs and agencies dispensing these services. In a study of home care agencies in California, Harrington and Grant concluded that the "home care financing, delivery and regulatory system is far more complex and fragmented than is commonly understood...." (1990: 451). The United States lacks a single or unified system of home care simply because it never adopted a national or comprehensive health care policy. Home care is mandated instead by many separate policies that evolved over the years.

Each of the resulting programs created its own administrative structure and operational procedures. Each also produced a separate definition of who qualifies for services. Programs coexist side by side but there is no mandate to coordinate them. States and local authorities attempt, at best, to institute a *de facto* accommodation. They fill gaps and help claimants who fall between the cracks by creating new or special programs. This further aggravates the prevailing fragmentation in the home care services field.

## PUBLIC POLICIES ON HOME CARE

There are at least 80 federal programs involved in long term care services but only 5 major ones are directly related to home care services.

The first is Medicare, authorized under Title XVIII of the Social Security Act. It is a federal health insurance program available to most persons over the age of 65 and to many of the disabled. It consists of two subprograms: Part A which covers hospitalization and rehabilitation costs for all persons receiving Social Security benefits, and Part B, a supplemental and elective insurance component for outpatient services, financed by monthly premiums. In fiscal year 1990, 30.0 million aged and 3.3 million disabled were protected under Part A, and 29.9 million aged and 3 million disabled under Part B (U.S. House of Representatives, Committee on Ways and Means 1990).

Medicare is the main federal payor of home care but it is primarily focused on the acute and short term medical needs of older persons, especially during the recovery that follows each hospitalization. These patients are entitled to an unlimited number of home health visits, with no cost sharing, provided they are homebound and in need of intermittent care. The request for care must come from a physician and the services can only be dispensed by a home health agency certified by Medicare. Medicare does not cover the needs of chronically dependent persons, nor those of persons suffering from Alzheimer's disease. It does reimburse, however, for hospice care, including support services for terminally ill patients in their homes.

The second program is the Social Services Block Grant (Title XX) of the Social Security Act. A primary goal of this program is to prevent institutionalization. States receive federal funds based on a population formula and may spell out their own service priorities. Home care thus competes with many other services for funding. A study by the American Association of Retired Persons found that the proportion of the Social Services Block Grant's budget allocated to home care throughout the states was consistently around 10 percent, and that home based services were the most frequently cited in 41 states. Most states reported, however, that they could not cope with the growing demand, and that long waiting lists were becoming a standard feature (Gaberlavage 1987).

The third main policy is the Older Americans Act, passed in 1965 with the intent of coordinating existing community services for the aged, as well as creating needed ones when not available. Its Title III covers a broad array of home care services: home delivered meals, personal care, shopping, and homemaker, home health aide, chore and escort supports. It is estimated that nearly 25 percent of the Older Americans Act funds are dedicated to home care, with increasing attention given to home delivered meals. Policy setting of service priorities is, however, decentralized: each state's office on aging, as well as each of the 600 local area agencies on aging, throughout the country, has the latitude to set its own objectives. Although the Act does not require an income test, funds tend to target those with the greatest social or economic need. Home care services under this funding mechanism must compete with other community programs such as adult day care, respite care and congregate meals.

Home care may also be covered under the Supplemental Security Income/Title XVI of the Social Security Act. At the option of the individual states, low income older persons qualifying for this federal income support may also receive supplemental payment for in-home services.

Medicaid is a joint federal and state public assistance program for the poor and medically indigent. It provides most of the public financing for institutional care but it is also emerging as a leading source of payment for home care services. Medicaid requires that home care include part-time nursing, home health aide services and medical equipment and supplies. Like Medicare, Medicaid originally limited its reimbursement to conditions requiring acute care only. However, as of 1981 Congress authorized the states to extend Medicaid home care services beyond medical related care. By waiving certain Medicaid regulations, states could also provide community and home care to dependent persons who would otherwise need institutionalization. Because this is a state administered and partially state financed program, there is wide disparity in the level of appropriations for home care. The seven states with the highest expenditures on home and community based care spent five times more per elderly person than the seven states with the lowest expenditures (The Pepper Commission 1990: 97). Overall, Medicaid expenditures on home care have been comparatively low and far below the spending on nursing home care. In addition, several states have created special home care services for population categories inadequately served by the main national programs.

Finally, the private sector has also stepped in to fill the gaps and pick up the slack. Prepaid health maintenance organizations and private long term care insurance provide some home care coverage. Life Care or Continuing Care Retirement Communities (CCRCs) offer housekeeping, meals and recreational services to their residents. These services are defined in a contract and residents pay an entrance fee, plus monthly payments adjusted for inflation. Because of the expense involved, only a small and more affluent segment of the aged population can afford the costs of a CCRC. As of 1987, there were about 120,000 persons living in some 680 life care communities (AAHA 1987).

Public programs utilize different strategies for delivering home care services: they may dispense the service directly; they may allocate the funds to the patients, so that these patients contract an individual provider or agency on their own, in a purely private transaction; and finally, they may enter into a third party arrangement. The latter is the most common procedure. It involves three participants. The first is the federal or state agency, which contracts with a fiscal intermediary. The second, the intermediary in question, is usually a not-for-profit organization that contracts, in turn, with the direct service providers, that is, the home care agencies. The fiscal intermediary reimburses these agencies for their services, but makes certain that the service consumers qualify and meet the eligibility criteria. Finally, the third level involves the home care agencies, which are independently operated but must be properly "certified," that is, they must meet a set of professional, administrative and quality standards in order to receive reimbursement for their services.

Both Medicare and Medicaid are open ended programs because they must pay all legitimate claims. They expect, however, that the fiscal intermediaries will follow established rules and ascertain that only valid, proper claims are reimbursed. These intermediaries end up enforcing the cost containment objectives of the federal and state programs.

United States policies mandating home care draw a statutory difference between "certified" and unlicensed providers. The first are formal agencies, qualified to receive reimbursement from the federal Medicare insurance program, as well as from Medicaid, the combined federal and state public assistance program. These certified agencies are subject to stringent operational standards and close scrutiny. The unlicensed category consists, in turn, of independent providers—both agencies and individuals—operating in a private and minimally regulated fee-for-service market. These providers are rapidly catching up with their certified counterparts, a trend that reflects both an increasing demand for services, and the fact that many patients are not found eligible to receive services from the certified sector.

Notwithstanding the fact that there are so many home care programs in the United States, they all have in common two self-evident features: first, the services take place in the patient's home, and second, they are linked to and blended with the help provided by families, relatives, friends and neighbors to a degree exceeding that found in any other level of long term care. It is this latter feature of informal participation, plus the fact that much of home care consists of unskilled and domestic tasks, that conspired for a long time against its acceptance as a formal human service of professional standing.

## HOME CARE AS AN ALTERNATIVE TO NURSING HOME SERVICES

Initially regarded as no more than an ancillary cottage industry, home care was gradually recognized as a valid component of the long term care continuum, but there is no consensus yet concerning its precise role and function. For some, home care supplements and finishes off the job initiated by other services, especially the acute care hospitals. Others instead harbor the rather ambitious expectation that home care can altogether replace other levels of service, particularly all or most of nursing home care.

The 1981 White House Conference on Aging took the latter course as it raised the banner of home care, in its rather imprecise plethora of versions, and hailed it as the alternative to the more costly institutional services. White House Conferences are convened by the President of the United States every ten years. They do not have formal legislative standing but they make recommendations that ultimately influence or become national policy. By identifying emerging needs and sifting out preferred service prescriptions for meeting those needs, delegates attending these conferences set themes and blueprints for action that government agencies must reckon with. The 1981 conference ended up proclaiming home care as the path to follow during the ensuing decade.

Home care did not surface, however, as an historical novelty in the course of the White House Conference in question. Its antecedents have been traced back to the hospital based home health services of the 18th century, and records of exemplary, albeit sporadic, program initiatives became quite common during the first half of the 20th century. The rather precipitous and relentless growth of home care, targeting dependent and disabled persons of all ages, probably began in 1966 when it was approved for fiscal reimbursement through the federal Medicare program. The causes of this expansion are, however, more complex and numerous.

One reason was the belief that home care constitutes an economically more efficient substitute or alternative to nursing home care.

A second cause is related to the patterns of federal and state financing of both hospital and nursing home care. Medicare, the federal health insurance program, instituted in 1983 a Prospective Payment System (PPS) which mandates a reduction of the average length of stay in acute care hospitals. In light of this economic imperative, hospitals have no choice but to discharge older patients in the early stages of their convalescence. Their eventual recovery in the community and at home hinges upon the availability of adequate home care service inputs.

At the same time, Medicaid, the federal and state public assistance program for health care, has instituted in several states a case-mix reimbursement system for nursing home care which limits access to nursing home beds for patients who do not require intensive skilled nursing care. The inevitable corollary of this policy has also been an increased demand for community based services.

Research evidence has not borne out, for the most part, the above mentioned assumptions and causal interpretations. To begin with, there is no conclusive or statistically significant evidence that home care leads to a reduction of nursing home utilization (Kemper et al. 1986). In fact, the number of persons needing nursing home beds may well increase in years to come. Murtaugh et al. concluded from an analysis of the 1982-1984 National Long Term Care Survey that 43 percent of individuals reaching the age of 65 in 1990 face a life time risk of nursing home institutionalization, as compared to 37 percent of actual utilization among older persons deceased between 1982 and 1984 (1990). True, the projected level of utilization may be affected by the availability of alternative long term care services, home care included, but even allowing for changing patterns of service delivery, the anticipated risk of nursing home placement, regardless of whether it will be for short or long term stays, remains substantially high. Home care services may well be tapping a different population, not necessarily all those who would otherwise be likely candidates for nursing home utilization.

The apparent reduction in the costs of services is an additional argument favoring home care over nursing home care, but there is less certainty as to how much cheaper it actually is. The New York State Long Term Home Health Care Program, also known as the "Nursing Home Without Walls Program," authorized in 1978 a wide range of community based services, provided that their costs would not exceed 75 percent of the average annual payment for nursing home services in the area where the patient resides. Senator Lombardi, author of the state bill that created the program, reported years later that the average cost for patient care had been consistently around 50 percent of the cost for institutional care (1986-87). Zawadski and Ansak found that spending for the outpatient services of the On Lok Community Care Organization for Dependent Adults (CCODA), in San Francisco, constituted only 57 percent of the Medicaid average individual reimbursement rate for skilled nursing care (1983). These and similar comparisons tend to indicate that home care costs between 50 and 60 percent of nursing home care.

These estimates may, however, be misleading unless all expenditure categories normally included in estimating nursing home costs are similarly factored in. The CCODA average cost per day, as the point in case, did not include housing and most of the food, which are routine components of the nursing home reimbursement rate. Allowing for these budget items, the gap between community and institutional care costs would not be that significant.

A third consideration relates to the assumption that Medicare's new Prospective Payment System (PPS) of reimbursement for hospital care has caused a greater demand for home care. The U.S. Senate Special Committee on Aging reports a 37 percent increase between 1983 and 1986 in the actual provision of services (1986). It is frequently stated that patients are often discharged too early from intensive care and surgical units, without a chance to heal or recover properly. As a consequence, some are readmitted to hospitals but most end up needing lengthier and professionally more intensive home care services.

Regrettably, the savings gained from the PPS system were not necessarily shifted to contend with the greater demand for home care, as common sense would dictate. Medicare was concerned with home care costs as well, which grew at the rate of 29 percent a year between 1980 and 1984, and consequently proceeded to cap costs at both ends, that is, hospitals and home care. In the case of home care it resorted to systematic denials of reimbursement applications, which rose by 133 percent during the 1983-1986 period. Medicare's fiscal intermediaries made those denials to certified provider agencies on medical or technical grounds. In the first instance, Medicare's agents often argued that the requested home care services were not necessary or had only custodial rather than rehabilitative merits. Any bureaucratic omission or oversight—a misplaced signature, an unfilled item on a billing form—constituted, in turn, sufficient reason for a technical denial.

Mechanisms for appeal were in place but both provider agencies and patients found the process too cumbersome and unrewarding. As a result, many certified provider agencies were denied reimbursement and some opted to withdraw their participation in the Medicare program. Many patients found themselves, in turn, forced to fully pay for the services, in the private market. Medicare thus succeeded in capping costs by excluding scores of the frail and dependent from eligibility. Medicare authorized the provision of service only in cases where the patient is homebound and needs skilled nursing care on an intermittent rather than continuous basis. Regrettably, the vagueness and ambiguity contained in the statutory definitions of both criteria made it possible for the arbitrary denials to occur.

## THE COST EFFECTIVENESS OF HOME CARE

Notwithstanding Medicare's attempt to hold the line, the use of community care and home care continued to expand, as have overall costs incurred by both Medicare and Medicaid (Bishop and Karon 1989). Between 1982 and 1989 home health care expenditures climbed 400 percent, from 1.8 billion to 9 billion dollars (U.S. Department of Commerce 1990). This is due to an increase in both the number of home health visits and the charge per visit. Under Medicare the average charge per visit doubled from $32.75 in 1980 to $65.71 in 1989 (American Association of Retired Persons, Public Policy Institute 1991). It is important to note that the majority of these visits under Medicare were for skilled nursing, and thus the increases may reflect the recipients' need for more professional care. As persons are discharged more rapidly from acute care hospitals, many of the treatments they would have ordinarily received there are currently offered in the home.

Under its 2176 Waiver, Medicaid allows states to provide home and community based care to persons who would otherwise be eligible under Medicaid for placement in a nursing home. One condition for using the waiver is that the provided services be "budget neutral," meaning that the states must show that the substitute services will reduce overall nursing home costs. To be most effective, the state programs must target those likely to enter a nursing home and the services must actually delay or avoid such entrance. A detailed study of two states using the waiver program, California and Georgia, indicated that even with a wide array of community services including case management, housing assistance, transportation, in-home services and respite care, neither state had achieved "budget neutrality" (Vertrees et al. 1989). Neither program significantly prevented or limited nursing home admissions. A possible explanation for this lack of effectiveness is inadequate targeting of the population at risk, and an inappropriate array of services. The findings from both programs may also suggest that community social services are not sufficient to deal with the severe medical and behavioral problems of persons entering nursing homes.

Ruchlin et al. (1990) reviewed the annual expenditures for older persons living in five community based settings, including those living in their own homes without case-managed home care, those with case management, and those in congregate housing. Individuals were assigned to one of four institutional risk groups. The results of the study showed that case-managed home care did not produce enough hospital and nursing home savings to cover its own costs. In fact, case-managed home care resulted in higher expenditures. One of the issues again raised in the study was that of targeting services toward those most at risk of nursing home placement if adequate savings are to be achieved.

These findings are similar to those of the National Long Term Care Demonstration which was a nationwide study evaluating the impact of case management and the expanded use of community services on institutional care in several communities (Kemper 1988). The evaluation of the Demonstration's effectiveness showed that care recipients and their families had increased use of home care, and experienced more satisfaction with the services and higher life satisfaction. However, the Demonstration did not show any significant decrease in nursing home placement, while overall costs were higher.

As more accurate outcome measures of the effectiveness of community care are developed, it may be essential to go beyond those associated with cost savings alone. A comprehensive and integrated system which responds to consumer needs, values and aspirations may be more important than cost savings. While targeting services toward the most impaired may be most effective in reducing nursing home admissions, efforts should also be geared to prevention. It is conceivable that offering various types of limited care to those requiring only low levels of assistance may further delay or prevent eventual nursing home placement. Moreover, as long as home care remains medically oriented, persons requiring social and supportive services will continue to be neglected and dismissed as ineligible. A survey of directors of home health agencies conducted in 1986 and 1987 found, however, that social supportive services were the most commonly requested types of assistance by consumers but such requests had to be largely turned down (Binney et al. 1990).

The greater use of home care is also related to the sheer increase in the number of older persons—this number doubled between 1960 and 1980—and the greater survivorship of the oldest cohorts among the aged, those 75 years of age and older (U.S. Senate Special Committee on Aging 1985-86). The costs, long waiting lists and difficulties of accessing institutional care are an additional reason for the greater appeal of home care.

The simplest and most straightforward reason home care is in such demand may, however, be the desire of older persons to remain in their own homes, even when disabled and incapacitated (McCauley and Blieszner 1985). Harris and Associates similarly found that 70 percent of older persons prefer to receive long term care services at home even when experiencing severe dependency and terminal illness (1982).

## POTENTIAL AND ACTUAL USERS OF HOME CARE

Although the net growth of home care services has been astounding by any measurable criterion, the number of older persons who are both potential and actual users of home care cannot be easily calculated. Estimates of the elderly population at risk are usually based on the prevalence of several disability factors. Consideration is given to the number of persons requiring help to perform essential personal care functions, or "activities of daily living," (ADLs), and also a set of home management tasks, or "instrumental activities of daily living," (IADLs). The former include activities such as walking, bathing, dressing, toileting and eating (Katz et al. 1963). The latter, in turn, involve more complex tasks such as shopping, managing money and preparing meals (Lawton and Brody 1969).

Depending on the number of impairment factors measured by both the ADL and IADL scales, Stone and Murtaugh concluded that the number of disabled but noninstitutionalized older persons may range between 411,000 and as many as 4,124,000 (1990). These figures, which constitute 1.5 percent, in the first instance, and almost 16 percent, in the latter case, of community based elderly persons in the United States, reflect potentially different eligibility criteria for the provision of home care services.

The lower number results from the application of a rather restrictive criterion which includes 3 or more limitations to activities of daily living (ADLs), for at least a 12-month period. The upper limit is obtained, in turn, from the utilization of a single indicator, be it an ADL or IADL limitation, known to have lasted for at least 3 months.

Stone and Murtaugh also provide an intermediate figure of 857,000 potential recipients of active home assistance, by adopting 2 or more ADL limitations as the threshold for eligibility. The authors caution, however, that the application of such a criterion may lead to a denial of services to cognitively impaired persons who are otherwise functionally self-sufficient. Rowland estimates that cognitively impaired older persons with less than 2 ADL limitations and living outside institutions number an additional half a million persons, but the particular needs of this latter group began receiving public policy attention only in recent years (1989). In adding both estimates, a less extreme measure of need of almost 1,400,000, or 5.10 percent of the aged population, is obtained, a figure almost identical to the number of older persons confined to nursing home care.

Estimates produced by earlier studies are close to Stone and Murtaugh's figures. Rivlin and Wiener arrived at a total of 4.9 million disabled elderly, a figure that results from adding 3.3 million with fewer than 3 ADL limitations and 1.6 million severely disabled who exceed 3 ADL limitations (1988). It is noteworthy that these authors found almost twice as many severely disabled elderly in the community as in nursing homes (1.6 million and 0.9 million, respectively). The vast majority of this group manage without resorting to institutional care simply because of the availability of uncompensated informal sources of support.

The above mentioned figures are estimates of the population at risk. What about the actual beneficiaries of community care and home care services? The 1982 Long Term Care Survey established that 1,190,000 of the 4.4 million noninstitutionalized aged persons receiving functional assistance were helped by formal services (Liu et al. 1985). Utilizing data from round 1 of the 1987 National Medical Expenditure Survey (NMES), Short and Leon (1990) concluded that more than a third—36.3 percent—or 2.0 million out of a total of 5.6 million of the functionally impaired aged utilized the following community and home delivered services: home care, senior center, congregate meals, home meals transportation and telephone monitoring. Home care was the most frequently used service, with 397,000 or 19.7 percent of all seniors with functional impairments benefiting from it. When disaggregating the 19.7 percent of home care users, it appears that 8.1 percent were attended to by homemakers, 4.9 percent by home health aides and 4.5 percent by nurses. It goes without saying that the majority of the aged with varying degrees of ADL and IADL impairments do not resort to the formal service system. Short and Leon also observed that more than half were obtaining informal help from relatives and friends, and over one third, or 34.6 percent, were relying exclusively on these informal supports.

## INFORMAL SOURCES OF HOME CARE

Most disabled older persons manage to remain in the community because of the assistance they receive from spouses, children, and other relatives and friends. These informal or uncompensated sources of support may well provide between 70 and 80 percent of all the care reaching the impaired elderly. Based on the 1977 National Nursing Home Population and the 1982 Long Term Care Survey, Manton and Liu have observed that for disabled men aged 65 to 84, wives constitute the leading source of personal caregiving, but that the reverse is not true, as disabled elderly women are assisted, for the most part, by children and other relatives (1984).

The majority of caregivers are women who provide more than occasional assistance. About 64 percent report that they have been providing care for at least one year, with most involved seven days a week for an average of 9 hours a day (U.S. Senate Special Committee on Aging 1989).

Many of these persons have actually altered their work schedules or even left their employment in order to assist their relative round the clock.

Estimates of the average age of these caregivers vary. The 1982 National Long Term Care Survey found it to be 57 years, although a more recent telephone sample study of households conducted for the American Association of Retired Persons (AARP) and the Travelers Companies Foundation reports a younger average of 49 years for primary caregivers (1988). As more people live longer into advanced old age, however, the average age of their caregivers may similarly follow suit and increase.

The importance of family support is further confirmed in that it is the absence of such assistance, rather than functional disability, which is most associated with nursing home placement. Nursing home residents are more likely to be without a spouse or without adult children than their peers in the community and to also have severe health problems which restrict their abilities for self-care (U.S. Senate Special Committee on Aging 1989).

There appears to be a hierarchical pattern of care in the utilization of informal assistance. Persons first turn to their spouses and then to their adult children in what has been called the "principle of substitution" (Shanas et al. 1968). When neither the spouse or an adult daughter is available, another relative is called upon to assume the responsibility and in their absence, neighbors or friends become involved.

Although there is generally one primary informal caregiver, most older persons receive help from more than one person in their network. Various relatives and friends generally assist with caregiving tasks. However, the presence of such persons does not necessarily guarantee that they actually relieve the primary caregiver. Research by Tennstedt et al. (1989) found that the assistance of these persons tends to supplement rather than complement the help provided by the primary caregiver. Moreover, if the primary caregiver is a spouse, he or she is less likely to receive any assistance from other caregivers. It is also important to note that even when secondary caregivers are involved, there is no substantial increase in the amount of assistance provided.

It is not, therefore, surprising that caregiving for indefinite and protracted lengths of time may produce psychological stress, fatigue, family conflicts and depression. Caregivers report at times that they are unable to continue working and are often cut off from friends. Their personal agendas seem to be put on hold and they can no longer live their own lives.

Attempts to meet the demands of both caregiving and work have been found to affect the health, finances, relationships and mental well-being of these employed caregivers (Neal et al. 1987; Sharlach and Boyd 1989). As a result, the caregiver may need as much support as the frail older person.

Studies continue to document the stresses associated with caregiving. However, not all impairments are found to be equally stressful. Patients whose conditions require constant supervision tend to cause both greater restriction and strain on their caregivers (Haley et al. 1987; Diemling et al. 1989). The types of stress encountered by caregivers have been categorized into primary and secondary stressors (Pearlin et al. 1990). Primary stressors are associated with the needs of the patient and the extent of caregiving that they demand. Impaired cognitive functioning and disruptive or problematic behavior are examples of primary stressors. Secondary stressors are those that result from family financial conflicts or employment demands.

However, as demanding as caregiving may be, it also involves certain rewards. Providing essential assistance can be gratifying in some instances as it is experienced as reciprocation for past affection and assistance (Motenko 1989). In addition, learning to cope with a difficult situation can potentially increase one's feelings of competence and mastery.

It would seem that formal home care may alleviate the caregivers' plight but this is not the case in all instances. In a study of Black and Hispanic caregivers of Alzheimer's victims that Monk et al. (1989) conducted in New York City, it was observed that receiving the regular help of home care workers does not lessen either the sense of burden or the feelings of depression among relatives.

Lawton et al. similarly found that respite services do not alleviate caregivers' stress (1989). Several interpretations may be ventured as to what may otherwise be regarded as a discouraging finding concerning the effectiveness or impact of home and community care.

First, home attendants may have been brought in at the point when the patient's condition was already very advanced and the caregiver was already profoundly stressed. Obtaining a few hours of relief each week did not, therefore, reduce the round-the-clock and relentless demands placed on the primary caregiver.

Second, informal caregivers continue to bear the lion's share of family responsibility for continuity of care. It may take more than a single service, no matter how important, to alleviate their burden. Stoller found, to this effect, that formal services do not necessarily reduce the informal caregivers' involvement (1989). In interviews that Stoller conducted over two periods with 135 community elderly and their caregivers, it was found that the introduction of formal services did not reduce either the amount or scope of care provided by the family. The formal services were found to supplement rather than replace the informal assistance.

A lack of substitution between formal and informal care was also found in the use of a case management system (Muscovice et al. 1989). Case managers allocated formal community based services to patients at risk of institutionalization based on need, without consideration of informal supports. The level and amount of informal care remained constant, regardless of the extent of formal care received. There was no reported substitution. In fact, offering respite care, counseling and training to caregivers may further strengthen them so that they can maintain their relative in the community for longer periods of time.

Hanley and Wiener, using the first wave of the National Long Term Care Survey, similarly concluded that paid home care does not weaken or reduce informal care (1990). The extent and quality of informal care were instead more influenced by the physical and financial needs of the patient than by the pesence and volume of the formal services received.

The previously reported study on Black and Hispanic caregivers (Monk et al. 1989) found, however, that the relations between formal and informal services may be far more complex and intriguing than anticipated.

As the use of informal supports increased among Blacks, so did their utilization of formal supports. This was not the case for the Hispanics where increases in the latter took place when the informal system weakened or remained stagnant. In the case of Blacks, it seems that the informal supports act as linkages to formal services. The more friends, neighbors and relatives are drawn to the helping tasks, the greater is the pooling of expertise and knowledge of community resources. Also, as the informal network expands, its many participants are more able to coordinate their schedules and free some of their time to negotiate the provision of formal services.

It is quite different in the Hispanic group where the use of formal services increased without a concomitant expansion of informal support systems. A plausible explanation is that some in the group are recent immigrants and have little of a dependable informal reservoir beyond their immediate families. Spouses and children apparently do not have backup secondary caregivers, at least in any appreciable numbers, to lessen their sense of burden.

An explanation which is more cultural in nature starts from the presumption that the immediate family would not, as a matter of principle, ask for help from relatives or neighbors. After all, it is seen as the spouse's and childrens' duty to go to any lengths, verging to the limits of self-sacrifice, to fulfill their familial obligations. It would appear to be more acceptable, however, that once the patient reaches an extreme degree of frailty, the family engage whatever formal community services can be located.

The same study established that immediate relatives tend to feel more depressed and burdened than caregivers who are more distant relatives, or not related at all to the patient. This was observed among both Blacks and Hispanics. Given, however, that the latter group included a proportionally larger number of close relatives, to the almost total exclusion of nonrelatives, it would seem to be a foregone conclusion that they would exhibit cumulatively higher scores regarding both a sense of burden and depression.

There are also certain similarities between the two ethnic groups in their use of formal services. Caregivers with poorer health resorted more often to formal services, as did those at the lower end of the socioeconomic ladder. The latter aspect may result from the fact that Medicaid, the public assistance program, includes home attendants and visiting nurses among the benefits for low income elderly. The use of formal supports tends to correlate with the extent of the victim's functional impairment, as measured with the ADL scale, while the use of informal supports was more significantly associated with cognitive and behavioral deficits. This specialization pattern may also be logically acceptable: relatives and friends can better handle behavioral idiosyncrasies and memory losses, but they probably need professional or paraprofessional help to deal with the physical demands of an incapacitated patient. Tasks apparently as simple as bathing or transporting a patient from bed to chair often exceed the caregivers' physical stamina.

There were also significant differences between the two ethnic groups. Among Blacks, the older the caregiver, the more frequent the use of formal services. Among Hispanics, the opposite tended to be the case, probably because the far more numerous younger caregivers are seeking relief in order to maintain a semblance of control over their lives. Furthermore, Blacks who manifest a greater sense of burden tended to increase the use of formal services but, surprisingly, to a very moderate degree. It is rather perplexing that among Hispanics there was even a slight reverse tendency: as the sense of burden intensified, formal services were utilized to a slightly lesser degree. What may be operating here is the fact that these caregivers are overwhelmed and isolated, and end up so absorbed with their daily obligations that they have no time to negotiate and obtain those formal services. Moreover, they may not even know where to begin to find out about them.

A major difference between the two groups relates to their sense of filial commitment. Hispanics were far more inflexible in their affirmation that children ought to care for their parents. Blacks seemed to temper their support for those norms with the realization that there are limits to a relative's capacity to care, and that once a threshold is reached, formal services become an inevitable necessity. Blacks, therefore, showed more consistency in their attitudes concerning filial responsibility norms. Hispanics seemed to experience more conflict and be torn in this respect, as they ultimately changed their views and agreed that seeking professional help was inevitable.

In essence, recent studies have not produced evidence of a clear-cut or consistent pattern of relations between formal and informal services. Nor do these studies seem to lend credence to the fear that once formal services are interposed, they end up replacing the informal supports. One important lesson that seems to surface, however, is that not all family caregivers are endowed with infinite resilience and endurance capacity and that even "strong" families need help themselves to simply carry on.

Furthermore, the actual pool of informal caregivers is bound to shrink as more women work full time. Also, the "baby boom" generation, that is, those born in the late forties and early fifties, had a lower fertility rate than their parents and grandparents. It follows that they will have less adult children to assist them when they reach advanced old age, around the second or third decade of the 21st century.

## HOME CARE PERSONNEL

The cost and quality of home care are closely associated with the availability, competence and commitment of the workers who deliver the services. Given the stringent cost containment requirements imposed by Medicare in recent years, many private service providers have taken the route of labor contracts and piecemeal payment for services. Rather than hiring a permanent workforce that enjoys stability, a measure of security, adequate remuneration and proper training, the trend has been just the opposite. Agencies thus opt for recruiting a temporary, free-lance and part-time roster of workers who can be called upon on a contingency basis. This is particularly the case among paraprofessional and unskilled workers whose wages are generally below those of their counterparts in other health service agencies.

It is not surprising, therefore, that the home care field is plagued with both personnel shortages and high turnover rates which have been reported to reach a level of 60 percent a year, in the case of New York City (Connell 1989). As a consequence, patients may be visited by anywhere from 3 to 20 workers in a single year. A 1988 evaluation of the Home Care Ombudsman Program in New York pointed out that dissatisfaction and conflicts with home care workers were the main complaint voiced by consumers (Shin 1988).

Although federal legislation requires the implementation of training and supervision standards for home health aides under Medicare, a study by the Office of the Inspector General of the U.S. Department of Health and Human Services reported in 1987 that the mandate in question had not yet been put into effect. It also found that supervisory nurses were not giving proper orientation to aides, and that on-site supervision was almost nonexistent (Office of the Inspector General 1987).

In order to improve the status of the paraprofessionals, Aalberts (1989) recommended that they work in teams, be given both standardized and specialized training for specific populations of patients, work a normal schedule of 40 hours a week, and receive special supportive services when having to deal with complex problems. Finally, Aalberts felt it essential to raise the status of the paraprofessional home care workers so that their roles more closely approach the importance of those of professionals in the same agency.

As a means of addressing the problems confronting home care paraprofessionals, the Ford Foundation funded three demonstration projects targeting the above mentioned issues of training and support, pay and benefits, status, and opportunities for advancement (Feldman 1989). The evaluation of the projects showed that supervisor support was essential to insure job satisfaction and that loneliness was a major source of stress. Training, however, was found to reduce the feelings of isolation and to contribute to reduced turnover rates. Moreover, workers dealing with problem clients benefited from getting special training and additional compensation. Moreover, early intensive training and follow-up support of new workers were found to increase their ties to the agency and to develop greater job commitment.

The experience of New York, which has the largest home care workforce in the country—60,000 persons—provides further insights into the problems inherent in the industry (Donovan 1989). Nearly all of the workers are minority women employed through 75 agencies which have subcontracts with the City of New York. These agencies hire, train, supervise and pay the workers. Health care benefits, worker training, and supervision are minimal, although home care workers have been unionized since 1986. In interviews with 404 workers, Donovan found high levels of psychological distress or demoralization particularly associated with inadequate case planning and a lack of sufficient training and supervision. Again, these findings highlight the need for significant improvements in the preparation and support of these paraprofessionals.

## QUALITY OF CARE

Home care is mandated by an assortment of seemingly unrelated public policies and operated by a variety of program structures that do not adhere to the same criteria of what constitutes quality of care. To date, there are no uniform national guidelines or standards of quality. Thus, although increasing numbers of older persons are receiving home care, there is no assurance that the service is appropriate or effective in meeting their needs.

A 1986 report by the American Bar Association brought to the attention of policy makers and service providers the quality problems inherent in the rapidly growing home care industry (U.S. Congress, House Select

Committee on Aging 1986). The risks of poor care, unreliable workers, neglect, abuse and exploitation as fundamental concerns in the current system were described along with recommendations for correcting them. Five years later, federal regulations and standards for governing home care agencies are still lacking. Although Medicare-certified agencies must conform to specific regulations, these apply only to their skilled services, but do not cover homemaker and personal care. Moreover, the unlicensed agencies are not covered by these regulations.

As of 1989, 39 states licensed home care agencies (Riley 1989). Most of these states applied the Medicare standards for licensing skilled nursing and specific therapeutic services. However, state licensure has not been found to assure higher quality home care standards or services than those found in non-licensure states.

A study of licensed and unlicensed home care agencies in California found similar problems in the services provided by each sector (Grant and Harrington 1989). Common shortcomings included difficulties with delivery and supervision of care, poor coordination of services, inadequate staff screening, supervision and training, theft and fraud, high rates of staff turnover, unprofessional or criminal conduct, the dispensing of medication and treatment by inappropriate personnel, inadequate clinical records, and failure to meet minimum training or education requirements. Licensure did not necessarily guarantee improved quality.

A thorough review of factors affecting the quality of care has found that home care clients require more intense and skilled care due to the more rapid discharges from hospitals under the Prospective Payment System (Applebaum and Phillips 1990). These patients are often very frail and at risk of abuse and neglect. They require far more sophisticated assistance than the paraprofessional worker is capable of providing. The majority of home care workers are untrained and poorly paid and motivated. High rates of absenteeism and turnover of staff further impinge upon the quality of the service.

Fiscal restraints on agencies also affect their efforts to maintain quality assurance standards. Direct supervision, regular meetings with workers, in-service training, and consultation are difficult to implement when costs and profits are the overriding concern of the privately operated contract agencies. Moreover, as the government itself seeks to put a lid on rising health care costs, even agencies that excel in the implementation of quality assurance standards may find it difficult to continue doing so while still allocating sufficient resources to the actual provision of services.

Quality assurance in home care is further hampered by the lack of standardized measures of care outcomes. Unlike assistance focused on acute conditions in which a cure or significant functional improvement can be used as an objective measure of the intervention's effectiveness, home care tends to focus on chronic conditions, to which analogous measures are not applicable. Consequently, quality assurance criteria tend to measure indirect factors such as personnel ratios and training, administration and organization, and the process by which the service is delivered to the patient. There is no evidence, however, to support the contention that these factors are linked to improved quality of patient care.

One means of measuring the actual quality of care is to involve consumers in both the design of the service plan and the measurement of its outcomes, to determine if the service they receive meets their expectations. Developing consumer input into the care process, as well as enhancing the patients' empowerment and rights, has been proposed as an important strategy to increase the quality of care (Sabatino 1989).

In recognition of the problems of quality control in the home care industry, the Omnibus Budget Reconciliation Act of 1987 mandated the establishment of state toll-free hotlines and investigative units to receive and respond to complaints regarding Medicare-certified agencies. Other provisions to assure quality of care contained in the same Act include improvements in certification procedures overseeing agency compliance with federal regulations and training requirements for home health personnel. The legislation also mandates states to develop sanctioning mechanisms, such as monetary penalties, suspension of payments and the appointment of temporary administrative overseers, as means of enforcing adherence to regulations. In addition, home health agencies must inform patients of their rights under Medicare regarding home health coverage. Unfortunately, these federal regulations pertain only to the Medicare-certified agencies and are not extended to the thousands of unlicensed ones.

Further efforts to assure quality care were mandated under the revised Medicaid provisions of the Omnibus Budget Reconciliation Act of 1990. Under the Act's new, expanded community based care provision, states will be responsible for surveying providers and certifying that all comply with federally established quality standards for service. Given that many of these providers are not Medicare-certified, the new procedures may help to extend the adoption of quality standards throughout the home care industry.

## INNOVATIVE PROGRAMS

The questions as to whether home care can in fact substitute for care in nursing homes and what the best approaches are for delivering home care services have been the foci of many experiments and demonstrations launched under the sponsorship of the federal and state governments, as well as private foundations.

Case management emerged in the early 1970s as the pivotal coordinative and cost reduction ingredient in the design of a series of home and community based experimental demonstrations. Kemper et al. (1987) noticed, to this effect, that only one out of 16 federally funded community care experimental projects failed to incorporate case management. Most of those initiatives relied upon an individualized or single professional approach to case management, although a minority also began experimenting with the utilization of multidisciplinary teams.

The ACCESS demonstration in Monroe county (New York State) was carried out from 1983 to 1985 with the intent to precisely compare those models (Eggert et al. 1990). It incorporated three service strategies. In the first, the "Centralized Individual Model," case managers exercised a monitoring function, relying on reports they received regularly from service providers, but they did not assess or reassess their charges, nor did they actually formulate the care plan. These tasks remained in the hands of the health care or certified home health agencies that visited and attended to the needs of each patient. The case managers were, for all practical purposes, "second liners," removed from the field. They provided advice and oversaw service delivery but could only react to their clients' new problems or situations after their occurrence.

The second strategy consisted of a "Neighborhood Team" and employed a more direct and continuous pattern of home visitations by a case management team that included a nurse and a social worker. They attended to each case on a direct basis. They conducted their own assessments and could anticipate crisis situations before they erupted, or in their earlier and more controllable stages. This Neighborhood Team model proved to be most cost effective: both hospital costs and home care utilization and costs were significantly lower (26 percent and 24 percent, respectively) than for the preceding "Centralized Individual Model." Mortality rates were similar for both groups during the first year—30 percent—but were lower for the Team model (11 percent, as compared to 16 percent) in the second year.

Finally, the third model was tested as a randomized, controlled experiment that ran from 1978 to 1981 and targeted homebound chronically and terminally ill patients who had an informal caregiver and wished to continue living at home (Zimmer et al. 1985). In this experiment, the treatment group received care from a "Home Health Care Team" (HHC) that included a geriatric physician, a social worker and a nurse, while the control group benefited from the prevailing types of community care. What set the HHC Team apart from the preceding Neighborhood Team was the greater distinction of roles among the participating professionals. For one thing, team members did not make joint visits. Furthermore, team members supervised and were more closely involved with the daily assignments of home health care nurses and aides.

The HHC Team proved to be most effective in reducing both hospital and nursing home utilization rates. Physician office visits were also lower but in-home health care visits, be it by the physician, social worker or nurse, were understandably more frequent. On the whole, the HHC Team was the most comprehensive and effective of the three case management approaches tested. The ACCESS experience began demonstrating the relative merits of different case management models and called attention to the need to identify which types of patients may derive greater benefits from the different methods of case management.

Coordination of services is one of the objectives of the "Living at Home Program" (LAHP), a demonstration operating in 20 communities across the United States. Initiated in 1987 by the Commonwealth Fund and the Pew Charitable Trust, it drew support from a coalition of 33 additional foundations and today constitutes the largest experiment concerning community based services under nongovernmental auspices. LAHP aims to determine whether cooperative, coordinated networks of health and social service providers can reduce duplication of and facilitate better access to existing home care services, as well as tailor services to unique local concerns and population needs. Initial evaluative results indicate that it has succeeded in targeting a very old population, with a median age of 80, that is poor, frail, female and living alone (Hughes and Guihan 1990).

Several state governments have also embarked in the reorganization of their long term care services and launched innovative home care initiatives aimed at reducing the use of institutional care. These developments are of more recent vintage, and followed in the footsteps of the long term care demonstrations of the 1970s and early 1980s.

Oregon initiated in 1981 the Assisted Living Program as an alternative to nursing home care, although nursing homes were retained as a service of last resort. To begin with, all long term care programs for the elderly and disabled were placed under the jurisdiction of a single state agency, the Senior Service Division. The result has been the doubling of the home care program and increases in adult foster homes (U.S. Congress, House Select Committee on Aging 1990).

Oregon's Assisted Living Program is based on a social model of care which builds upon each person's strengths and capabilities. Individuals live in their own apartments in a complex where 24-hour staff assistance is available. The program provides many of the intermediate care services normally offered only in a nursing home. All residents have a care plan uniquely designed to meet their individual needs as they have defined them, and as interpreted by their families and staff. The emphasis is on promoting personal choice and autonomy rather than dependence.

Pilot testing of the model has shown an improved level of functioning for residents and higher levels of life satisfaction when compared to persons in intermediate care nursing facilities. Moreover, the cost of care is only 80 percent of the equivalent care in an intermediate facility. This is due to the fact that there are less staff requirements and residents are obliged to function as independently as possible.

The state of Illinois has also subsumed all of its long term care programs under the state's Community Care Program. All program participants must meet the criteria for nursing home admission and those not eligible for Medicaid must have less than $10,000 in liquid assets. Three direct services are offered: adult day care, homemaker help and chore services, with additional care planning and case management. All assessment and case management is conducted by local Community Care Units under contract to the Department of Aging, with a third of these units being home health agencies (Justice 1988). The provider agencies are selected based upon quality measures designed by the state.

The state of Maine provides a wide array of community services to persons assessed as needing nursing or boarding home care. Local program managers design individual care plans and packages centered around the needs of the clients. The most frequently used service is personal care assistance, often involving paying neighbors or friends for the care. This approach is particularly unique in that it both incorporates and builds upon the informal support network.

In Wisconsin, the Bureau of Long-term Support administers community long term care programs throughout 72 counties (Ball 1989). The program is built around a care management system that serves all persons requiring long term care. Income requirements are that persons would become eligible for Medicaid within six months of entering a nursing home through a "spend down" of their resources. The state offers guidelines for county agencies, but within these guidelines there is much latitude for care management and designing services to meet individual needs. Care managers may purchase many types of services that would assist their clients to remain independent. As in Maine, this may involve the hiring of relatives or friends to provide assistance.

Particularly unique to the Wisconsin system is the emphasis on consumer participation. Guidelines mandate that consumers be represented in state and local advisory committees, so that their opinions and preferences be taken into account in the design of policy and services.

Florida, which has the highest proportion of persons over 60 of any state, has developed Community Care Programs for the elderly located in each of the 11 state health districts. The programs must include case management and at least three of the following services: homemaker and chore services, respite care, adult day care, medical transportation, mini day care, home health aides, home nursing, personal care, and medical therapeutic services (U.S. Congress, House Select Committee on Aging 1990). The intent of the program is to assist functionally impaired elderly to live in the community, to reduce nursing home use, and to develop cost effective service delivery. To date, the program has been found to increase the quality of life for participants and is reported to be cost effective.

## NEW POLICY DIRECTIONS

The Congressional Bi-Partisan Commission on Comprehensive Health Care recommended that quality assurance in home care center around a case management system (The Pepper Commission 1990: 120). Officially renamed "The Pepper Commission" for its first chairman, the late senator Claude Pepper, the Bi-Partisan Commission was created by the United States Congress in 1988 to find long term care solutions for the frail aged and severely disabled persons. At the end of its work it recommended that eligibility for home care should be determined by a state or local government, or a federally funded non-profit assessment agency, using standardized assessment methods and criteria. Furthermore, it proposed that case managers design an "Individualized Care Plan" for each patient and determine the number and types of services required. They will also conduct periodic reassessments, to insure that services are performed according to both established standards of care and cost containment considerations. In particular, the case manager will have the authority to operate a budget that covers all services needed by the patient.

The Commission identified the following home and community based care services under the jurisdiction of a case manager: home health care; physical, occupational and speech therapy; personal care (feeding, transferring and personal hygiene); homemaker help (meal preparation, laundry and housework); grocery shopping and transportation; medication management; adult day care; respite care for caregivers; training and supportive counseling for family caregivers.

The Pepper Commission's recommendations have not yet been fully adopted, but partial elements improving home care services have already been sanctioned as law by the United States Congress. They include a five-year expansion of Medicaid, to become effective in July 1991. Under the new terms, home care services will be available to any person with two out of three impairments in the ADLs for which they require assistance (bathing, dressing, toileting, eating). An important revision is the inclusion of persons unable to perform these activities due to a primary or secondary diagnosis of Alzheimer's disease.

Another significant change concerns Medicaid's requirement of "budget neutrality." According to The Pepper Commission's recommendations, states would no longer have to provide evidence that services offered in the home are less costly than care in an institution.

Participating states will have to use the uniform assessment instruments to be instituted by the federal government by July 1991.


## CONCLUSION

The demand for home care services has been mounting relentlessly in the United States, but the country lacks a coherent system of home care services. There is instead a virtual non-system, a staggering diversity of federally and state mandated programs which do not adhere to similar quality criteria and do not coordinate their operations. Services remain unavailable to many, and those lucky enough to be eligible are not necessarily satisfied with either the number of hours of service they receive, or the worker's performance.

Provider agencies experience, in turn, great difficulty in recruiting personnel. Given the low reimbursement rates they receive from public programs, these agencies cannot offer compensation, training, support and supervision incentives commensurate with those offered by other health services. Medicare and Medicaid have instituted operational guidelines for their certified agencies but there has been inconsistent or ineffectual enforcement of those guidelines. The main thrust has been toward cost containment. As a consequence, there is virtually no qualitative difference between the certified and unlicensed agencies.

Home care services have long had to contend with a pronounced historical orientation toward nursing home care. The decades of the seventies and eighties witnessed a gradual move away from that institutional bias. To begin with, home care services grew in volume, and there was also a greater experimentation with innovative models for delivering these services. Public policy wavered, however, between the recognition of home care as an intrinsically valid link in the long term care continuum, on one hand, and the illusion, on the other, that home care can fully replace nursing home care at a fraction of its cost.

Home care has indeed potential advantages over nursing home care but there is no assurance that it can be less costly, if implemented according to desirable professional standards. The recommendations of The Pepper Commission constitute a decisive move both in the direction of such standards and in the recognition of home care as a needed service, in its own right. The Commission's emphasis on uniform assessment and case management procedures may well constitute the first steps toward a more simplified and rational system of home care services. This is the policy and planning agenda as far as home and community care are concerned for the 1990s and beyond.

## References

AAHA-American Association of Homes for the Aging (1987). "Continuing Care Retirement Communities: An Industry in Action." Washington, D.C.: AAHA Publications.

Aalberts, N. (1989). "Training home care professionals." *Caring* (February): 26-27.

AARP and Travelers Companies Foundation (1988). "National Survey of Caregivers, Summary of Findings." October. Washington, D.C.: American Association of Retired Persons.

American Association of Retired Persons, Public Policy Institute (1991). "Medicare's Home Health Benefit: Eligibility, Utilization, and Expenditures." 1, January. Washington, D.C.: American Association of Retired Persons.

Applebaum, R., and P. Phillips (1990). "Assuring the quality of in-home care: The other challenge for long term care." *The Gerontologist* 30: 444-451.

Ball, C. (1989). "Long Term Care Management: A Policy Analysis of Four Exemplary Models." Washington, D.C.: American Association of Retired Persons, Public Policy Institute.

Binney, E., C. Estes, and S. Ingman (1990). "Medicalization, public policy and the elderly: Social services in jeopardy?" *Social Science and Medicine* 30: 761-771.

Bishop, C., and S. Karon (1989). "The composition of home health care expenditure growth." *Home Health Care Services Quarterly* 10: 139-175.

Connell, N. (1989). "Home care paraprofessionals: Undervalued, underpaid and increasingly unavailable." New York: Community Council of Greater New York.

Diemling, G., D. Bass, A. Townsend, and L. Noelker (1989). "Care-related stress: A comparison of spouse and adult-child caregivers in shared and separate households." *Journal of Aging and Health* 1: 67-82.

Donovan, R. (1989). "Work stress and job satisfaction: A study of home care workers in New York City." *Home Health Care Services Quarterly* 10: 97-114.

Eggert, G.E., B. Friedman, and J.G. Zimmer (1990). "Models of intensive case management." *Journal of Gerontological Social Work* 15 (3/4): 75-102.

Feldman, P. (1989). "Reducing turnover among paraprofessionals." *Caring* (February): 28-29.

Gaberlavage, G. (1987). "Social service to older persons under the Social Services Block Grant." Washington, D.C.: American Association of Retired Persons.

Grant, L., and C. Harrington (1989). "Quality of care in licensed and unlicensed home care agencies: A California case study." *Home Health Care Services Quarterly* 10: 115-138.

Haley, W., E. Levine, S. Brown, J. Berry, and G. Hughes (1987). "Consequences of caring for a relative with senile dementia." *Journal of the American Geriatrics Society* 35: 405-411.

Hanley, R.J., and J.M. Wiener (1990). "Will paid home care destroy informal support?" *The Gerontologist* 30 (Special Issue): 242A.

Harrington, C., and L.A. Grant (1990). "The delivery, regulation and politics of home care: A California case study." *The Gerontologist* 30 (4): 451-461.

Harris, L. and Associates, Inc. (1982). "Priorities and expectations for health and living circumstances: A survey of the elderly in five English speaking countries." New York.

Hughes, S.L., and M. Guihan (1990). "Community based long term care: The experience of the Living at Home Programs." *Journal of Gerontological Social Work* 15 (3/4): 103-130.

Justice, D. (1988). "State Long Term Care Reform: Development of Community Care Systems in Six States." Washington, D.C.: National Governors' Association.

Katz, S., A.B. Ford, R.W. Muskowitz, B.A. Jackson, and M.W. Jaffe (1963). "The Index of ADL: A standardized measure of biological and psychological function." *Journal of the American Medical Association* 185: 94-99.

Kemper, P. (1988). "The evaluation of the National Long Term Care Demonstration: Overview of the findings." *Health Services Research* 23: 161-174.

Kemper, P., R. Applebaum, and M. Harrigan (1987). "A systematic comparison of community care demonstrations." Madison, W.I.: University of Wisconsin. Institute for Research on Poverty. Special Report Series, 45, June.

Kemper, P., R.S. Brown, and G.J. Carcaguo (1986). "The evaluation of the National Long Term Care Demonstration: Final Report." Princeton, N.J.: Mathematica Policy Research.

Lawton, M.P., and E.M. Brody (1969). "Assessment of older people: Self-maintaining and instrumental activities of daily living." *The Gerontologist* 9: 179-186.

Lawton, M.P., E.M. Brody, and A.R. Saperstein (1989). "A controlled study of respite service for caregivers of Alzheimer's patients." *The Gerontologist* 29: 8-16.

Liu, K., K. Manton, and B. Liu (1985). "Home care expenses for the disabled elderly." *Health Care Financing Review* 7 (2): 51-58.

Lombardi, T., Jr. (1986-87). "Nursing Home without Walls." *Generations* 11 (2): 21-23.

Manton, K., and K. Liu (1984). "The future growth of the long term population: Projections based on the 1977 National Nursing Home Population and the 1982 Long Term Care Survey." Paper presented at the Third National Leadership Conference on Long Term Care Issues, Washington, D.C., March 7-9.

McCauley, W., and R. Blieszner (1985). "Selection of long term care arrangements by older community residents." *The Gerontologist* 25 (2): 188-193.

Monk, A., J. Lerner, A. McCann-Oakley, and C. Cox (1989). "Families of Black and Hispanic dementia patients: Their use of formal and informal support services." Final Report to the Andrus Foundation-American Association of Retired Persons. New York: Columbia University School of Social Work, August.

Motenko, A. (1989). "The frustrations, gratifications, and well-being of dementia caregivers." *The Gerontologist* 29: 166-173.

Murtaugh, C.M., P. Kemper, and B.C. Sillman (1990). "The risk of nursing home use in later life." *Medical Care* 28 (10): 952-962.

Muscovice, I., G. Davidson, and D. McCaffrey (1989). "Substitution of formal and informal care for the community-based elderly." *Medical Care* 26: 971-981.

Neal, M., N. Chapman, and B. Ingersoll-Dayton (1987). "Work and eldercare: A survey of employees." Paper presented at the Annual Meeting of the Gerontological Society of America, Washington, D.C.

Office of the Inspector General (1987). "Home health aide services for Medicare patients." Washington, D.C.: Department of Health and Human Services.

Pearlin, L., J. Mullan, S. Semple, and M. Skaff (1990). "Caregiving and the stress process: An overview of concepts and their measures." *The Gerontologist* 30: 583-595.

Riley, P. (1989). *Quality assurance in home care*. Washington, D.C.: American Association of Retired Persons, Public Policy Institute.

Rivlin, A.M., and J.M. Wiener (1988). *Caring for the disabled elderly: Who will pay?* Washington, D.C.: The Brookings Institution.

Rowland, D. (1989). "Help at home." Baltimore, M.D.: The Commonwealth Fund, Commission on Elderly People Living Alone.

Ruchlin, H., J. Morris, C. Gutkin, and S. Sherwood (1990). "Expenditures for long term care services for community elders." *Health Care Financing Review* 10 (Spring): 55-65.

Sabatino, C. (1989). "Homecare quality." *Generations* (Winter): 12-16.

Shanas, E., P. Townsend, D. Wedderburn, H. Friis, P. Milhoj, and J. Stehouwer (1968). *Old People in Three Industrial Societies*. New York: Atherton Press.

Sharlach, A., and S. Boyd (1989). "Caregiving and employment: Results of an employee survey." *The Gerontologist* 29: 382-387.

Shin, E. (1988). "The ombudservice for home care workers." New York: Community Council of Greater New York.

Short, P.F., and J. Leon (1990). "Use of home and community services by persons ages 65 and older with functional difficulties." Washington, D.C.: National Medical Expenditure Survey Research Findings #5, Department of Health and Human Services, Publication No. (PHS) 90-3466.

Stoller, E. (1989). "Formal services and informal helping: The myth of service substitution." *The Journal of Applied Gerontology* 8: 37-52.

Stone, R.I., and C.M. Murtaugh (1990). "The elderly population with chronic functional disability: Implications for home care eligibility." *The Gerontologist* 30 (4): 491-496.

The Pepper Commission, U.S. Bi-Partisan Commission on Comprehensive Health Care (1990). "A call for action." Final Report. Washington, D.C.: U.S. Government Printing Office, September.

Tennstedt, S., J. McKinlay, and L. Sullivan (1989). "Informal care for frail elders: The role of secondary caregivers." *The Gerontologist* 29: 677-683.

U.S. Congress, House Select Committee on Aging (1986). "The Black Box of Home Care Quality." Washington, D.C.: U.S. Government Printing Office.

U.S. Congress, House Select Committee on Aging (1990). "Housing for the Frail Elderly." Washington, D.C.: U.S. Government Printing Office.

U.S. Department of Commerce (1990). "Health and Medical Services." U.S. Industrial Outlook 1990. Washington, D.C.: U.S. Government Printing Office.

U.S. House of Representatives, Committee on Ways and Means (1990). Green Book. Washington, D.C.: U.S. Government Printing Office, June 5.

U.S. Senate Special Committee on Aging (1986). "Aging America: Trends and Projections." Washington, D.C.: U.S. Government Printing Office.

U.S. Senate Special Committee on Aging (1989). "Aging America: Trends and Projections." Washington, D.C.: U.S. Government Printing Office.

Vertrees, J., K. Manton, and G. Adler (1989). "Cost effectiveness of home and community based care." *Health Care Financing Review* 10: 65-78.

Zawadski, R.I., and M.L. Ansak (1983). "Consolidating community-based long term care: Early returns from the On Lok Demonstration." *The Gerontologist* 23 (4): 364-369.

Zimmer, J., A. Groth-Junker, and J. McCusker (1985). "A randomized controlled study of a home health care team." *American Journal of Public Health* 75: 134-141.

# two

Home and Community-Based
Services for the Elderly in
the United Kingdom

*John Baldock*

## COMMUNITY CARE IN THE UNITED KINGDOM

Community care in the United Kingdom is in a state of great flux and
uncertainty. The pattern of services and provision that developed after the
Second World War is to be thoroughly reformed in a series of stages
beginning in April 1991. This follows the National Health Service and
Community Care Act 1990 which itself was the consequence of a series of
reports and enquiries into the provision of community care. Thus this
contribution cannot report on an established system of social care for the
elderly but rather on an extensive debate and critique of existing provision,
on the results of a number of experimental innovations that contributed to
that debate and on the intended, but as yet uncertain, new structure of
services.

What is happening in the United Kingdom is not so much the shift from
one system of care to another but rather the attempt to construct a system
out of the disorder and unpredictability that currently exists. This is
sometimes difficult for those in other countries to accept. They often have
an image of welfare in the United Kingdom that assumes that the elderly are
protected by comprehensive universal services. This image is largely
derived from the reputation of the National Health Service. However, as
will be explained later, the NHS has never played more than a marginal part
in the supply of personal home care services for the elderly in their own
homes. The differences between the British social care problems and those
found in the United States, for example, are not as great as some might
imagine. North American commentators, particularly those in the United
States, often point out that the provision of care there is characterised by a
"non-system," that is to say that care has to be put together from a wide

variety of uncoordinated and independent sources (Wylie and Austin 1978: 16; Arnold 1987: 27). The same is true in the United Kingdom.

The implicit postwar promise of a comprehensive safety-net of support for the frail and disabled has never been fulfilled. Public home care services have rarely reached more than a fraction of those in need. The remainder have either been supported informally by their families, have entered residential or hospital care or have simply been neglected (Henwood and Wicks 1984). Now, in the United Kingdom as elsewhere, demographic pressure, economic constraints and changing public expectations have together made the existing ad hoc non-system unsustainable and the search is on to construct a genuine, if pluralistic, system of care.

While economic and ideological factors are important, the key to the current pressure for change in the provision of services is demographic, the growth in the numbers of the old needing care. In absolute terms the numbers are not great but relatively the United Kingdom, like many other industrial societies, is currently experiencing rapid increases in the numbers of the elderly who require some help to get through the day. The two categories estimated below are a good indication of a) those who will need help on a daily basis and b) those who will need almost constant surveillance.

Table 2.1    Elderly  people  (000s)  GB

|  | 1981 | 2001 | Change |
|---|---|---|---|
| a) Unable to bath unaided | | | |
| 65-74 | 270 | 242 | -28 |
| 75-84 | 288 | 334 | +46 |
| 85+ | 199 | 356 | +157 |
| All 65+ | 757 | 932 | +175 |
| b) Unable to get out of bed unaided | | | |
| 65-74 | 71 | 64 | -7 |
| 75-84 | 60 | 70 | +10 |
| 85+ | 58 | 105 | +47 |
| All 65+ | 189 | 239 | +50 |

Henwood and Wicks 1984: 16

These increases, this contribution will argue, have pushed the existing system of care, already very inadequate, over a threshold of political and social acceptability. One response has been to force government to initiate a substantial reconstruction of public provision which emphasises a mixed economy of support for the elderly outside institutions and in the community.  Another, closely related consequence, has been to stimulate innovation and experimentation with new ways of supporting the frail elderly.  Together these responses imply a very different, and possibly better, world of care for the elderly of the future.  But the risks of the changes now in train are considerable.

## THE CURRENT PATTERN OF PROVISION

A distinctive feature of the services available to the elderly is that there is no single source or organisation to which they can go to get help.  Rather there is a mixture of sources, which can supply different services, under different degrees of obligation and for different reasons.  Consequently, what any one old person is actually getting is more a matter of chance, accidents of time, place and opportunity, than any other factor.

Institutional care, in hospitals, nursing homes and residential homes, has never been an important part of the British way of caring for the dependent elderly.  In 1984 only some 8.5% of those aged 75+ were in some public or private institution (Audit Commission 1986).  This figure has not changed very much over the last 70 years, ever since the inheritance of Victorian poor law and the workhouse began their decline.

In particular, the UK does not use hospitals and medical facilities to care for the aged to the same extent as other industrial countries.  This is a result of the way the National Health Service has been able to contain the use of hospital for all age groups.  For example, in the UK about 100/1000 of all ages are admitted annually to hospital for acute care.  The figure for those over 65 is 170/1000.  Comparable figures in the US are 160 for all age groups and 390 for those over 65 (Zwick 1985).  Only about 2% of people aged 75+ are in hospital at any one time (Audit Commission 1986).

The low use of medical services reflects their scarcity and the fact that the NHS is not a system that responds directly to consumer demand.  Centrally-determined and cash-limited budgets mean that the volume of services is almost entirely supplier-determined.  There are few financial incentives for doctors and hospitals to provide the elderly with more.  Many, whose conditions are not immediately life-threatening, are told they must wait, sometimes years, for treatment.  This ability of the hospital service to control its expenditure on the elderly in a way that is almost independent of need and demand means there is little incentive to transfer money to supporting a cheaper home care sector in the way that there is in countries where hospital care is paid for by insurance funds.  Neither is the shifting of funds to community care helped by the fact that the National Health Service, which funds hospitals, is budgetarily quite separate from local government which pays for most home care services.  The budget controllers in the hospital service are very reluctant to lose control of funds to the community care sector.  Governments have attempted to encourage the movement of resources across this divide by means of a number of special programmes but so far the sums involved are relatively very small indeed.

## Financial Support for the Frail Elderly

The state supports the dependent elderly living in the community partly by providing them with income and partly through the direct provision of care services.  Except for the social insurance-based retirement pension, none of these forms of care amounts to a social right.  They are all dependent on needs and means tests conducted by the professional suppliers.  In many cases the rules governing these tests are broad and vague, effectively making the benefits discretionary ones.  This professional rationing is inevitable given that the supply of public funds available for community care of the elderly is far too small to allow universal entitlements.  In particular, there remains the problem discussed below that it is often far easier to get state support for expensive residential care than it is to get help with home care.

Financial support available to the elderly in the community consists of: the retirement pension, means-tested income support with special premiums for the very old and the disabled, housing benefit, attendance allowances and, for those who provide care, the invalid care allowance.  Small reductions in liability for direct income tax are available to all the elderly whose incomes are sufficient to be taxable.  Those who financially support their elderly relatives may also claim small income tax allowances.  There are no statutory requirements for employers to allow employees to take leave to care for the elderly.  The attendance allowance and the invalid care allowance (both described below) are the recognition that the social security system gives to the financial costs of caring.

A central problem for the elderly who wish to remain in their own homes is that these benefits are both low in value and quite difficult to obtain: subject to strict tests of need and of financial means. It is often easier to obtain state support for the fees of private residential and nursing homes. Institutional care payments are available from the social security system, without any test of need, to all residents who have assets of less than £3000. They are currently between £190 and £250 a week depending on the type of home (though this is usually lower than the actual fees—often well over £250 a week—leaving the old people or their families to find the difference).

A further problem for many of the elderly is that means-tested help with living expenses, housing costs and residential care is only available to those who have largely spent their savings. Full benefit is usually only available to those with less than £3000 in savings (in 1991). For those with between £3000 and £8000 the benefits are sharply tapered. This rule disqualifies many hundreds of thousands of elderly people from state help and encourages a "spend-down" or "pauperisation" effect.

Furthermore, state payments for residential care are means-tested but not needs-tested like the community care benefits. The only requirement is acceptance by a public or private home. Consequently, at a time when it is in principle government policy to encourage people to remain at home as long as possible, the fastest growing item in expenditure has been subsidies to residential care (Audit Commission 1986). By the end of 1988 social security expenditure on residential care in private-sector homes was costing almost £1000 million a year, a 100% increase in 2 years (Brindle 1988). Expenditure on this form of demand-determined care was effectively out of control and seriously undermining the government's policy commitment to care in the community.

Some benefits are paid only to those amongst the elderly who have recognised care needs. The most important of these is the *Attendance Allowance* which is tax-free and can be paid to any person, irrespective of any other income, who is judged to need regular help with daily living. The need assessment is made by a doctor on the basis of a home visit. Those judged to need constant attention, both day and night, receive the full rate, £41.65 a week in 1991. Those who require help only at night get the partial rate of £27.80 a week. In 1990 about 700,000 elderly, 7% of the 65+ population, received the attendance allowance (Horton and Berthoud 1990).

Perhaps the most innovative benefit of recent years has been the *Invalid*

*Care Allowance*, introduced in 1976. This benefit is paid to those who give up full-time work in order to care for a disabled dependent. Initially it was payable only to men and single women. Married women were excluded on the assumption that their caring did not involve a forfeit of earnings. This exception was ruled illegal by the European Court in 1986 and some 85,000 married women are expected to benefit. Up to 1986 only about 10,000 people were receiving the allowance. However, although the invalid care allowance is an important recognition in principle of the costs of caring, in practice it provides a poor substitute for lost earnings, paying only £31.25 a week in 1991.

The rules governing state payments to the elderly and their carers are complex and the take-up of the benefits remains low compared with the numbers living in the community. Financial support for domiciliary care has developed in an ad hoc way as governments have realised the advantages of allowing the dependent elderly to remain in their own homes. However, there are still strong financial incentives to place the elderly in residential care. The "community care benefits" are subject to stringent needs tests which mean that only the most severely dependent and their carers are eligible. In addition, the amounts paid are relatively small. Even where all possible payments are being received, the amount would usually be less than half what the state would pay if the old person went into a residential home.

## Social Support for the Frail Elderly

Table 2.2 is an attempt to give an idea of the range of services available, the variety of sources from which they may come and the chances that someone 65 or over may be receiving them.

What the table essentially demonstrates is that public services are relatively marginal to the lives of most of the elderly most of the time. The main reason is, of course, that most do not need or want help. However, we do know, for example, that some 24% of people 75 and over cannot go out of their houses on their own and that 17% cannot get up and down stairs (GHS 1985). Their principal sources of help are informal, from family and kin.

The chief forms of service available to support the elderly in the community are: home helps, home nursing, luncheon clubs and day care, meals on wheels, care attendant and sitting services, respite residential care

Table 2.2    Use of home care services by people 65+ during the previous month, 1985

|  | 65-74 % | 75+ % |
|---|---|---|
| Casualty or outpatient dept. of hospital | 21.3 | 12.9 |
| Doctor at surgery | 27.2 | 17.8 |
| Doctor at home | 11.3 | 11.9 |
| Home nurse | 3.5 | 8.4 |
| Home help | 4.2 | 13.5 |
| Day centre or lunch club | 6.9 | 7.1 |
| Meals on wheels | 0.8 | 5.1 |

GHS 1985

and social work support. Since these are nearly all services that are the responsibility of local government, their quantity, quality and range vary enormously across the country. The chief ones are outlined below:

The most common form of assistance is the *home help*. These are almost always women, usually employed part-time by the local social services department. Home helps call on the elderly (and other disabled) for a regular number of hours each week and assist with a whole range of household tasks: cleaning, laundry, shopping and sometimes cooking. They are much less often involved in personal care tasks like dressing and bathing. By no means all the elderly will receive a home help; this is the case for currently only about 7% of the over 65s (SSI 1987). Both need and ability to pay are assessed by a home visit. Although less than 10% overall of the cost of the service is met from user charges, about half of recipients will have to pay something. The chance of getting home help and the amount received vary enormously across the country. Some local authorities spend nearly twice what others do per head of population (Audit Commission 1985). Large numbers of high-need elderly do not get the service at all, often because they are helped by their families. Those who do receive it get limited and partial assistance. Two or three hours a week is most common. There is a tradition in the working of the service which emphasises "cover," reaching as many people as possible, rather than "intensity," providing enough service to make a substantial difference to a person's quality of life. Consequently, in most cases the home help service is insufficient to ensure that the high-need elderly can continue to live at home. This is changing, however. Unable to expand overall expenditure, an increasing number of authorities are redesigning their home help services so as to focus more intensely on the most needy—those on the margin of requiring residential care. These policies mean that the service must be withdrawn from many who hitherto would have expected to receive it.

*Home nursing services* are provided by the local health authority and traditionally there have been problems of cooperation between them and local government which provides most of the other domiciliary services. Elderly people at home are most likely to be dealt with by a "district nurse." These are qualified nurses who work in teams together with some support from junior nurses and auxiliaries. About 20% of the elderly will receive care from a district nurse during the year; about 6% will be seen in a month (OPCS 1981; 1982). However, the help received will be fairly limited, largely of a medical nature such as the giving of injections, changing of dressings and possibly help with bathing. Visits are relatively brief, about 20 minutes or so. Most district nurses are attached to GP practices and in most cases, 70%, visits follow a referral from a GP. The next most common reason for referral is when an elderly person leaves hospital (OPCS 1982). As a result, the district nursing service is largely a source of partial help at times of acute, almost emergency need.

After home helps the most common service the elderly at home are likely to receive is a place at a *day centre or day hospital* (Tester 1989). At any one time about 6% of the over 65s benefit in this way. In practice very few of those attending are likely to be under 75. Day hospital places, reaching about 1%, do not differ greatly from day centres except that the routine provision of baths and simple medical attention, giving of drugs or physiotherapy, is more common. Whether an elderly person is attending a day hospital or a day centre run by the local authority or by a voluntary organisation is often a matter of accident and what is available in their vicinity. Day care is not a precisely targeted service. Many of the most needy do not attend. Indeed the more immobile are less likely to be willing or able to manage the journey to the centre. Travel to day hospitals is usually by ambulance and to day centres by "mini-bus." A high proportion of day centres are run by voluntary organisations, particularly by the national charity Age Concern, though a substantial proportion of their financing (usually about 75%) comes from grants and fees paid by the local authority. The central feature of the day centre routine is the provision of lunch and some of those attending may come simply for that. Most luncheon clubs take place in a day centre. Like many of the domiciliary services, day care is only of partial help to the dependent elderly and their carers. Attendance on more than two days a week is rare, allowing each day centre place to be shared over the week between four to five elderly persons. The elderly are often returned home as early as 3 or 4 o'clock in the afternoon and the centres do not run over the weekends.

Some 3% of the elderly, 5% of the over 75s, receive meals delivered to their own homes—"*meals on wheels*" (GHS 1985). Many of the recipients are those living on their own. Again, however, the service is not comprehensive in that the deliveries will not occur over weekends and most receive them on only two or three weekdays. The meals, pre-cooked and chilled for reheating or hot meals in insulated containers, are most often delivered by volunteers in their own cars or special vans. These deliveries do provide a limited opportunity to check whether the old person is all right. However, again, many of the highly dependent do not receive this service; it is not particularly popular. About a third of the cost of the service is obtained from charges to the users.

*Care attendant and sitting services* are increasingly common but national data are not available. The detailed characteristics of these schemes vary across the country but the broad outlines are similar. Their main function is to relieve the informal, family carers of disabled and elderly people. Care attendants may be volunteers, sometimes younger retired people, or they may receive a small payment for their time. They look after the dependent person while their carer goes out, usually for 4 to 5 hours but sometimes overnight as well. The care attendant is usually trained and prepared to do all the tasks that the normal carer does. Although most referrals come from the state services, these schemes are almost always run by voluntary organisations. The best known model is the Crossroads Care Attendant Scheme, the first having been set up in Rugby in 1974 (Bristow 1981). Sitting schemes tend to be even more informally organised. They are often run by local associations of carers. They are an equivalent of baby sitting but for elderly dependents instead. Volunteer sitters come round for an evening or for a few hours in the day while the permanent carer goes out.

*Respite residential care*, sometimes known as short-stay residential care, is where an elderly person goes into residential care for an occasional short stay, often while their principal carer goes on holiday, or where the old person goes into a home on a regular basis, say one month out of every three. Almost all of the 3000 or so residential homes in England accept residents on this basis. Indeed more than half the receptions into homes are for short stays. However, only about 2% of the residents at any one time are short stay. That means that in an average home there may be only one or two short-stay residents at a time. There are also a very few homes that specialise in short stays. Although the system offers considerable relief to carers, but often with problems when the old person returns home, this is a service which is not particularly liked by the old people or by the homes themselves. Both find it disturbing to regular patterns of life (Allen 1983).

*Social workers* are largely employed by the local government social services departments. There are about 25,000 of them (full-time equivalents) in England (HPSS 1988). However, as well as being responsible for the care of the elderly, they must provide care for other needy groups in the community: children and families, the mentally ill and the disabled. It can be estimated that about 35% of social worker time is spent on care of the elderly (Audit Commission 1986: 97). This means that there is only about the equivalent of 1.2 social workers to every 1000 over 65, or about 3 to every 1000 over 75. In the best areas these figures might be doubled by the provision of unqualified care assistants. The consequence is that social workers tend to intervene in the lives of the elderly only at crisis points when a key care decision must be made, usually about entry into residential care or when support arrangements must be made for someone returning home after a time in hospital. Social workers cannot provide much in the way of direct, routine care, and where they do so they are likely to be allocating their time very inequitably, ignoring many needy cases. In recognition of this there has long been a debate about whether social workers should be the key care organisers or case managers for the elderly and a number of local experiments into how this might be done have taken place. The recent "Griffiths Report" (1988) supported this central managerial role for social workers but it has not yet become a significant reality. At present social workers enter the lives of the dependent elderly very infrequently compared with doctors or home helps and there is no clear public image of their caring role.

## The Family and Community Care

It has long been understood by researchers in this field that by far the largest part of care for the elderly in the community has been provided by families (e.g. Townsend 1963). However, often little account was taken of this reality by public policy. Numerous studies have shown how poorly integrated social services are with informal care and how insensitive they can be to the needs of carers (Pitkeathly 1989; Lewis and Meredith 1988; Qureshi and Walker 1989). There is some evidence that the provision of public support tends to be inversely related to the supply and commitment of informal care, particularly when that care is provided by women (Parker 1990; Twigg et al. 1990). This knowledge about the central role played by informal carers only began to play a central role in policy debate in the 1980s and it did so for two reasons.

The first was that the issue was taken up by feminist social researchers who began to document in detail the work and burden of caring (Ungerson, ed. 1990). Secondly came the realisation on the part of government and policy makers that quite small reductions in the supply of family care could have substantial costs for the public sector if it had to fill the gap (Audit Commission 1986). As a result, more recent policy documents like the Griffiths Report (1988) and the White Paper, *Caring For People* (Cm 849, 1989) have been far more explicit about the need to work with and support the family in its caring role.

Until quite recently, data on the amount of family care for dependent adults was uncertain because it was based on the very small samples obtained by individual researchers. Lately, however, this has been corrected by two very large scale studies. In 1985, the General Household Survey, which is a national sample of over 12,000 households, included detailed questions on caring for dependent adults (Green 1988). It was discovered that one adult in seven (14% or over 6 million people in Great Britain) was supplying "some regular service for a sick, handicapped or elderly person living in their own or another household." Three percent of people gave 20 hours a week or more to this caring role. Although women were more likely to be carers than men, and in particular were more likely to be doing heavy caring, the gender divisions were not as great as some had previously expected. The value of this caring work has been estimated as between £15-24 billion a year, more than the state expenditure on the National Health Service (Family Policy Studies Centre 1989).

These findings have been confirmed and supplemented by the National Disability Survey which has looked at the sources of support for disabled people living in the community (OPCS 1990). It was found that only 7% of the disabled are in institutions and that the vast majority are supported by their families.  Disability was rated along a scale of 1 to 10 and amongst those in the severest categories, 9 and 10, 86% were cared for informally in private households.  The formal sector was found to be supplying very little help with self care (4%), or with household activities (12%).

This raw demographic data needs to be put into the context of a more sociological understanding of the changing role of the family in modern Britain.  The surveys are snapshots in time, indicating those involved in caring in one week or one month.  What they imply is that the chances of any adult becoming the carer of another adult at some point in their lives are very great and are increasing.  High rates of marriage and family formation throughout the postwar period coupled with substantially increased life expectancy mean that the three-generational and even the four-generational family is common.  The different generations in these families may not live together in the same households but there is much evidence that regular contact and support between the generations remain very high (Willmott 1986).  For example, amongst women with children who work, well over half of the consequent substitute childcare is done by grandmothers (Martin and Roberts 1984).  This caring is almost always a product of kinship and it is becoming even more explicitly central to the planning of public policy at a time when the family as an institution is undergoing rapid change and is clearly under strain.  It is not certain that traditional social definitions of family obligation and particularly of women's obligations to care will be sustained in the future.

The divorce rate in Britain is one of the highest in the world; four out of ten marriages now fail (Haskey 1990).  One child in four now lives in a reconstituted family or with a lone parent (Kiernan and Wicks 1990). It is not clear that these children will feel the same obligations to care for their elderly parents, nor that their parents will expect it.  It must be said that research does still appear to show that a majority still accept that children have a duty to care for their elderly parents (Finch and Mason 1990).  This is reflected in the remarkable statistic that in Britain, outside institutional care, 23% of single women over 80 live with their children (CSO 1987). Finch and Mason found that 57% of their sample of adults disagreed with the proposition that children had no obligation to care for their parents, but at the same time 39% did agree with this view.  It seems that cultural ideas about caring obligations relate almost solely to children and parents (very few extend this obligation to other members of the family), that these ideas are not universal throughout the community and that they are changing.

In particular, there is evidence that filial obligations to care are not seen as absolute and uncontingent (Finch 1989). Rather, they are to be assessed in terms of a daughter or son's other obligations and duties. The rule that children should care for their parents is not incontestable but is perceived as a starting point for negotiation within families. Furthermore, over half the sample in Finch and Mason's study believed that where there was an available alternative to family care, such as state care or paid-for care, then that was to be preferred. These contingent definitions of family obligation are particularly under threat from the growth of married women's employment. In Britain today 75% of married women with children aged over 10 are in work (GHS 1989). This is not just a product of economic necessity. It is clear that many women today regard employment as a right and do not accept traditional assumptions about a woman's "natural role" in relation to home and care. This view is likely to receive material confirmation in a society where low birthrates mean an inevitable decline in the number of young people available to enter the labour market. Economists project that in Britain in the 1990s eight out of ten new jobs will have to be filled by women (Moss 1988). There are real reasons to believe that many more women will have other commitments to weigh against their "obligation" to care.

The role of the family in the care of the elderly is therefore complicated, varied and ambiguous. Traditional assumptions and practices remain strong and important. Family care remains by far the most important form of social care for old people. On the other hand, public policy makers need to be very careful about relying on these institutions. Family practices are much more varied than they used to be. The values of kinship obligation have to compete with others to do with work and independence. Patterns of household formation are similarly more varied and the consequent arrangements more fragile and, in that sense, less reliable. Public policy about caring must operate in much more varied and uncertain territory.

## Voluntary Provision

It appears to be the received opinion in other countries that in Britain voluntary organisations play a significant part in the provision of personal care services.  In some senses this is true.

There is a long tradition of volunteering in Britain.  Particularly amongst certain sections of the middle classes, contributing some of one's time to participation in a voluntary organisation is almost a cultural norm. It should be remembered that in some other societies this sort of activity would be largely under the auspices of the churches.  Indeed, in Britain too, if one consults any of the directories of voluntary organisations, one finds that church-based societies predominate in the lists of those concerned with the welfare of the elderly.  However, Britain is a secular society: less than 4% of the population attend a church on a regular basis, and consequently most volunteering is secular too.

The chances of a dependent old person in the community receiving some help from the voluntary sector remain surprisingly low.  In most small towns there will be a volunteer bureau which helps to direct those wishing to do voluntary work to suitable organisations.  However, only a small part of this volunteering impulse will be directed at the elderly, despite the fact that they constitute one of the largest groups in need.  Their care is still seen primarily as a private matter and a family responsibility.  Of those elderly living in the community who need regular help with the performance of some activity of daily living, only 2% receive informal assistance from someone outside their family (GHS 1985).  One of the principal aims of those voluntary organisations in this area is to relieve family carers. Nonetheless, a recent study has estimated that of the 4.5 million informal carers of the elderly in Britain only 4% received regular voluntary assistance and, in the case of those carers who were living in the same household as the old person, the figure was only 1% (Green 1988).

The most established part of the voluntary sector's contribution to the care of the elderly is in the provision of residential and nursing homes.  In 1986 there were over 1000 voluntary homes for the elderly providing for 25,121 people (compared with 101,704 in the state sector and 77,557 in the private, for-profit sector) (HPSS 1988).  Amongst these institutions are some of the best and most innovatory.

In the community the major contribution of the voluntary organisations is not to care in the home but to offer day care: the provision of day centres, lunch clubs and transport to and from them are the predominant activities. These services are often run on behalf of, or in partnership with, the local authorities and are substantially funded by them.

As well as these established areas of activity, the voluntary sector does play an important role in the generation and testing of innovatory ideas. Most of the schemes described later began as voluntary initiatives.

Self-help groups of informal carers of the elderly have emerged increasingly over the last decade. As this is a distinctively unbureaucratised part of the voluntary sector, it is difficult to assess its size and impact. The Carers' National Association, a very small organisation with, until recently, only one paid organiser, has encouraged carers to set up local groups. These are sometimes initiated by local social workers or representatives of Age Concern. The carers will usually ask one or two local social service professionals to join the voluntary management committee. The function of these local groups is to allow members to compare notes, exchange information and to lobby local social service providers. They often organise a cooperative sitting service as well. However, it is clear that only a very small proportion of carers become involved in these groups and there is some evidence that they tend to be the most articulate and informed, and often middle class (Ungerson 1987: 33-4). Paradoxically, therefore, these organisations may generate inequalities in access to domiciliary care services, allowing their better-informed and less-isolated members to obtain a relatively privileged position. A recent national survey has confirmed the view that very large numbers of carers carry out their task with no outside support at all. This is particularly true of elderly people caring for a spouse: 70% did so with no outside help (Green 1988).

In recent years the voluntary organisations have increasingly found themselves pulled into financial partnerships with government. This has been partly a result of the availability of short-term, special project funds where government prefers to contract out the administration and provision of service rather than commit itself directly to the employment of staff. It has also been partly a consequence of the availability of funds primarily directed to occupying and training the unemployed. This has been a mixed blessing for the voluntary organisations. On one hand, it has provided them with funds and the opportunity to experiment with new services. On the other hand, they have found themselves sacrificing their autonomy and have risked providing rather unpredictable services to fragile clients. Government employment priorities and funding have tended to change rather abruptly and the voluntary organisations have been given almost no role in the planning and design of these programmes (Brenton 1985).

In short, while the voluntary sector plays a high profile role in both the provision of services, particularly the more innovatory sort, and in the policy debates about the care of the elderly, one must be careful not to exaggerate their impact upon the daily lives of most frail old people. The primary sources of home care remain family carers and, to a much lesser extent, the state. Where gaps occur, the voluntary sector attempts to step in and fill the space. But it is far too small relative to the size of the problem to do so always or to be relied upon to do so.

## Private and For-Profit Home Care Services

This is a subject of increasing discussion amongst the policy research community (e.g. Leat and Gay 1987; Midwinter 1986). However, the 1985 General Household Survey reveals that only 1% of the elderly needing help with an activity of daily living had used paid help in the last month (GHS 1985).

Completely private, ad hoc arrangements between client and paid carer are by their very nature undocumented. However, while there is a tradition of paying someone to help with housework, this does not readily extend to the provision of personal care tasks: help with toiletting, dressing and eating. Certainly there is no evidence that such paid assistance is widespread.

There is increasing evidence of the setting up of private-care agencies, often by former nurses or social workers (Midwinter 1986). Again there is an existing tradition, that of the private nursing agency offering (usually quite expensive) home nursing for invalids. However, what is observed here is the extension of these activities to the provision of personal care services: a service somewhere midway between simple housework and skilled nursing. Some of the private agencies aimed at the elderly offer a very wide range of services from house maintenance, housework and shopping to night attendance, personal care and nursing. The appearance of these agencies is taken to indicate that there is now money to be made where previously only expensive, medical services were profitable. It is argued by some that this trend will develop as more of the elderly retire on generous pensions, as the reservoir of informal carers shrinks for demographic and employment reasons and as the public home care services target their resources more selectively.

The principal problems of the British home care services may therefore be summarised:

*Low intensities of service*: Public services tend to sacrifice really useful levels of care to coverage of a larger number of clients but at a low level of input. In practice, the most common source of help is from informal family helpers, most often wives and daughters. These are often very intense caring relationships and may involve most of the hours of the day.

*Territorial variations in the supply of services*: A major problem with national figures of service use is that they hide huge variations between different parts of the country. This is very marked in the case of domiciliary care. One local authority might be spending seven times as much as another on day care and nearly four times as much on meals on wheels (Audit Commission 1985). Services are seen to be very weak in deprived inner cities, so much so that one commentator has doubted whether community care facilities can be said to exist in inner London (Roberts 1982).

*Poor targetting*: A persistent problem in the delivery of all Britain's health and social services has been a failure to reach those in the greatest need. This is particularly true of domiciliary services where case finding mechanisms are weak or non-existent. The services only reach those who ask or who, by chance, they have come to know (SSI 1987: 15).

*Fragmentation of services, little coordination in their use*: With so many sources, and varied points of origin, it is clear that resources spent on the domiciliary care system will only be used efficiently and effectively if there is a high degree of cooperation and coordination. Unfortunately, this is not the rule. None of the principal professional groups, general practitioners, community nurses and social workers, sees care of the elderly as their primary responsibility and none has the power nor the incentives to coordinate care.

In short, the principal problem with the British domiciliary care services for the elderly is that they were not initially evolved in order to deal with the very frail. It was always implicitly assumed, quite wrongly, that once people reached the point where they needed daily personal care, they would go into an institution. The domiciliary services evolved as "off the shelf," partial services which would be more or less universally available to those who asked for them. Case management would be by the consumer or their carer. Demographic changes have rendered this model irrelevant.

The growth in numbers of severely dependent people in the community, many of them on their own and unwilling to move from their homes, has created the need for services of a new and different kind, more comprehensive, more intensive and better organised.

## THE EVOLUTION OF THE POLICY DEBATE

"Community care" has been an avowed aim of all British governments since the 1950s. However, the reality has been slow to follow. The term was first extensively used in connection with the care of the mentally ill and the intention to close down the large asylums inherited from the nineteenth century. This was a slower process than initially envisaged but by 1990 80% of the places in those institutions had been closed, and the vast majority of the mentally ill now live in the community but receive very uncertain support (House of Commons 1985).

As the growth in the numbers of the frail elderly increased rapidly after 1970, so the focus of policy debate shifted to how they might be cared for outside institutions, where most of them were already. The most prominent manifestation of this debate was a steady stream of government documents about the problem. These government publications took a number of forms: white papers indicating broad policy intentions, reports of special committees either from within government (the Social Services Inspectorate and the Audit Commission) or funded by it (The National Institute of Social Work and the results of commissioned research from universities and other special units). The first White Paper (the British term for a fundamental statement of government policy) on the elderly was published in 1981, *Growing Older* (Cmnd 8173). This argued that not only was the community, their own homes, the best and most desirable place for the elderly to live, but that for the most part their support should not come from the state but from the informal and voluntary sectors: "These spring from the personal ties of kinship, friendship and neighbourhood. They are irreplaceable. It is the role of the public authorities to sustain and, where necessary, develop—but never to displace—such support and care. Care in the community must increasingly mean care by the community" (Cmnd 8173: 8.1).

However, little practical change followed from these broad policy intentions. By the mid-1980s the pressure of numbers combined with severe constraints on public expenditure meant that public care provision had tended to become no more than a reactive crisis service which was responding unpredictably and inefficiently. The care services began to come under the gaze of accountants rather than social scientists. A series of investigations by central and local government auditors revealed that not only was little spent on community care compared with institutional support, but that what money was spent was very poorly spent (Audit Commission 1985, 1986; National Audit Office 1987; Public Accounts Committee 1988). Many of the most needy in the community were getting little or nothing: public authorities had no clear targetting or case finding mechanisms. Little was known about the benefits of the services that were received. In particular, there was little evidence that they prevented entry into institutions. At the same time the auditors demonstrated that public subsidies for residential care through the social security system were effectively out of control and that very large sums were being spent expanding a form of care which public policy was dedicated to reducing.

The government response was, in 1987, to commission a report on community care from Sir Roy Griffiths, former managing director of the Sainsbury's supermarket chain and the man responsible for an earlier and far-reaching report on the National Health Service.

March 1988 saw the publication of the Griffiths Report and this short document of 28 pages will eventually lead to major changes in social policy for the care of the elderly and other dependent groups in the community. The report's remit was "to review the way in which public funds are used to support community care policy and to advise ... on the options for action that would improve the use of these funds as a contribution to more effective community care." The option of advising increased expenditure was therefore explicitly cut off. However, Griffiths was careful to point out that he did not recommend any reduction in expenditure and, in a number of places, he remarked on the scarcity of resources relative to the size of the tasks.

The report is in fact largely a list of recommendations. Griffiths saw the fundamental fault of the existing system as the lack of precise accountability for the performance of key care tasks. Firstly, no single state bureaucracy has ultimate responsibility for the provision of community care. Secondly, within the bureaucracies it is rare for specific individuals to have responsibility for ensuring the provision of services to particular clients. The report recommended an almost legalistic fixing of responsibility to particular departments and officials. "My intention is to pinpoint responsibility for arranging the provision of resources in the community " (Griffiths 1988: para. 6.13).

That responsibility was to be very firmly pinned on the local authority social services departments. It was not primarily a responsibility to provide the services themselves but to ensure that care is provided by someone. The local authorities were: to "identify people with community needs in their area," to ensure that all other public authorities consider these cases and provide services where appropriate, to develop and sustain informal and voluntary care, and to encourage the use of private services. Where individuals need a high level of services, the local authorities should appoint "care managers" to oversee continuous assessment and provision of services. Griffiths reflected the evolution of the policy debate to date by giving content to the present government's ideological preference for pluralist and, where possible, market provision of services.

The government's response to the Griffiths Report did not emerge until December 1989 with the publication of the White Paper, *Caring for People* (Cm 849). This was quickly followed by the necessary legislation in the National Health Service and Community Care Act 1990, and the date initially set for the commencement of the new system of community support for dependent people was April 1, 1991. Since then the government has announced that financial and organisational constraints mean that many of the changes will have to be delayed and introduced over a number of years.

The core recommendation from Griffiths accepted by the government was that, where possible, government money currently available to support people in residential institutions should also be available to care for them in their own homes. To this end, money will be transferred from central government to the local authorities whose social service staff will be required to assess the needs of all old people asking for help and on the basis of these assessments to allocate resources either to domiciliary support or to the provision of care in an institution.

It is this double power, both to assess needs and to supply the funds and services to individuals, that has received much criticism. It is not clear how citizens' entitlements to service and rights of choice and appeal are to be protected. Nonetheless, despite the facts that the speed of implementation and the exact nature of the new arrangements are still unclear, they do in principle promise a more varied and effective system of support: a variety of providers, public, voluntary and private, will be encouraged to supply the new market for care; assessments of need will be more systematically carried out; and carers are explicitly recognised as central to the caring system.

In addition, local authorities will be required to ensure in cases of high need that a case manager is identified who has overall responsibility for coordinating services and ensuring they are supplied. The case manager could be a carer but, where necessary, local authority social workers will have to fill this role. Thus the white paper and the subsequent legislation have made targeting and the management of resources at the level of the individual the central tasks of community care.

## INNOVATION AND EXPERIMENTATION IN HOME CARE

Since the beginning of the postwar British welfare state, but increasingly over the last 15 years, the major service providers to the elderly have tended to generate innovations as alternatives where their prime services could not meet demand.

Housing departments provided visiting wardens and alarms to check regularly on old people in their own homes in the same way as if they had entered sheltered housing.

Social services departments set up "good neighbour" schemes which would check regularly on old people who were not eligible for a home help or whose home helps could not visit often enough. For more needy clients, schemes were set up which aimed to sustain them in their own homes at the level of care they would have got in an old people's home. These schemes have a variety of names: "neighbourly helps," "care aides," "care attendants," "augmented home help," "intensive home help" and "community care schemes."

Hospital staff recreated the equivalent of hospital care, both long-term and short-term, in people's own homes and set up home care schemes that would allow them to release people into the community more quickly after treatment.

These schemes tend to be partial in their nature. That is, they are rarely comprehensively available to all an agency's relevant population. Even when the schemes cease to be merely pilots or experimental, they are not usually available to everyone who might be eligible but remain very local. Only rarely have the small schemes described here been followed by their adoption, top-down, as services available to everyone.

## Types of Innovation

The archetypal bottom-up innovation in Britain generally emerges at the very local level, even at the level of the individual case, when existing services simply fail to meet even minimum expectations. The three most common care problems that old people face are that:

i.  none of the available services provides what they need (e.g. companionship, moral support, out-of-hours emergency service);

ii.  they require a coordinated mixture of the existing services (e.g. social care with a health input, housing with a social care input);

iii.  they need to move back and forth between these care sectors (usually between care at home and care in a hospital).

The innovator is a lively individual who works for one of the major suppliers of care: the social service, the health service, the housing department or a voluntary organisation. She encounters clients for whom the services she can provide are not a sufficient or an ideal solution. Neither can she insist that a part or the whole of one of the other services be provided. This condition can occur not only when services are stagnant or contracting. It can happen when they are expanding. Hence, bottom-up innovations were common even during the expansionary phase of care services. Two solutions are available to the innovator:

i.  use some of the resources already within her control to construct a new service that fills the gap;

ii.  win the support of one or some of the other suppliers in the construction of a new combination of existing services. This usually requires considerable skills in persuasion.

In both cases the use of resources in this way means they will not be available for the uses they were previously put to. Some, possibly less needy, clients may lose out.

Thus the two most common types of innovation here are relatively informal joint teams of front-line workers from health and social services or the creation of new forms of care that will fill the gaps.  Social services typically fund care attendants or helpers who will provide personal care more intensively or who will attend in unsocial hours.  Housing departments provide street wardens or care attendants.  Voluntary organisations set up sitting services or recruit gap-filling care workers.

In fact, the flexible care attendant, care assistant or paid volunteer is one of the most common consequences of service innovation, particularly for the dependent elderly.  A frail old person at home needs help with whatever needs doing, whenever it has to be done.  In short, they require time and flexibility.  Both of these are expensive for established organisations.  In order to ration scarce labour, they only do particular things at certain times.  In consequence, the core achievement of many innovations is actually no more than the discovery of a cheaper supply of labour.

The key problem with these bottom-up initiatives is that it is very difficult to tell whether they add to the overall efficiency of the care system.  They are micro responses to local care vacuums.  Whether funded out of existing base budgets or some sort of "new money," they inevitably have an opportunity cost for the existing mainstream services and their clients.  At the very local level it is usually difficult to assess relative costs and benefits and, anyway, in practice no attempt is usually made to do so.

Top-down innovations have very different motivations behind them.  Generally, they only occur when managers cannot raise budgets fast enough to satisfy the demand (or expressed need) for their services.  Therefore, they rarely occur during times of fast base-budget growth when managers tend to respond to growing need simply by expanding the existing service even if it is inappropriate for some clients.  Once budget growth falls behind the growth in need, three kinds of solution present themselves:

i.   The manager can target an existing service more accurately, thus excluding some lower-need people who have hitherto been getting the service.  This solution tends to divert pressure to other parts of the care system.  For example, in Britain hospital managers have unilaterally cut the number of geriatric beds, arguing that old people should only be in hospital when they have a medical rather than a social need.

ii.  The manager, if responsible for several linked services, may attempt to sharpen the boundaries between them and shift clients towards the more cost-effective service.  Hence some social service managers have been reducing residential care in order to increase funding for their domiciliary services.

iii. A manager may create a new, more cost-effective service and shift clients to it. A hospital may develop a "hospital-at-home" scheme; a social services department may develop a new "intensive" or "augmented care" service. Such services may well involve the cooperation of providers from other services, for example, social workers and home helps, and therefore be similar to the bottom-up innovation ii.

Not included in this list is an increasingly popular form of "quasi innovation" in Britain: one that just shifts the costs of existing care to another budget. For example, local authorities are turning their residential homes into "independent" housing associations whose costs can then be substantially covered by the residents claiming rent from the social security budget.

## Case Management Schemes

It may surprise readers in America, where there has been long experimentation in case management and now some disillusionment with its potential (Callahan 1989), to learn that the most influential innovations in Britain have been those that use this approach and that they are to some extent seen as a method of cost containment. The White Paper which introduced the reforms currently taking place stated:

> Case management provides an effective method of targetting resources and planning services to meet specific needs of individual clients. The approach has been successfully employed in a number of schemes and projects, some of the best known of which are in Kent, Gateshead and Durham. Case management systems have been an important feature of a number of the Department of Health's Care in the Community pilot projects. The government believes that the wider introduction of the key principles of case management would confer considerable benefit, and will seek to encourage their application more widely (Cm 849, 1989: 3.3.3).

Given the centrality of the schemes mentioned, it is appropriate to describe them in some detail.

## The Kent and Gateshead Community Care Experiments (1977-86)

These have been the most influential of all the recent British initiatives and have led to many imitations in different parts of the country. The object of the scheme, which was closely studied by a team from the nearby University of Kent (Challis and Davies 1986), was to test the feasibility of home care for very frail old people, usually living on their own, and who normally would have been candidates for institutional care.

From the clients' point of view the objective was to supply care in the community at least as good and comprehensive as residential care. From the social services departments' point of view the object was to experiment with a system of service provision which would ensure the performance of the key care tasks in the most efficient, effective and reliable ways. The principal way of achieving this was the creation of the role of "case manager" within an organisational framework which would, it was hypothesised, provide the incentives necessary for the optimum performance of that role.

During the experimental periods, care was provided for highly dependent elderly people (97 in Kent, 90 in Gateshead). They were matched with control samples of similar elderly people. For the experimental group the system of "case management" replaced the normal system of care that would have operated. Normally the elderly people would probably have received some of: the community nursing service, the home help service, day centre or day hospital care, meals on wheels, social worker visits, voluntary care and informal care by family or friends. However, none of these would have necessarily been available and almost all of them would have been supplied according to their own independent criteria and timetables.

Under the scheme, on the other hand, a single social worker was to oversee all the client's needs. Each social worker had about 30 cases to manage. A key instrument was the development of a chart which mapped out the client's week with the days on the vertical axis and on the horizontal axis the critical periods of the day such as getting up, lunch time and going to bed. Using this simple chart it was possible to identify who was providing for the person's needs and when there were critical gaps.

The case managers were made cost sensitive by allowing them a budget, per client, of up to two thirds of the cost of a residential place.

A good deal of the budgets were consumed by the provision of the existing standard social services: home helps, day centre places, aids and adaptions.  However, the social workers were able to coordinate and vary this provision in more planned and innovative ways.  In almost all cases, meals on wheels were not used and more sociable solutions were evolved, such as meals cooked by a neighbour or by the old person themselves but with help.  In addition, the clients continued to receive National Health Service resources where these seemed suitable and could be obtained.

The major innovation that occurred was the payment of small fees to local people to act as regular "helpers" in the care programme.  "The actual fee paid was agreed between the social worker and the individual helper and varied according to the task to be done, the characteristics of the elderly person, the time the task was done and the circumstances of the helper. Payment was not for time but for the performance of a specific task. Helpers ranged from those with previous caring experience, either as nurses or home-helps or merely informally in their own families, to those, such as young housewives or the recently bereaved, with room in their lives that they wished to fill with a worthwhile activity.  The helpers were usually not in a position to enter the labour market.  The tasks to be undertaken were made explicit in a 'letter of agreement' that clarified the expectations of the social services in return for the fee."

In achieving its basic objectives the scheme was successful.  Most of the experimental sample were able to remain in their own homes for substantially longer than the controls.  In the case of the Kent experiment what was most striking, and unexpected, was the increased longevity of the experimental sample.  "This difference was statistically significant; that is to say the differences are unlikely to have occurred by chance and may be attributed to the effects of the alternative forms of care."  However, this effect was not repeated in the Gateshead experiment.

In terms of admission to residential homes there was also a relative advantage for the community care scheme.   This was, in a sense, to be expected: the object of the experiment was to keep people at home. However, this was not at the expense of their well-being, was certainly in accordance with their wishes and was a pattern that was maintained, albeit to a decreasing degree, to the end of the four years.

In terms of admission to hospital care there was slightly more use by the experimental sample in the third and fourth years. This was because for some the fact of remaining for much longer in their own homes meant that when the time did come for institutional care their physical condition made long-term hospital care the only feasible option. In this way the impact on the hospital service was changed and delayed but not reduced. By the end of the fourth year the proportions of the original samples in institutional care were similar but, due to their longer life expectancies, twice as many of the community care cases remained in their own homes.

Table 2.3    Kent. Location of matched pairs of cases over 4 years

| | Year 1 CC | Year 1 CG | Year 2 CC | Year 2 CG | Year 3 CC | Year 3 CG | Year 4 CC | Year 4 CG |
|---|---|---|---|---|---|---|---|---|
| | % | | % | | % | | % | |
| Own home | 69 | 34 | 50 | 20 | 35 | 12 | 23 | 11 |
| Res. care | 12 | 27 | 20 | 34 | 22 | 31 | 15 | 20 |
| Hospital | 4 | 5 | 3 | 3 | 8 | 1 | 5 | 3 |
| Died | 14 | 33 | 26 | 40 | 32 | 53 | 53 | 63 |
| Moved away | 1 | 1 | 1 | 3 | 3 | 3 | 4 | 2 |
| Total no. | 74 | | 74 | | 74 | | 74 | |

CC = community care (experimental group)
CG = comparison group (standard provision)

Gateshead. Location of matched pairs after one year

| | Community care % | Comparison group % |
|---|---|---|
| Own home | 63 | 36 |
| Res. home | 1 | 39 |
| Hospital | 7 | 4 |
| Died | 28 | 20 |
| Moved away | 1 | 1 |
| Total no. | 90 | 90 |

The costs of the care were carefully controlled by giving the case managers budgets equal to only two thirds of the cost of residential care in the area. This cost constraint was averaged over the whole of each case manager's caseload, allowing them to go over the limit on one case so long as others below the limit compensated for this effect.

The elderly did not remain in their own homes to the detriment of their well-being. The experiment was able to demonstrate advantages in the quality of life of the cases in the experimental sample both in terms of their felt well-being and professional assessments of their circumstances. The methods and criteria used in these evaluations were complex and are thoroughly described in Challis and Davies (1986).

## The Darlington (Durham) Community Care Project (1985-88)

One of the chief limitations of the Kent and Gateshead community care experiments was that they were solely innovations initiated and run by the local authority social services departments, and the crucial health services were not integrated into the provision. Instead, the case managers had to do their best to secure the cooperation and understanding of the home nursing service, the GPs and the hospitals. This they often succeeded in doing, but there were instances where health and social services found themselves working at cross-purposes and effectively. The Darlington project involved the integration of health and social care services under one management and the creation of a new breed of home care assistants able and willing to carry out health care, personal and social care tasks and housekeeping.

In this scheme, instead of selecting elderly people at risk of residential care placement, the sample was made up of very frail people who were already in an institution, the Darlington hospital, where they were chronically dependent, long-term patients. The objective was to improve the quality of care and the degree of satisfaction of the old person and their family compared with both long-stay care and the standard home care services. The domestic and caring tasks were undertaken by a single worker: the home care assistant. Again, the cost of home care was budgeted at case level and to be no more than hospital care and preferably less—about 66%.

101 highly dependent old people (65 female, 36 male) were discharged from Darlington hospital to enter the project during the period of the evaluation. They were selected on the basis that they were too frail to return home under normal circumstances but that they were mentally alert. Nonetheless, about a third were later found to have or have developed an appreciable amount of mental confusion. "Only 6% were mobile unaided. 22% were chair or bed-bound. Only 35% were fully continent. Instability was a severe problem for 45% and a third exhibited levels of confusion

indicative of organic brain disease" (Challis et al. 1989).

The outcomes for the 101 cases were compared with 113 cases in a control group population of old people in hospital in neighbouring Durham.

38% of the cases were discharged to live alone in their own homes, 57% to spouse or family care and 6% to non-family care. Support was provided from early morning to going to bed largely by the 83 specially trained home care assistants. These carried out all necessary tasks where possible and irrespective of whether they were housework, personal care or minor medical attention. The project was able to persuade the home nurses and physiotherapists to train the care assistants and delegate some of their more routine tasks.

Each of 3 groups of about 18 assistants was directly responsible to a service manager who performed the day to day case management role for the clients. This is the same key role described in the Kent and Gateshead experiments (case finding, assessment, care planning, monitoring, reviewing). The service managers were also required to design services that produced an average cost of two thirds of hospital care. In practice, the bulk of support was provided by the home care assistants. The service manager was in turn accountable to two tiers of supervisory groups—the multiprofessional project team and the overall Joint Coordinating Group. In this way an integrated acceptance of responsibility by both health and social services was obtained and reliable coordination was ensured.

The project was reasonably successful in the achievement of all of its goals. It was found possible to maintain at home people whose dependency normally means they are in hospital.

**Table 2.4    Destinational outcomes**

| Location | Experimental group | | Control group | |
|---|---|---|---|---|
| | 6 months | 12 months | 6 months | 12 months |
| At home | 67 | 57 | 13 | 10 |
| Hospital | 2 | 2 | 81 | 53 |
| Nursing home | 1 | 2 | 5 | 11 |
| Res. care | - | - | 2 | 4 |
| Dead | 31 | 40 | 12 | 35 |
| | 101 | 101 | 113 | 113 |

The higher death rate amongst the experimental sample is significant. It is partly explained by the fact that 14 of those recruited into the sample were known to be terminal cases who wished to die at home. However, increased stress and slower access to medical care cannot be ruled out.

It was shown to be possible for many tasks that are usually regarded as the responsibility of separate occupations (home helps, nurses, care assistants) to be successfully and more efficiently performed by one person. This in itself is not surprising. Informal, family carers usually mix tasks in this way, but it is unusual to get paid care workers to do so.

A range of scales were used to measure morale and disability outcomes for the two samples. It was found that the experimental sample of old people scored as well or better than the control sample while the scores for the morale of their family carers were markedly higher.

The costs of the experimental home care compared favourably with the institutional alternatives. The experimental project costs were about £196 per week compared with acute hospital costs for the control group of £382. However, the housing costs of home care, largely borne by the clients or their families, were not taken into account. Thus, a large proportion of the savings in community care are achieved by shifting accommodation costs from the public sector to private individuals.

Lastly, the experiment succeeded in adding a new, innovative form of care to that currently available in the Darlington area. In particular, tasks not normally done by service professionals, but essential to the dependent old at home, were performed reliably and effectively. A system of administrative cooperation between health and social services that worked at the level of the individual client was demonstrated.

## The Care in the Community Initiative (1983-88)

The Darlington scheme was itself part of a larger group of projects specifically funded by the British government in order to demonstrate to local authorities and health services what could be achieved in the community care of not only the elderly but also other groups such as the mentally ill and the physically and mentally disabled. These projects are together known as the Care in the Community Initiative. They are built upon the belief that progress in closing long-stay hospital beds and moving care to the community will be faster if it is demonstrated that long-term institutional patients can actually be moved out of hospitals into other forms of care. The Care in the Community pilot projects demonstrated the movement of dependent people out of long-term institutions to an intermediate form of care between hospital and home, mainly very sheltered housing. These projects were generously funded and involved considerable capital spending in the form of new buildings. They have been monitored by the PSSRU (Personal Social Services Research Unit) at the University of Kent which has published both an interim and a final report which describe the philosophy behind the initiative and the methods used to evaluate it (Renshaw et al. 1988; Knapp et al. 1990). The government allocated £19 million to funding 28 projects which from 1983 to 1988 moved some 900 people out of hospitals and permanently closed down those beds. Most of those moved were not the elderly but the mentally ill, the physically disabled and the mentally handicapped. However, seven of the projects involved the elderly or the mentally infirm elderly. Six (Coventry, Winchester, Camberwell, Hillingdon, St. Helens and West Cumbria) moved a total of 135 old people out of long-stay hospitals into very sheltered housing or small group homes. The largest of the new units was for 30 people (St. Helens). Generally the new living arrangements involved separate flatlets or group living by no more than 10 people. In all cases the old people shared the same health and community services supplied to others in the area. The seventh project involving the elderly was the Darlington project, already described.

The final report on the 28 projects was submitted to the Department of Health in June 1989. Its findings are complex and can be summarised only crudely here:

1.  The demonstration projects showed that it is possible to move highly dependent residents of long-stay institutions into community-based housing and to support them with intensive domiciliary services a) without significant measurable losses in welfare and with some limited gains and b) that it is possible to do this within the average costs of the institutional places closed down—usually at about 75% of previous costs.

2.  The main obstacle to shifting resources in this way is the start-up cost: the initial investments in staff and buildings that have to be made before patients can be moved. It will usually be necessary for central government to fund these initial investment costs.

The remarkable feature of the case management schemes described so far is their success in not only achieving levels of welfare at least as acceptable as those achieved in institutional care but also their ability to do so at lower costs. This has not been the general finding in the United States (HCF 1987; Kemper et al. 1987). There it was generally found to be the case that where lower costs were achieved it was because the people recruited by the experiments were not those who would have gone into institutional care in any case. The problem then is that any more generalised provision of case management is likely to raise the overall costs of the care system by drawing into it people who would not otherwise have received support and there may be relatively little impact on rates of institutionalisation. While this effect must remain a possible explanation for the British findings, it seems unlikely given the care with which the samples were selected and the fact that in some cases the clients involved were already in institutions. However, another effect noted in the US literature is perhaps important here, the importance of the free, or nearly free input of informal family care work into the experiments. This is clearly significant in the British cases where "paid volunteers" have been an important effect of case management (Baldock and Ungerson 1991). This potential of case management, carried out by publicly employed professionals, such as social workers, to construct a lower cost mix of public and private care is clearly one of the attractions in a system such as the British one where there is an established, if inadequate, public care service upon which, in the last resort, costs are likely to fall.

Another possible explanation of success in case managed community care is that the projects that have positive results are those that in some way recruit those elderly who put so high a valuation on staying at home that they are prepared to accept, and not see as diswelfare, situations and circumstances that others might find intolerable. This was one of the conclusions of a study designed to test the absolute limits of home care by selecting not only the most frail but also intellectually confused people.

## The Ipswich and Newham Home Support Projects (1984-86)

The aims of these were (i) to support elderly dementia sufferers at home at "acceptable" levels of welfare and (ii) to explore the limits of home care (Askham and Thompson 1990).

"Acceptable meant: effective coordination of social care with nursing and hospital care; care to include the dimension of emotional support the lack of which often precipitates entry to a hospital; care to be an integrated package covering all needs; care to provide for the five "i's" of need—immobility, instability, incontinence, intellectual impairment, informal carers; the service providers to be aware of the costs of the care supplied."

Samples were constructed in Ipswich (a provincial town) and Newham (in inner city London) from elderly referred to psychogeriatric services with OBS (organic brain syndrome) scores of 3 or more. The elderly were allocated to either action (95) or control (71) samples. They were assessed at 6 months and 1 year in terms of destination and measures of confusion and of satisfaction with their situation. In addition, detailed interviews were carried out with all "reliable witnesses" on family, support, housing circumstances, physical and mental health and changes and events since referral.

Two "development officers," one in Ipswich and one in Newham, spent up to £200 a week on providing care services to the clients (compared with estimates of £220 for a psychiatric hospital place and £165 for a residential home). After thorough investigation of what the clients and their family carers, where there were any, wanted and needed, the development officers case-managed packages which included existing domiciliary services where they were suitable (this involved considerable negotiation and continuous monitoring) and filled the gaps with the services of local paid carers. These carers were carefully selected and paid on an hourly basis to cover all needs not otherwise dealt with. In this sense the service differed from the Kent community care model where the paid carers were contracted to perform specific tasks. In Ipswich and Newham the carers were encouraged to claim for as many hours of support as had been necessary. A paid carer worked with only one client at a time.

The projects were not able to keep more people at home for longer.

Neither were any significant differences found in the levels of disablement between the two groups. It was found that in both samples the degree of mental disablement and the degree of physical disablement did not determine whether a client stayed at home. Some of the most extreme cases along both these dimensions remained at home up to 12 months. Case analysis revealed the crucial factors were double incontinence, aggression and wandering. Neither informal carers nor paid carers could cope well with these.

Table 2.5    Keeping people at home

|  | Ipswich | | Newham | |
|---|---|---|---|---|
|  | Action | Control | Action | Control |
| At home (6 months) | 35% | 76% | 46% | 44% |
| At home (1 year) | 22% | 53% | 26% | 6% |

The differences between the action and control samples became apparent only from case by case analyses. The key difference was the ability of the project to keep at home those who had very high OBS scores (8+), who had no informal support *and who wished to stay at home.* 7 such cases were maintained for 12 months in the action sample. There were no similar cases in the control sample.

The weekly costs, borne directly by the service providers, of care for those maintained at home for 12 months or more varied between £100 and £150 a week, not including the housing costs. These figures are appreciably below the costs of institutional care.

This study was deliberately designed to test the limits of home care and therefore selected the most disabled candidates that appeared. One disadvantage of this was that many of those selected were removed to hospital or residential care or died within a few days and before the project inputs could begin. This was particularly true in Ipswich where the availability of institutional care was high. What the study did show was that in those cases where an old person wished to stay at home, irrespective of their disabilities, it was possible to replicate the best quality informal care. But neither the project nor informal carers could cope well with aggression, double incontinence or wandering and, even with the best home care available, formal or informal, many at this level of need prefer to enter an institution. But not all.

## Schemes Which Use Informal Resources

It is not only case managed schemes that have come in many cases to depend for their success on the input of informal care. Earlier it was pointed out that many of the developments in innovative community care in the UK are "bottom-up" responses to the scarcity and inadequacy of the existing provision. The dominant solution here too is to create, encourage or incorporate voluntary and informal caring. In one sense this is simply to extend the status quo. It is already true that state and for-profit organisations do not take on the main responsibility for the care of a dependent old person at home.  We know that this is largely carried out by the more than 4 million informal carers of the elderly, a million of whom will be spending 20 hours a week or more on the caring task (Green 1988). Where informal care is not available, a very dependent old person will, in rare cases, receive comprehensive home care from the statutory services or, much more likely, enter a residential home.  The main contribution of the voluntary sector to home care is to offer various kinds of relief and support to informal carers and thereby compensate for the often observed fact that the statutory services tend to focus on the elderly on their own rather than those with carers (Qureshi and Walker 1989).  Indeed, where the state is involved in the support of informal carers, this tends to be indirectly through the financing of voluntary initiatives aimed at carers.  An excellent survey of services available to carers and of initiatives to improve them is provided by Twigg et al. (1990).

This traditional division of labour between the state and the voluntary sectors in their contribution to home care may be changing.  A number of studies have observed that the marginal benefits won by the state home care services may be greater where they assist the carers of dependent old people rather than old people on their own (Levin et al. 1989; Bebbington et al. 1989). It may well be more efficient for the state to care for carers than to do the home care itself.  However, so far it has not done so and the rest of this section concentrates on voluntary rather than statutory initiatives to help carers.

Judith Oliver, former director of the Carers' National Association, has succinctly and comprehensively described the main needs of carers (Oliver and Briggs 1985).  They are: early identification, information and advice, comprehensive medical and social assessment, continuing back-up and review, and regular relief from caring.  There are initiatives, mainly voluntary, across the country to tackle one or more of these.

The most common method of support for informal carers is to offer them a respite from their responsibility.  Respite care may be for anything between a few hours and several weeks.  It may take the form of a substitute carer coming into the home or the old person being taken to be cared for elsewhere.  There are hundreds, possibly thousands, of such schemes across the country and most of them are run by voluntary organisations though often with a subsidy from local government.

The most common form of respite is provided by "sitting services." A skilled and trusted substitute comes into the home to care for the old person while the chief carer goes out. Sitting services are run by all sorts of local, usually voluntary, organisations. The archetypal form is the Crossroads scheme. Begun in Rugby in 1974, this is one of the few innovations of recent years that has become more or less available across the country. The national voluntary Crossroads organisation has its headquarters in Rugby and supports several hundred local schemes.

At the local level each scheme provides for a catchment area of about 50,000 people and usually consists of a voluntary management committee employing a coordinator (usually an ex-nurse) who supervises a team (averaging 6) of paid care attendants. The schemes are funded for the most part either by the local health authority or the social services department. The help provided often extends to far more than the provision of a simple sitting service to the regular provision of substitute care by a Crossroads care attendant so that the chief carer can go out or even just sit back and relax for a time.

Although it is aimed at all carers of disabled people, 65% of Crossroads clients care for people over 65. Help is usually given for the same period each week and the average session is 5 hours. 20% of sessions are at night. The care attendants will deal with lifting and incontinence and aim to carry out any function normally performed by the carer.

The EEC funded a study of 14 schemes between 1977 and 1980 (Bristow 1981). This study produced some evidence that the schemes reduce overall demand for residential care. It is clear that in individual cases they make the difference between the carer being able to continue or not. These findings are confirmed by an evaluation of Crossroads schemes in Essex (Cooper 1985) which also looked at the possibility of statutory services replicating the input of Crossroads care attendants and the likely cost. It concluded that public services that generated the same outcomes would be likely to cost up to twice as much as the voluntary ones and that carers had little confidence that they would offer the same flexibility and reliability.

There are numerous variations on the theme of the sitting services. In Sutton, Surrey, the local social services provide carers with the cash to allow them to buy in their sitters from neighbours and friends. Some sitting schemes allow carers to go away for longer—up to a week in the case of the York "In Safe Hands" service. Others allow for unplanned or emergency respite. For example, the Hillside Centre in Plympton, Devon and the Family Support Unit in Middlesborough allow known users to phone up for immediate respite carers. There are no reports of this sort of on-demand facility leading to excessive or unmanageable over-use. The chief problem with carers is their reluctance to use help rather than their abuse of it.

An alternative to the sitter coming to the client's home is for the old person to go and spend time in the replacement's home. This can take the form of respite care for several days or even weeks. The original and most famous of these "Family Placement Schemes" is in Leeds. Respite care in residential homes for the elderly is another and long-established way of relieving carers when they go on holiday or simply routinely every few months though it is not really an innovation, having been in existence, if only on a limited scale, for many years.

This idea has been taken further in what are known as "assisted lodgings in private households" which are not entirely voluntary since some payment is made, though at levels which are often well below what would be commercially viable. These are schemes which place old people in private "foster homes" for a fee. In recent years these schemes have tended to favour short-term placements and are largely a form of respite care. However, long-term or permanent placements have existed on a very small scale since the 1960s.

Thornton and Moore (1980) looked at 15 schemes providing long-term placements in the late 1970s and discovered that they were genuinely an alternative to residential or even hospital care. The old people involved were likely to exhibit high dependency, including confusion and incontinence. The level of care provided in foster homes was high. The caring was almost always done by a middle-aged woman, often an ex-nurse or care worker. People willing to foster an old person were discovered through local newspaper advertisements. None of the schemes reviewed appeared to have any difficulty recruiting foster carers. It was in fact more difficult to find the clients to be placed with them. Payment was from a variety of sources: social security, social services and the clients themselves.

As to costs, Thornton and Moore concluded "the major cost advantage of assisted lodgings over residential institutions is that places can be created without the need for large amounts of capital expenditure. The amount paid to carers often compared favourably with the cost of keeping a client in a home or hospital, but this ignores the other costs of operating the schemes and when these are taken into account the comparison becomes less favourable." In the 1980s long-term placements, always very few and of small scale anyway, appear to have gone into decline because changes in social security rules have made it easier for professionals and families to place old people in private residential homes. It is also possible that some of the people who might previously have provided placements have gone on to run their own private residential homes. However, when the Griffiths and White Paper proposal that social workers manage social care budgets is implemented, it may be that there will be a revival of long-term assisted lodgings as a better option for some clients and a more effective use of resources for budget-holding social workers.

The voluntary sectors' work with informal carers has been largely concerned with developing mechanisms through which they can help each other. The Carers' National Association has encouraged the establishment of carers support groups across the country. Carers can meet to discuss their burdens, discover they are not alone and learn of the available local help. It has become clear that these operate best if there is a skilled professional input, usually from social service and nursing staff, to guide discussion and add the appropriate information.

Even though these groups are now common, it is very likely that most carers do not know of them. This is partly because the population of carers of the elderly is a constantly changing one. Very basic publicising and information drives have to be mounted frequently to reach the continuous flow of new and unprepared recruits to the world of caring (Richardson et al. 1989). Both local social services departments and carers groups have found it very worthwhile to mount Carers' Information Days at local centres (carers often cannot travel far). It may be important to advertise these using some other term than "carer" since many do not know that this is what they are.

The broadcast media is a powerful way of reaching needy carers, and television in particular can show the actual work of caring which is otherwise a private and hidden industry. In Britain, after many years of near invisibility, the flow of television programmes aimed at carers is increasing.

In some parts of the country voluntary organisations have set up permanent carers centres with employed staff available to offer advice and various forms of practical help. A telephone help line may be a central part of this service.

These various carer support schemes are generally not evaluated in any systematic way. This is partly because the resources are not available to do so and partly because it is assumed that their very use demonstrates they are effective. The calculus of cost effectiveness is to a degree contrary to the ethos that drives these innovations. Whether they allow carers of old people to continue for longer is not the point. The object is to ease their burden. Indeed many of the initiatives explicitly state that one of their aims is to make known to carers what the alternatives to home care are and to allow those bearing intolerable burdens to stop doing so.

Moore and Green (1985) studied 13 voluntary schemes designed to assist caring relatives, 8 of which primarily helped carers of the elderly. The size of their sample and the variety of types of help and client precluded a technical evaluation. However, their case study method provided a classic statement of the conclusions which are ubiquitous in the literature about this sort of innovation:

1. Voluntary carer support schemes reach a tiny proportion of the potential clientele in a neighbourhood. Case finding is difficult, there being no ready-made lists of likely users. The most obvious source of referral is the statutory services but in practice these pass on few and often unsuitable people. A great deal of effort has to go into publicity, with limited returns, though the services do reach some people not in touch with existing services. There is very little overlap with existing services, but neither is there much collaboration.

2. Volunteers are surprisingly easy to find. One problem is maintaining their commitment in the absence of suitable cases. However, the volunteers' role rarely extends in practice to the heavy personal care tasks that are the drudgery of caring. This is partly a consequence of the volunteers' expectations and partly due to the carers being reluctant to ask anyone else to do these tasks. The help that these voluntary schemes offer is limited to very partial forms of relief.

3. The users who continue to use services declare themselves pleased with what they get but what is offered is rarely very precisely suited to their needs. They fit the help offered as best they can to their particular cases. On the whole they find the voluntary provision more reliable than statutory services. It is the limited range and flexibility of these schemes that may, in part, explain

why a large proportion of carers who learn of them do not go on to use them. For a substantial proportion of carers part of the problem was that the services offered largely aimed to relieve them temporarily of their caring role while what they wanted was assistance and support in carrying it out. For example, they might not wish to leave their home while the volunteer took over.

4. There is considerable confusion, ambiguity and variation amongst users and providers about whether they want to pay or be paid for the services. This is a complex area where different social norms and expectations overlap and contradict one another.

One way round the problem of fitting help to carers' needs has been demonstrated by the Bexley Community Care Scheme. A core idea behind the scheme is that only carers know exactly what they need since they are, inevitably and necessarily, the case managers for their frail old person. The scheme aims to empower the carers by supplying them with money, contacts and information (Chambers 1986; Maitland and Tutt 1987). In particular, much energy is put into obtaining funds, from the social security system and from charity, to assist the carers in employing neighbours as helpers. By making the carer the employer and purchaser of assistance they are given control and greater ability to get exactly the help they need.

Research has not demonstrated that carer support schemes can or should prevent or delay entry into residential care. However, it is clear that public money is going into these innovations because health and social service policy makers see them as an economic alternative to other more expensive forms of care. Whether carer support schemes will in the long run save the state money is a very complex question. Clearly by informing millions of their financial and social service rights, the carers movement could greatly increase demands on public benefits and services. It is at least in the interests of the state to play a part in its evolution and help avoid the unlikely possibility that it develop into a protest movement against caring.

As has already been pointed out, carers initiatives have been seen in Britain as principally a part of the voluntary sector. Public funding is usually short-term and presented as seed-corn or pump-priming money. There lies a problem. Only some carers will benefit from the sorts of innovations described in this section. They are not uniformly or predictably available. They are a system of home care bound to generate complex inequalities in benefit and predictability. They clearly should be an addition to, rather than a substitute for, a standard, predictable, national system of home care.

## CONCLUSION

With the implementation of the Community Care Act 1990, which will be phased in from April 1991 to April 1993, care of the elderly in Britain moves into a form very different to that which has existed since the Second World War. It is almost possible to say that a revolution in care is taking place. The argument for some sort of change is very strong. The care services that currently exist have been shown by numerous studies to be inadequate and poor value for money. They are certainly unable to meet the challenge of the rapid growth in the numbers of very old and frail elderly that is currently taking place. Secondly, it has become necessary for public policy to respond to the well-established wish of most people to remain in their own homes for as long as possible and to be cared for at home.

However, the shift to community care is being combined with another shift in public policy about which there is much less of a consensus in Britain: the shift to the mixed economy of welfare. The frail elderly have been put on the front line of a major and risky change. In all the policy documents associated with the current changes the government has made it clear that it will not spend more public money in order to make community care work. Indeed, relative to the growth in numbers of those aged 75 and over, it is fairly clear that public expenditure will fall. The slack must be taken up by the non-state sectors: private (for-profit), charitable (not-for-profit) and family and neighbourly care. What evidence is there that these sectors will be able to generate more care resources and that they will be able to work well together? Here, as this chapter has attempted to show, the policy makers have pinned their hopes on highly contestable evidence about the strength and reliability of the non-state sectors and on a very limited number of experimental innovations in case management.

### References

Age Concern (1979). *Good Neighbour Schemes, 4 case studies.* London: Age Concern (Information Department, 60 Pitcairn Road, Mitcham, Surrey, CR4 3LL, England).

Allen, I. (1983). *Short-stay Residential Care for the Elderly.* London: Policy Studies Institute.

Arnold, Diane (1987). "The brokerage model of long-term care: a rose by any other name." *Home Health Care Services Quarterly* 8.2: 23-43.

Askham, J., and C. Thompson (1990). *Dementia and Home Care: a research report on a home support scheme*. Mitcham: Age Concern England (obtainable from Age Concern England, Dept. BL4, 1268 London Road, London, SW16 4EJ, £12.95).

Audit Commission (1985). *Managing Social Services for the Elderly More Effectively*. London: HMSO.

Audit Commission (1986). *Making a Reality of Community Care*. London: HMSO.

Baldock, John, and Clare Ungerson (1991). "What D'ya Want if You Don' Want Money?" In M. Mclean and G. Groves, eds., *Women's Issues in Social Policy*. London: Routledge.

Bebbington, A.N., B.P. Davies, B. Baines, H. Charnley, E. Ferlie, M. Hughes, and J. Twigg (1989). *Resources, Needs and Outcomes: a comparative study of services for the elderly in ten local authorities*. London: Gower.

Brenton, M. (1985). *The Voluntary Sector in British Social Services*. London: Longman.

Brindle, D. (1988). "Social security bill for nursing home places 'exceeding £1bn'." *The Guardian*, 6 October.

Bristow, A. (1981). *Crossroads Care Attendant Schemes*. Crossroads Assn., Rugby.

Callahan, James J. (1989). "Case management for the elderly: a panacea?" *Journal of Ageing and Social Policy* 1.1/2: 181-95.

Challis, D., and A. Davies (1986). *Case Management in Community Care*. Aldershot: Gower.

Challis, D., R. Darton, L. Johnson, M. Stone, K. Traske, and B. Wall (1989). *Supporting Frail Elderly People at Home: the Darlington Community Care Project*. Canterbury: University of Kent.

Challis, D., R. Chessum, J. Chesterman, R. Luckett, and K. Traske (1990). *Case Management in Social and Health Care: the Gateshead Community Care Scheme*. Canterbury: University of Kent.

Chambers, P. (1986). "Paid neighbours improve care for frail elderly." *Geriatric Medicine* 11: 42-5.

Cm 849 (1989). *Caring For People: community care in the next decade and beyond*. London: HMSO.

Cmnd 8173 (1981). *Growing Older*. London: HMSO.

Cooper, M. (1985). *Hard-won Reality: An Evaluation of the Essex Crossroads Care Attendant Schemes*. Braintree, Essex Social Services.

CSO (1987) Central Statistical Office. *Social Trends No. 17*. London: HMSO.

DHSS (1981a). *The Primary Health Care Team*. London: HMSO.

DHSS (1981b). *Care in Action*. London: HMSO.

DHSS (1981c). *Growing Older*. London: HMSO.

Family Policy Studies Centre (1989). *Family Policy Bulletin No. 6*, Winter. London.

Finch, J. (1989). *Family Obligations and Social Change*. Oxford: Polity Press.

Finch, J., and J. Mason (1990). "Filial Obligations and Kin Support for Elderly People." *Ageing and Society* 10: 151-76.

GHS (1985). "Elderly People in Private Households—1985." In *General Household Survey 1986*. London: HMSO, 1989.

GHS (1989). *General Household Survey 1987*. London: HMSO.

Green, H. (1988). *Informal Carers: General Household Survey 1985*. OPCS, Social Survey Division, series GHS No. 15, supplement A. London: HMSO.

Griffiths (1988). *Community Care: Agenda for Action, A report to the Secretary of Social Services by Sir Roy Griffiths*. London: DHSS, HMSO.

Haskey, J. (1990). "Marital Breakdown." In *Population Trends*, Autumn. London: HMSO.

HCF (1987) Health Care Financing Administration. *Health Care Financing: Evaluation of Community-Orientated Long-term Care Demonstration Projects*. Publication No. 03242, Department of Health and Human Resources, Baltimore.

Henwood, Melanie, and Malcolm Wicks (1984). *Forgotten Army: family care and elderly people*. London: Family Policy Studies Centre.

Horton, C., and R. Berthoud (1990). *The Attendance Allowance and the Costs of Caring*. London: Policy Studies Institute.

House of Commons (1985). *Community Care with Special Reference to Adult Mentally Ill and Mentally Handicapped People*. Vol. 1, Social Services Committee. London: HMSO.

HPSS (1988). *Health and Personal Social Service Statistics 1987*. Department of Health. London: HMSO.

Kemper, Peter, R. Applebaum, and Margaret Harrigan (1987). "Community care demonstrations: what have we learned?" *Health Care Financing Review* 8 (4): 87-100.

Kiernan, K., and M. Wicks (1990). *Family Change and Future Policy*. York: Joseph Rowntree Memorial Trust.

Knapp, M., P. Cambridge, C. Thomason, R. Darton, and J. Beecham (1990). *Care in the Community: evaluating a demonstration programme*. London: Gower.

Leat, D., ed. (1986). *Creating Care in the Neighbourhood*. A shortened version of Abrams et al., *The Neighbourhood Care Action Programme*, 1986. London: Advance.

Leat, D., and P. Gay (1987). *Paying for Care: a study of policy and practice in paid care schemes*. Research Report No. 661. London: Policy Studies Institute.

Levin, Enid, Ian Sinclair, and Peter Gorbach (1989). *Families, Services and Confusion in Old Age*. Avebury: Alderlshot.

Lewis, J., and B. Meredith (1988). *Daughters Who Care: daughters caring for mothers at home*. London: Routledge.

Maitland, N., and N. Tutt (1987). "Bexley's Trump Card." *Social Services Insight*, 18 September: 16-17.

Martin, J., and C. Roberts (1984). *Women and Employment: a lifetime perspective*. London: HMSO.

Midwinter, E. (1986). *Caring for Cash: the issue of private domiciliary care*. London: Centre for Policy on Ageing.

Moore, J., and J.M. Green (1985). "The contribution of voluntary organisations to the support of elderly relatives." *The Quarterly Journal of Social Affairs* 2 (1): 93-130.

Moss, P. (1988). *Child Care and Equality of Opportunity*. Consolidated Report to the European Commission, Brussels.

National Audit Office (1987). *Community Care Developments, a report by the Comptroller and Auditor General*. House of Commons paper 1987-8, No. 108. London: HMSO.

Oliver, J., and A. Briggs (1985). *Caring; the experience of looking after disabled relatives*. London: Routledge and Kegan Paul.

OPCS (1981) Office of Population, Census and Surveys. *Access to Primary Health Care*. London: HMSO.

OPCS (1982) Office of Population, Census and Surveys. *Nurses Working in the Community*. London: HMSO.

OPCS (1990) Office of Population, Census and Surveys. *Disabled Adults: services, transport and employment*. Disability Survey Report No. 4. London: HMSO.

Parker, G. (1990). *With Due Care and Attention: a review of research on informal care*. Second edition. London: Family Policy Studies Centre.

Pitkeathly, J. (1989). *It's My Duty, Isn't It?* London: Souvenir Press.

Public Accounts Committee (1988). *Community Care Developments, 26th report*. House of Commons 1987-8, No. 300. London: HMSO.

Qureshi, H., and A. Walker (1989). *The Caring Relationship: the family care of elderly people*. Basingstoke: Macmillan Education.

Qureshi, H., D. Challis, and B. Davies (1989). *Helpers in Case-Managed Community Care*. London: Gower.

Renshaw, J., R. Hampson, C. Thomason, R. Darton, K. Judge, and M. Knapp (1988). *Care in the Community: the first steps*. London: Gower.

Richardson, A., J. Unell, and B. Aston (1989). *A New Deal for Carers*. Informal Caring Support Unit. London: Kinf's Fund Centre.

Roberts, J. (1982). *Community Care in London—a pipe dream?* London: School of Hygiene and Tropical Medicine.

SSI  (1987) Social Services Inspectorate. *From Home Help to Home Care: an analysis of policy, resourcing and service management*. London: DHSS, HMSO.

Tester, S. (1989). *Caring by Day: a study of day care services for old people*. London: Centre for Policy on Ageing.

Thornton, P., and J. Moore (1980). *The Placement of Elderly People in Private Households: an analysis of current provision*. Department of Social Policy and Administration Research Monograph. Leeds: University of Leeds.

Townsend, P. (1963). *The Family Life of Old People*. Harmondsworth: Penguin.

Twigg, J., K. Atkin, and C. Perring (1990). *Carers and Services: a review of research*. London: HMSO.

Ungerson, C. (1987). *Policy is Personal: sex, gender and informal care.* London: Tavistock.

Ungerson, C., ed. (1990). *Gender and Caring: work and welfare in Britain and Scandinavia.* Hemel Hempstead: Harvester Wheatsheaf.

Willmott, P. (1986). *Social Networks, Informal Care and Public Policy.* Research Report No. 655. London: Policy Studies Institute.

Wylie, Mary, and Carol Austin (1978). "Policy foundations for case management: consequences for the frail elderly." *Journal of Gerontological Social Work* 1.1: 7-17.

Zwick, D. (1985). "Home Care Services for the Elderly: the English way." In L. Reif et al., eds., *International Perspectives on Long Term Care.* New York: Hayworth Press.

# three

## Home-Based Care in Canada and Quebec: Informal and Formal Services

*Frédéric Lesemann*
and
*Daphne Nahmiash*

Canada has undergone a major shift in the relationships between the diverse actors contributing to the welfare of the population through public services, private resources and informal supports, as in most industrialized countries experiencing a rapid development in their social policies during the past thirty years.

This process of redefining priorities is especially evident in the area of services to seniors and the expansion of home-based care. A result of political and fiscal pressures, the situation is particularly acute in a country which is facing an enormous deficit. Seniors wish to remain in their own homes and institutionalization represents more than a last resort. Major health care reforms are presently under way in several Canadian provinces. They are usually characterized by a trend which is redirecting some of the specialized institutional care services toward simple, locally-based community services.

This chapter aims to provide some basic information about demographic trends in Canada and organizational modes of delivering home-based services to seniors. It will summarize, as well, some of the home care literature relating to the links between family and informal care and public services.

## BASIC SOCIO-DEMOGRAPHIC TRENDS AND THE ORGANIZATION OF HOME CARE SERVICES

The Canadian population is still relatively young compared to other industrialized countries, even though it is aging rapidly.  In 1991, 11% of the population (2.8 million people) were over the age of 65.  It is interesting to note that this percentage corresponds to that of Sweden and Great Britain during the 1950s.  The average growth rate of the senior population varies considerably from province to province.  It has already reached 4% in Ontario and is up to 5% in Quebec.  As one might expect, this growth rate is having an impact on the health care system.  Aging differs according to gender: in 1991 there were 85 men per 100 women among seniors in the 65-69 age range but only 57 men per 100 women in the senior population group aged 80 and over.

The economic situation of older Canadians is relatively satisfactory. 82% of older men and women reported that they were either very or reasonably satisfied with their income in 1991 (Statistics Canada 1991).

Most seem equally satisfied with their state of health: almost two thirds of seniors aged 65-74 said they were in good or excellent health and 57% of seniors over 80 reported themselves to be in good health (Statistics Canada 1991).

Family and community bonds are strong.  According to the same national survey, 50% of people aged 65-74 provide moral support to others and 35% provide home help for others.  These percentages decline to 35% and 19% respectively for seniors over 80 years of age.  92% of those over 65 state they have one or more close friend or relative.  More than 80% of these close friends live in the same town or municipality.

From a historical point of view one must remember that social and health care services are the responsibility of the provincial governments when considering how services are organized in Canada.  Fiscal arrangements have been negotiated with the federal government, including equalization mechanisms between rich and poor provinces.  They attempt to establish a cost sharing process for the various programs between the different levels of government.  This financial participation has enabled the federal government to play a major role in the orientation, evaluation and standardization of the various provincial programs and in establishing norms and standards at a national level.  In 1957 the national universal hospital insurance plan was created and subsequently, in 1968, the universal health insurance system was set up. The historical development of these programs has broadly influenced the prevailing health care system in Canada, as a medical, hospital-oriented acute care system.

As Chappell (1989: 21) states: "The involvement of the federal government has helped create a health care delivery system with a medical emphasis. This is perhaps best demonstrated by the role played by physicians within the systems."

Non-medical and non-hospital health programs are considered low priority as are preventative and community-oriented programs. Social services, housing, transportation and home support programs—basic to home care—have never been adequately financed because they were not considered to be health services in the strict sense of the term. They were not considered to be social services either as those services were only for low income people subsequent to a means test. According to Marshall (1989: 7): "Reflecting the medical and hospital emphasis of Canadian health and medical care, while it is estimated that 85% of persons aged 65 or older see a physician at least once a year, only 8% receive meals on wheels, 3.5% receive transportation services, 4.3% homemaker or home help services, 4.3% assistance with shopping and banking, and 2.7% nursing or other medical calls at home."

In Canada home care services were first developed in the 1970s, illustrating the small percentage of seniors up to this time as well as the orientation of the health care system and the absence of national financing mechanisms for home-based services. On the other hand, the rate of institutionalization of the elderly was very high, reaching as high as 24% in some provinces for those aged 80-84 and 50% for those over 85. This high rate of institutionalization has declined considerably since 1976 for those aged 65-74, stabilized for 75-84 year olds and risen rapidly for those 85 and over. Consequently, the institutional clientele has completely changed in the past fifteen years, transforming the existing senior residences into long-term care hospitals. The decline in institutional care for those under 80 years of age has been compensated for by the development of home care services.

In 1977, the federal government introduced new block grants to develop universally admissible extended care services. However, the majority of provinces developed services of a medical nature. Manitoba, Quebec and Saskatchewan responded to both health and social needs through the development of homemaking services, meals and other forms of home support. In response to the great demand for services, Quebec had to establish a waiting list sometimes lasting up to several months which constituted a form of triage and established priorities based on the urgency of the request and the heaviness of the case and included the application of an informal means test. Those requesting services who had means were referred to private agencies. The province of Saskatchewan developed a method of allocating services on the basis of risk and need.

In the development of community-based services the provinces had considerable flexibility. In spite of this Chappell states in 1989 (p. 25) that the services are still "primarily discussed as add-ons to the existing medical care system with little discussion of changing that system." Furthermore, in six out of ten provinces, Ontario included, requests for home care must be referred by a doctor for professional health care. In the other provinces, including Quebec, the needs of users are assessed by non-medical professionals from the home care teams (Shapiro 1991: 23). However, the community-based teams, such as those in Quebec, are being continually pressured to resolve the ongoing crises of the institutional milieux.

Home care services are usually organized by multidisciplinary teams of professionals and paraprofessionals. These teams deliver home-based services to enable people to stay in their homes for as long as possible and help them improve their functioning whilst retaining their autonomy. The services have a coordinating role, are complementary to family resources and mobilize resources available in the community. In light of this, several provincial governments and the federal government offer financial support to local volunteer organizations so that they can play a role in enabling dependent people to stay in their homes and in their neighbourhoods. The funding is for the organization of concrete help and services and activities to promote social reintegration.

Thus one of the main characteristics of Canadian home care services is their dependence on hospital institutions and this is one of the key problems confronting these services in the past decade. Moreover, it is the constant theme of the publications and research studies on home care, presented in the next part of the chapter.

## HOME CARE LITERATURE: HOSPITAL-BASED OR HOME-BASED CARE

In our review of the Canadian research and publications on home care during the past ten years we found three key themes, which can best be described in reference to the main objectives, philosophy and disciplines involved in the studies. The first theme relates to the literature produced by both levels of government. It promotes a new philosophy of health care. It no longer states that the population's health can be improved by increasing hospital investments and the number of doctors. The recognition of the role of prevention and the awareness of the social dimensions of health care are both considered as factors which determine good health. It is also evident that the state of dependence brought on by the aging process includes both medical and social dimensions. Coming to grips with this phenomenon means not only changing the way we perceive aging as illness but also changing the orientations of our health care system.

*Aging: Shifting the Emphasis* (Canada 1986b) and *A Framework for the Development of Home Care in Canada* (Canada 1986c) are federal publications characterized by these new orientations. They are largely inspired by the public health philosophy promoted through the World Health Organization (W.H.O.). These documents formulate guidelines for the organization of health care using W.H.O. principles to promote the improvement of the adverse social and environmental conditions which are the cause of the problems rather than advocating the improvement of the service system itself. Isolation, insecurity, violence and inequity are intimately associated with a deteriorated state of health. The approach for the elderly is to promote all forms of social reintegration and the creation of social bonds. For others it is the promotion of family and community bonds to improve their well-being. Housing conditions are equally important in this approach proclaimed mainly by health specialists in the fields of epidemiology and public health.

A second category of studies is written and produced by health economists and portrays home care services as a substitute for institutional and hospital-based services. Questions are posed about how home care services can best relieve the hospital burdens. Questions are asked about efficiency and cost reduction from the global system which perceives home care to be an important element within this system. In this massive body of literature studies can be found which evaluate hospital-based home care programs established as an extension of hospital care. This is the approach adopted and recommended by the Canadian Medical Association, favouring hospital-organized home care as a mechanism to improve the integration of home care services with hospital care (Marshall 1989: 34). Other studies describe Extra-Mural Hospitals or hospitals-without-walls, whose prime objectives are to reduce hospital stays and meet the needs of beneficiaries whose health condition does not require the technological support of a hospital (Desrosiers and Gaumer 1987: 59). Day hospitals are also widespread in Canada, providing assessment, surveillance and rehabilitation therapy services to elderly people on a daily basis or several times per week on an outpatient basis. Respite services for family caregivers are often associated with these programs. Intensive home care services (ranging from 5 to 35 hours per week) are offered as supplementary services to prevent and delay institutionalization. They sometimes result in the selection of the least appropriate cases to be taken care of at home and aim to increase the efficiency of highly specialized equipment (Joubert et al. 1991). Significant studies have been conducted by the consulting firm of Price Waterhouse upon the request of the provincial governments of Ontario and Manitoba which evaluate the cost efficiency of their respective home care programs (Price Waterhouse 1988a, 1988b). The conclusion of these studies is that home care programs must be articulated more directly with cost efficiency studies and those studies which attempt to reduce the cost of institutional hospitalization.

Nevertheless, at least three authors question the contribution of hospital-based home care programs in terms of their functioning and their ability to reduce costs. The national *Report on Home Care* (Canada 1990) states that "home care by itself cannot achieve savings for the system as a whole because of the well-documented tendency for institutional services to operate at capacity regardless of whether or not some of their functions have been displaced to home care. Without clear policies aimed at reducing costs for the system as a whole, the more efficient and effective home care becomes the more costly will all components of the health system become. This may be termed the paradox of efficiency. For ... home care to succeed in reducing the total system costs depends entirely on coordinated approaches to funding of all relevant sectors" (p. 18). Shapiro et al. (1987) and Kane and Kane (1985) similarly conclude: "The only forseeable scenario by which substantially increased efforts directed toward community care would seem likely to reduce total long-term care costs is as part of a deliberate strategy to dramatically reduce the supply of institutional beds. This could be done most simply, but not easily, by removing a nursing home bed from the funded pool each time a well-supported client is enrolled. Alternatively, one could pursue a longer-range investment strategy by committing the system to more community support and constraining any new growth in nursing home beds. Either approach must contend with the political and social realities, which currently push persons into institutions" (Kane and Kane 1985: 253). On the other hand, Béland (1985) and Contandriopoulos et al. (1984) state that opening new home-based services and programs does not contribute to reducing hospital costs because such programs discover new needs and promote new demands which then have to be met.

A third category of studies emphasizes home-based, community-based services and informal support networks. The notion of community and neighbourhood volunteers is an integral part of the services. Individuals and families are recognized to have varied and unique needs which are at the base of the service system. In the research an enormous amount of attention is devoted to family dynamics, caregiving issues, respite resources, and relationships between formal and informal systems. These studies are produced by sociologists and social and community workers and rely on qualitative as well as quantitative methodologies. The "home-based" approach is based on the recognition that "home is the central site—the major workplace—where lifelong illness is managed on a daily basis.... The major concern of the ill and their families is not merely nor primarily managing an illness, but maintaining the *quality of life*, as defined specifically by them, despite the illness...." (Strauss and Corbin 1988: 47). It is also evident from studies that the needs, expectations and ways of dealing with illness for the dependent person as well as for caregivers are inherently different from one individual to another. Heterogeneity rather than homogeneity, singularity and specificity rather than generality characterize the field of home care for the elderly. This means for policy makers that heterogeneity must be recognized by program planners (Chappell 1989: 87; Shapiro 1989: 27; Havens 1989: 12).

This particular research approach pays attention to so-called "informal" home care. Numerous studies have explored this area, dealt with in the third section of this chapter.

Another important aspect from the research involves respite resources for caregivers. Respite care is usually referred to as any source of relief for caregivers or the frail person in or outside the home. Family support groups have also been created to relieve caregivers' stress. Lesemann and Chaume (1989) determined that an important number of persons attending such groups are highly educated, middle class individuals and frequently do not live with their dependent. They are able to express themselves verbally with ease and this style of communication is probably familiar to them.

Studies in this type of research are also concerned with the quality and condition of housing arrangements, often emphasizing the inadequacy of housing options and environments as a possible reason for institutionalization. Housing is one of the essential elements in the provision of quality community-based care, since people have generally spent a significant part of their lives within their four walls and these have become part of their life experience and their identity.

Studies of the socio-economic status of home care beneficiaries highlight the relative poverty of a sizeable number of elderly people, especially very old women. Thus poverty represents a strong indicator of potential use of home care services which can contribute to the prevention of physical or mental deterioration. In this context Shapiro (1989: 11) comments that "it would be unreasonable to have a policy which acts as a disincentive to use ... [of] the most important and least expensive service in terms of helping individuals and families cope at home...; if some people who need the service refuse a needs test or refuse to pay for service they need, what have we gained if they deteriorate to the point of requiring institutionalization?"

Some studies highlight the importance of the varied ethnic and cultural preferences prevalent in a country with such high immigration rates as Canada. Ethnicity becomes increasingly important with age because it is associated with identity, status and tradition, providing a continuity from the past to the present. This premise raises questions about who should organize and deliver services and implies that needs are multifaceted and defined not only by age but also by culture and related resources (Driedger and Chappell 1987; Ujimoto 1987).

Coordination of services is a central theme of home care studies in this third category of research. It signifies the reinforcement of informal support networks, and specifies the need for formal services complementary to those supplied by family and community resources. The role of professional case manager is usually determined as involving "a flexible approach to service delivery and a constantly up-to-date knowledge of changing community resources" (Havens 1986: 98). Coordination is thus planned according to the care needs of the caregiver-care receiver pair and not purely from a cost-effective point of view as is the case with hospital-based services.

## ANALYSIS OF THE RESEARCH STUDIES RELATING TO FAMILY PRACTICES AND INFORMAL NETWORKS

The institution-based approach has direct repercussions on the orientation of family support practices and the role of informal networks and community resources.

The majority of studies question these practices from the point of view of the service system by evaluating in what way and to what degree such conditions and practices relieve and complement the existing services. How do they supplement these or evaluate the need to create new services in order to respond to new needs? A considerable part of the research contributes to the support of this perspective and its main objective is to identify the diverse types of problems experienced by the elderly. The clientele is thus defined essentially by their deficits and difficulties alongside other identified population groups. A completely different research approach characterizes a limited number of studies. These are based on a system of reference other than the service system and are generally oriented toward the observation of informal or natural care networks. We will now proceed to an analysis of some of the studies from both approaches.

## Research Based on the Service System Approach

Generally these studies attribute a positive image to the act of caring, which is presumed to be classifiable, measurable and capable of replication. They are most often based on experimental methodology with control groups; they measure the various selected indicators and, when possible, establish significant correlations between variables. Their legitimacy lies in their ability to contribute toward a better knowledge of the clients served, a greater effectivity of existing programs or the elaboration of new programs.

The data is collected through questionnaires or surveys.

An example of this type of recent study was the survey done in 1987 of 2,000 Quebecers. The survey was part of the health and social service commission studies (Jutras, Veilleux and Renaud 1989: the title of their work may be translated as "Unknown partners: caregivers of dependent seniors"). The results of this survey show the role of women in the helping process and the impact of this process on family and professional life. They examine the "burden" associated with being a primary caregiver, living with a dependent and participation in activities of daily living; the "burden" is even greater when the caregiver does not work outside the home. The family seems to be the main partner in the public service system and, according to the opinions expressed, community resources appear to be non-existent. This kind of study is characterized by a series of recommendations to government policy makers based on the results of the survey.

There are numerous studies based on needs, behaviours or problems confronting individuals giving care to dependents. Béland (1988: 261), in his summary of the research in the area of social gerontology conducted in Quebec from 1975 to 1987, estimates that the psycho-social perspective is dominant and represents a good third of publications. These are followed by demographic aging studies and program evaluations of services to the elderly, especially those connected with home care (ibid.). As has been stated, questions about family support abound in these studies. Quebec is not the only province which places importance on such studies, as similar issues are to be found in the vast majority of studies in other Canadian provinces and the United States. Garant and Bolduc (1990) have recently completed a review of the Quebec, Canadian and American literature on "Dependent seniors, their caregivers and the links with the public service system" (p. xvii) which represents a program evaluation of the response to the needs of seniors requiring long-term care. Almost 200 studies were analyzed. The main conclusions from this study were as follows:

- The lack of involvement of families and the abandoning of their dependents is a myth. Today, more than ever, the family constitutes the most important source of help (p. 11). As long as the person's health condition is not too deteriorated, the family network functions as a model of reciprocity: one gives as many services as one receives. The family rather than the social and health services system is the principal source of help when the state of health of one of its members deteriorates severely (p. 12).

If we take into account the new demographic pressures, lifestyles, the changing role of women and housing conditions, we cannot assume that families will be able to continue their caring role in the future as in the present.

- Caregivers are mainly women and for the most part are assuming their responsibilities alone without any help from the public system (p. 38). Family support is characterized by its diversity: it consists of emotional support, financial help, mediation between the formal service system and the senior, multiple concrete services and the assurance of a continuous presence. The objective burden is very heavy and the length of the helping situation is very long. It is a constant source of stress and emotional tension. There is also a financial strain. Support for persons suffering from dementia is especially difficult and by far the most stressful.

- Motivation for caregiving revolves around two concepts: love and affection on the one hand, responsibility, debt and guilt on the other. Psychological bonds, family solidarity, reciprocity and social norms constitute the gamut of motives which caregivers experience, knowing that their decision to help their dependent is more the consequence of successive events than a real choice (p. 68). Cohabitation between parent and child also has non-negligible financial dimensions.

- Bonds between the informal helper and formal help seem indispensable and one cannot suffice without the other; they are reciprocal and each is specific and interchangeable. Formal help tends to consider informal help as a complementary resource. Formal services do not promote the disengagement of the caregiver (p. 93). However, when formal services are insufficient caregivers may become demoralized and social bonds may be destroyed rather than reinforced (p. 98).

- Garant and Bolduc's study concludes with a series of recommendations proposing research and actions to promote home care, improve the quality of life of dependent people and stimulate the development of a complementarity between the formal service system and the informal network (p. 127).

Chappell (1989) has similarly reviewed the literature in this area. Her results are almost identical. She claims even more strongly that caregivers only use formal services as a last resort after all informal supports have been used (p. 17). When caregivers ask for help they are often at the end of their rope and their dependent's health is severely impaired. The dependent may even be in the terminal phase of the illness.

## Research About Lifestyles and Family Responsibilities

These studies are not really oriented toward the service system rationale or the professional and organizational perspective. The data collection is characterized by systematic observation, case reviews and life stories, using qualitative methods of analyzing conversations and social processes. The interactions between family members, informal and formal helpers, health care personnel and researchers are generally at the core of these studies.

This section will be introduced by a study which refers to two types of the research mentioned. Based on the first type, there is an evolution to the second. Lesemann and Chaume (1989) surveyed approximately 200 primary caregivers of severely dependent people in Montreal to determine the home care conditions and problem solving strategies from the informal as well as the formal network. The study was conducted through questionnaires and interviews. The authors were surprised at some of the results. Firstly, a caregiving relationship appears to be a relatively typical phenomenon with emotional and moral dimensions originating from a complex history of family relationships. As it is generally presented in the specialized literature, it is an extremely relative phenomenon. Cases which are medically heavy may be perfectly acceptable for the helper if the intrafamilial dynamics are experienced positively. The inverse is also true: light cases may be perceived as intolerable. The bottom line is that each case is individual and particular and any attempt to portray the potential objective thresholds of breakdown of caregivers is illusory.

Another result noted by the researchers is the difference between the assessment by the home care professionals of the degree of dependence of the beneficiaries of care as compared to that of the caregivers regarding their dependents. Participants were recruited by the researchers from lists of heavily dependent clients provided by the home care establishments. They were described in general by their caregivers as lightly dependent using the same criteria as the professional providers. This difference is interpreted by the researchers as an illustration of the relativity of perceptions about the strategic behaviour of those requesting services. The latter may have felt they had to insist on the heaviness of the case to the evaluators in order to obtain services, whereas from the researchers they had nothing concrete to gain and they wished to appear to be in control and affirm their dignity. In other words, all seemed problematic in the first situation whereas all seemed well in the second.

This report introduced a variable of social stratification in terms of the educational level and age of the caregiver. It seems that older people and caregivers who are less educated are also more tolerant and ready to assume almost any limits of care. On the other hand, those more educated and younger clearly establish their limits and require public services when those limits are reached, however variable and subjective the limits may be.

Thus the researchers who began this study from the point of view of exploring the crisis in the welfare state, as to how it displaces its burden to family caregivers, found families characterized by the uniqueness of their relationships and respective practices. These families count on the state to play an essential role over which they exercise control. Thus two different rationales coexist in the field of home-based care: one that of the family, the other that of the institution; the former is characterized by its autonomy, the latter by its distance.

Interest in the work of caregivers and their motives for caring is particularly notable among researchers with a feminist approach. Aronson (1988), for example, expresses interest in the experience of women giving and receiving care. In her study, there seems to be a conflict for the women questioned between the need for care and security and the sharing of values such as independence and self-sufficiency. Furthermore, Guberman, Dorvil and Maheu (1987) have produced, from a limited number of cases, a striking portrait of female caregivers and very dependent or demented elderly people, as well as some young handicapped people. In a later study in 1991, the authors Guberman, Maheu and Maillé attempted to comprehend the meaning of technocratic terms such as "taken care of by the milieu" for dependent people (p. 11). They state that "presuming that to take care of someone is not a natural process, actions influenced by a multiplicity of social factors such as love, affection ... are not the only element" (p. 12). The research study shows the diversity and fragmentation of the tasks accomplished (p. 78) and their stressfulness, the limited support received from the social service system, and the isolation of the caregivers and their families (p. 117).

The motives for caregiving usually spring from a feeling of affection for the person, although a number of women state they do not feel any affection for their dependent (p. 173). The role of caring is a central theme for a number of women. "It goes beyond filial sentiments and extends to all members of the family, even to outsiders who are involved in caregiving. What's important is to serve, to feel useful, to help" (p. 187). On the other hand, the feeling of obligation and duty exists, although less frequently (p. 190). Moreover, the decision to assume care may come from a range of factors, precipitating events and motives which may interact and be transformed by time (p. 219).

Rosenthal (1987) has completed a study of 400 families in Hamilton, Ontario from a different perspective. She explored the intergenerational relationships in the helping process. The results indicate the great significance of the family as a source of emotional, social and concrete support. A spouse and particularly a wife is the most important caregiver to an elderly person. The family is very active and the great majority of dependent people can count on the presence of a member of their immediate kin. The majority of seniors questioned claimed they prefer not to live with their children and find it normal that they pursue their careers, whilst 89% claimed they could count on a child living within a proximity of an hour and a half from their home. Three quarters stated they had received a visit from a child during the week prior to the study. The quality of relationships between parents and children seems improved when parents are in good health. Manifestations of dependence lead somewhat to a deterioration in the quality of the intergenerational relationships. Help between generations is clearly marked by reciprocity. People aged 75 and over are found to help their children, particularly in the area of emotional support.

This research study shows the great capacity of women, as opposed to men, to nurture family bonds and the family network. In an emergency situation a family member is most often solicited, even if only to contact the health care system. Most family members, in their attempts at maintaining bonds of solidarity between generations, seem to develop a number of specialized roles. These can be assimilated in the form of a "family division of work" (p. 330) in which the functioning mechanism is assured by the informal leadership role of one member in particular, most often female and recognized by the others as a central person, a source of strength for the family.

To terminate this brief summary of research about family practices in the area of caregiving we turn to the work of Corin (1984) and Corin et al. (1984) in which the social networks and the socialization patterns of the elderly are described.   The studies are based on an explicit, initial, epistemological hypothesis that: "Older people use a series of socialization strategies in their social relationships" (Corin 1984: 184); this view differs from the classical or objectivist study of social relationships which would have produced a very different portrait.  The portrait would have been a much more deficient one of the socialization of elderly people showing the problems they experience and their deterioration, and would have been largely influenced by the reduction of aging to a biological process (p. 158). The study talks about constructing a dynamic approach to the social life of the elderly and the meaning they attribute to it (p. 160).  Hence originates the natural support system considered as a form of actualization of social relationships in their daily life (p. 160).  This perspective points out that a support network is more often developed by women than men, that women's networks are often more extensive than men's, that relationships with one's parents often pass on to the women, and that children and parents have an active, continued and long-term relationship, whereas friends and neighbours are only sporadically involved in relatively autonomous activities of dependent people.

Living alone in an urban milieu tends to incite one to develop networks of friends and neighbours or to live with someone if one no longer has a spouse.   However, being single or a widow seems to define exclusive domains: single people are friends with singles, married couples with other married couples (p. 183).  In rural areas members of social networks are closer than elsewhere; networks consist of friends and relatives. Nevertheless, in both urban and rural milieux, wealthy and poor neighbourhoods, kin relationships are very important, permitting care substitution between children and their parents (p. 175).

In terms of types of strategies employed, an especially active type of socialization (contacts, activities and exchanges) is associated with the absence of contact with the formal system; in fact, direct contact with formal resources or with strategies relating to them tends to be associated with a pronounced disengagement (Corin et al. 1984: 98).  Diverse forms of socialization lead to diverse strategies of service utilization.  If we take into account the specificity and quality of socialization developed by individuals, we are led to modify those representations of informal resources which are somewhat systematized and recognize the uniqueness of the behaviour and strategies of the diverse informal actors.

## CONCLUSION

This review has enabled us to illustrate some of the major issues involving the organization of home care services in Canada in a context of economic and fiscal restraint for both provincial and federal governments. The first issue from the three types of research studies identified concerns about links between the service systems and the medical-hospital institutions. We have noted that these systems are under considerable pressure to resolve the financial constraints of the large hospital institutions. Such pressure is unnatural for services which promote a different rationale for care and caregiving. It discourages a family and community dynamic which would pursue objectives of health, quality of life and well-being rather than respond to pathological problems and services which are caught up in the spiralling of costs. If the institutional rationale does not undergo a major shift, the relief provided by the home care system to its clientele may only be temporary. Such is the paradox or "perverse effects" of efficiency portrayed by some authors.

The second issue concerns the relationship of the service system to informal care and family practices. Firstly, this approach is linked in analogous terms to the abovementioned debate: the majority of studies relate to the present service system. They explore to what extent and under what conditions families and informal networks can contribute to a service system which, as we have established, is presently in a situation of crisis. Secondly, an epistemological shift leads us to make an intellectual break with the demands of the system, permitting us to examine family practices in order to discover their real dynamics, unsuspected strengths and the considerable contribution they are making to the welfare of our society. With this knowledge, we can correct our false notions and prejudices and relativize claims made by planners and institutional administrators to regulate the realm of family and community relationships in the name of problem solving associated with the aging process.

A number of countries are concerned about the stress the aging population might have on the health care system in the immediate future.

Our review of the literature leads us to suggest that in Canada we have similar concerns. In addition, we have concerns about reorienting our system which is subject to pressures from professional, organizational and commercial interest groups, so that the area of aging brings to light a potential organizational, political and moral deficit.

## References

Aronson, J. (1988). *Women's Experiences in Giving and Receiving Care: Pathways to Social Change*. Ph.D. dissertation, University of Toronto.

Béland, F. (1985). "Les demandes, les besoins et la planification des services aux personnes âgées." *Service social* 34 (1): 14-29.

Béland, F. (1988). "La recherche en gérontologie sociale au Québec : une originalité obscure ou une obscurité méritée?" *Revue canadienne de vieillissement* 7 (4): 257-292.

Canada (1986a). *Achieving Health for All: A Framework for Health Promotion*. Ottawa: Supply and Services Canada.

Canada (1986b). *Aging: Shifting the Emphasis*. Ottawa: Health & Welfare Canada.

Canada (1986c). *A Framework for the Development of Home Care in Canada*. Ottawa: Health & Welfare Canada.

Canada (1990). *Rapport sur les soins à domicile/Report on Home Care*. Ottawa: Approvisionnements et Services, Santé et Bien-être social Canada.

Chappell, N.L. (1989). *Formal Programs for Informal Caregivers of the Elderly on Supporting Elder Care*. Winnipeg: University of Manitoba.

Contandriopoulos, A.P. et al. (1984). *Les services d'aide à domicile et l'utilisation des ressources du système de soins*. Montreal: GRIS, Université de Montréal.

Corin, E. (1984). "Manières de vivre, manières de dire : réseau social et sociabilité quotidienne des personnes âgées au Québec." In *Troisième âge et culture*, Questions de culture. Quebec City: IQRC.

Corin, E. et al. (1983). *Le fonctionnement des systèmes de support naturel des personnes âgées*. Vol. 1. Quebec City: Laboratoire de gérontologie sociale, Université Laval. Mimeo.

Corin, E., J. Tremblay, T. Sherif, and L. Bergeron (1984). "Entre les services professionnels et les réseaux sociaux, les stratégies d'existence des personnes âgées." *Sociologie et sociétés* XVI (2): 89-104.

Desrosiers, G., and B. Gaumer (1987). *L'occupation d'une partie du champ des soins de première ligne par l'hôpital général*. Quebec City: Commission d'enquête sur les services de santé et les services sociaux. Synthèse critique no 17.

Driedger, L., and N. Chappell (1987). *Aging and Ethnicity, Toward an Interface*. Toronto: Butterworths.

Garant, L., and M. Bolduc (1990). *L'aide par les proches : mythes et réalités*. Quebec City: Direction de l'évaluation, Ministère de la santé et des services sociaux.

Guberman, N., H. Dorvil, and P. Maheu (1987). *Amour, bain comprimé ou l'ABC de la désinstitutionalisation*. Commission d'enquête sur les services de santé et les services sociaux. Quebec City: Les Publications du Québec.

Guberman, N., P. Maheu, and C. Maillé (1991). *Et si l'amour ne suffisait pas; femmes, familles et adultes dépendants*. Montreal: Remue-ménage.

Havens, B. (1986). "Boundary Crossing: An Organizational Challenge for Community-Based Long-Term Care Services Agencies." In A.O. Pelham and W.F. Clark, eds., *Managing Home Care for the Elderly*, 77-98. New York: Springer.

Havens, B. (1989). *Funding Issues: Rationalizing Costs When Resources are Scarce*. Ottawa: Canadian Association on Gerontology.

Joubert, P., A. Laberge, J.P. Fortin, M. Paradis, and F. Desbiens (1991). *Évaluation du programme québécois de services intensifs de maintien à domicile*. Quebec City: Centre hospitalier de l'Université Laval. Mimeo.

Jutras, S., F. Veilleux, and M. Renaud (1989). *Des "partenaires" méconnus : les aidants des personnes âgées en perte d'autonomie*. Montreal: GRASP, Université de Montréal.

Kane, R.L., and R.A. Kane (1985). *A Will and a Way, What the U.S. can Learn from Canada about Caring for the Elderly*. New York: Columbia University Press.

Lesemann, F., and C. Chaume (1989). *Familles-providence : la part de l'État*. Montreal: St-Martin.

Marshall, V.W. (1989). "Models for Community-based Long Term Care: An Analysis Review." Ottawa: Health & Welfare Canada. Unpublished.

Ontario (1987). *Health for All Ontario*. Panel on Health Goals for Ontario. Toronto: Government of Ontario.

Price Waterhouse (1988a). *Review of the Manitoba Continuing Care Program*. Toronto.

Price Waterhouse (1988b). *Operational Review of the Ontario Home Care Program: Final Report*. Toronto: Report to the Ministry of Health.

Richardson, B.G. (1990). "Overview of Provincial Home Care Programs in Canada." *Forum* (Fall): 3-10.

Rosenthal, C.J. (1987). "Aging and Intergenerational Relations in Canada." In V.W. Marshall, *Aging in Canada*, 2nd ed., 311-342. Markham, Ontario: Fitzhenry and Whiteside.

Shapiro, E. (1989). *A Cross-Canada Tour of Home Care*. Nova Scotia Conference on Home Care.

Shapiro, E. (1991). "Un tour d'horizon du soutien à domicile au Canada." In *Actes du Forum sur le soutien à domicile*. Montreal, March 21-22.

Shapiro, E. et al. (1987). "Do Nursing Homes Reduce Hospital Use?" *Medical Care* 25 (1): 1-8.

Statistics Canada (1991). *Vieillissement et autonomie*, September.

Strauss, A., and J.M. Corbin (1988). *Shaping a New Health Care System*. San Francisco: Jossey-Bass Inc. Publishers.

Ujimoto, K.V. (1987). "The Ethnic Dimension of Aging in Canada." In V.W. Marshall, *Aging in Canada*, 2nd ed., 111-137. Markham, Ontario: Fitzhenry and Whiteside.

# four

## Care for the Elderly in the Netherlands: New Policies and Practices

*Marja A. Pijl*

In this chapter we will discuss recent developments in care for the elderly in the Netherlands. First we will give some background information on the elderly and on relevant policies. We will then discuss some specific concepts related to care. Changes in policy and the development of new concepts have led to a variety of experiments and innovations, many of them accompanied by research. We will describe some of these. We will end the chapter in making a critical assessment of the present situation by presenting some new vistas which may be of importance for the more distant future.

## RELEVANT DATA ON THE ELDERLY AND RELATED POLICIES

### Some Data on the Elderly

The Netherlands is a small but densely populated country of 15 million inhabitants. At present 12.8% of the population is 65 years or over. It is expected that the percentage of elderly will gradually increase until a high point is reached in 2035 when 23.4% will be 65 years or over. Life expectancy at birth is 73.5 years for men and 80.1 years for women. Therefore there are many more elderly women than elderly men: in 1990 there were 533,000 women of 75 years or over and only 278,000 men in the same age group. The higher the age the more often people live in a single person household. However, this changes after the age of 85, when there is a sharp increase in the number of persons living in institutions. The following table is based on figures given in a recent government White Paper (WVC 1990).

Table 4.1    Men and women living in single person households, with other persons, and in institutions in 1987 (in percentages)

|  | Single person household | Living with other persons | In institutions | Total |
|---|---|---|---|---|
| **Men** | | | | |
| 65-69 | 11 | 88 | 2 | 100 |
| 70-74 | 13 | 84 | 3 | 100 |
| 75-79 | 18 | 76 | 6 | 100 |
| 80-84 | 24 | 61 | 15 | 100 |
| 85+ | 24 | 43 | 33 | 100 |
| **Women** | | | | |
| 65-69 | 33 | 64 | 2 | 100 |
| 70-74 | 45 | 51 | 4 | 100 |
| 75-79 | 50 | 39 | 10 | 100 |
| 80-84 | 46 | 31 | 24 | 100 |
| 85+ | 28 | 24 | 47 | 100 |

The number of persons aged 65 and over with a foreign nationality is still relatively low. In 1989 their number was just over 15,000. This figure does not include persons having come from Surinam or the Antilles who hold Dutch nationality. The number of elderly persons (65 and over) of Surinamese origin is estimated at 6,000 and of Antillian origin at 1,000. It is to be expected that there will be a considerable growth in the near future. When we look at the 55 and over age group the figures for foreign nationals and persons coming from Surinam and the Antilles are respectively: 38,000, 15,000 and 3,000. There are no reliable data on the number of refugees and gypsies.

In 1985 the average gross income of elderly persons was Dfl. 28,740 per year. The State Pension, which every person over 65 receives, accounted for 57% of the elderly's income, whereas 26% came from work related pensions and 18% came from other sources (such as capital). The amount of the State Pension for 1991 is fixed at Dfl. 1,428 gross per month for a single person and at Dfl. 996 gross per month for each of two cohabiting partners. The amount of the State Pension is fixed yearly at a level which is considered to be the social minimum. Looking more closely at incomes one finds that 17% of all households with a head of family aged 65 or over have an income which is not more than 105% of the social minimum. Single persons and persons aged 80 and over in particular are found among those who live on the social minimum. In other words, many of those living on the social minimum are elderly women, living by themselves.

Elderly persons who are not institutionalised mostly live in normal houses or apartments. 7% of the age group 65-74 and 19% of the age group 75 and over live in houses especially designed for the elderly. Elderly persons own their homes less often than the younger age groups. 63% of the elderly population live in rented housing. The quality of the rented housing, especially for the age group 75 and over, is lower than average. Elderly tenants pay a considerable amount of rent: on the average this represents 20% of their income, even though many of them receive a subsidy towards rental costs (SCP 1990).

The elderly who are institutionalised live in nursing homes or residential homes. The latter used to provide primarily accommodation with some services. As admission criteria for the residential homes have become much stricter the differences between residential homes and nursing homes seem to be gradually disappearing.

The present day elderly have had considerably less education than coming generations. In 1985 53% of persons aged 55 and over had had no more than elementary school. When we differentiate for gender we find that 41% of men aged 55 and over and 62% of women aged 55 and over had no more than elementary education. It is expected that in 2010 these figures will be much lower: in that year 20% of men aged 55 and over and 31% of women aged 55 and over will have had elementary education only (SCP 1990). The enrollment of the elderly in educational courses is less than half the rate of the age group 30-54. As far as data on gender are available they show that two thirds of the elderly participants in adult education are women.

There have been considerable changes in participation in the labor market over the last two decades. The following table illustrates this.

As can be seen participation of women in the labor market has increased. For a long time the rule was that women with children stayed at home and cared for the family. Gradually this pattern is changing. Women are now encouraged to stay at work while raising a family or to re-enter the labor market after some years at home. This change of norms has had its effect on the age group 50-54. The table also shows that men leave their jobs at an earlier age than before. This is partly due to early retirement schemes, but a more important reason is disability. 38% of men aged 60-64 receive a disability pension (WVC 1990). Of those aged 65 and over only 1.6% are employed.

Table 4.2    Labor participation according to age and gender, 1971-1989 (in % of the corresponding age group) (SCP 1990)

|  | 1971 | 1980 | 1989 |
|---|---|---|---|
| **Women** | | | |
| 50-54 | 23 | 25 | 31 |
| 55-59 | 19 | 18 | 19 |
| 60-64 | 13 | 10 | 7 |
| **Men** | | | |
| 50-54 | 93 | 86 | 84 |
| 55-59 | 87 | 74 | 67 |
| 60-64 | 74 | 46 | 25 |

Political involvement among the elderly is low. Although a high percentage participate in elections (in 1986 more than 95% of the age group 65-84 did so), they are underrepresented in elected bodies such as Parliament and provincial and municipal councils. Since 1973 there has been a decrease in elderly people's contacts with their political representatives, such as their members of Parliament, burgomaster, alderman or member of the municipal council. In 1973 26% of persons aged 65 and over reported having had contacts with a local politician. In 1986 this percentage was only 12. In a survey held in 1989 70% of the age group 65 and over said they agreed with the statement that they did not have any influence on government policy.

On the other hand there has been a growing participation of the elderly in voluntary work. Over the last 10 years the percentage of time spent on voluntary work has gone up from 2.1 to 2.9.

Finally we want to mention that 30% of non-institutionalised men aged 65 and over and 31% of the corresponding category of women are members of an association for the elderly.

## Policy for the Elderly

Policies are developed in many places. One can distinguish between sector policies (such as housing, social security, education, health) and policies for certain categories (such as youth, elderly, handicapped, migrants). The problem with policies for categories is that they are usually built on elements of sector policies. Their effectiveness depends on the willingness of policy makers in these various sectors to tune in to the policies for categories. The most recent White Paper on policy for the elderly was signed by no less than five ministers, the Minister of Social Welfare, Health and Cultural Affairs (WVC) being the minister primarily responsible. There are not only national policies: there are also provincial and municipal policies. As a consequence of the recent trend to decentralise, more powers have been given to provincial and municipal government.

There are many private associations in the Netherlands. This is part of the social history of the country. For a long time both the Protestant churches and the Roman Catholic church have had an important influence on social life. Therefore many associations were set up on a denominational basis. After the second world war the government began to subsidise these organisations. Originally the government did not interfere with their policies but as the subsidies grew, government influence grew as well. Gradually many organisations have changed, lost their religious orientation, merged and become professionalised. So far, most of the professional care in the Netherlands is given by fully subsidised, private organisations, not by government agencies. Although the organisations, because of their financial dependence, have lost much of their power and autonomy they still play a role in policy making on the national, provincial and local level.

Reflecting on recent developments in the social sector the Social and Cultural Planning Office has come to the conclusion that there is overproduction of policies in the Netherlands. In its latest biennial report (SCP 1990) the following analysis is presented of policy making on the national level. Even though the government is striving for a greater efficacy this does not lead to less policy making. On the contrary, in some sectors there is an increase in policy measures. Policy overproduction has different appearances: goals that have not been attained are not discarded but are further refined. Budget cuts often lead to more regulations because smaller budgets come to target more specifically designated groups.

Politicians seem to have an immanent and continual urge to develop new policies. They do not seem to bother about the practicability of their ruling, nor do they wait until earlier measures have been fully implemented. New policy leads to new rules on top of the existing ones. In some sectors such as the care sector and education the adaptability and flexibility of large and complex organisations are overestimated. Do not these policies overshoot the mark? The Social and Cultural Report concludes that fundamental choices need to be made concerning governmental interference.

Having made these preliminary remarks we will now take a closer look at policy for the elderly. A good overview is given in the special section of the Social and Cultural Report (SCP 1990) dealing with the elderly. It is only since 1970 that the government has a specific policy for the elderly. That does not mean that there were no laws specifically meant for the elderly before that date. In fact, the law that can be considered as the precursor of the State Pension dates from 1919. Improvements were made in 1947 until the State Pension was introduced in 1957.

When the government started to subsidise private organisations in the care sector the government did not at first interfere with their policy, but limited itself to a certain control over prices and quality. Whatever measures were taken had mostly to do with the financial situation of the elderly and with the need for protection of some of the elderly. That is why the government made money available for residential homes for the elderly.

The first White Paper on policy for the elderly (1970) characterises the elderly as persons who are faced with losses in many spheres of life. One of the main policy goals is easing some of the hardships of the most vulnerable among the elderly. A second important goal is to maintain the independence of elderly persons.

The second White Paper (1975) continues in the same line. It contains measures to counteract deprivation and to promote independent living. The government puts a limit to the number of residential homes and makes money available for sheltered housing and home help. It is then that the government begins to act on the kind and volume of private services. The same White Paper also launches the idea of the closed circuit of services, which means that there should be a coherent system of services which can deal with the total range of the elderly's needs. For every need there has to be a specific service. The Social and Cultural Report remarks that the issue of the interrelation of services is primarily a problem of policy making and not so much a problem of the elderly.

In the next White Paper (1982) a similar policy problem attains a central place: cost containment. At that time it has become evident that a strong increase in the number of elderly is to be expected. Calculations of the financial consequences of this demographic trend are felt to be alarming. From then on the core element of policy for the elderly is financial policy. Later government papers (1986 and 1988) do not come up with new motives for policy for the elderly. Gradually a distinction is being made between different groups of elderly: younger elderly, older elderly, elderly women, elderly migrants.

At the end of 1990 a new White Paper is published. It consists of one central paper and no less than 13 accompanying publications, some of them dealing with more specific policies (such as prevention or the position of elderly women), others reporting the results of commissioned research. What is new? The government chooses to define the elderly as persons aged 55 and older. Research has pointed out that the age group 55-65 has more or less the same pattern of life as the age group 65-75, due to the fact that people leave the labor market at an earlier age. The government states that policy for the elderly is more than care policy. Integration and participation of the elderly need to be stimulated. Dutch society makes too little use of the experience and wisdom of the elderly, according to the government. Policy for the elderly is considered to be complementary policy, that is to say in those instances where policies geared to the general population prohibit participation by the elderly, complementary policy for the elderly needs to be developed in order to enable them to participate.

Preconditions for participation are: a sufficient income, adequate housing and good health.

In the White Paper the following priorities are stated:
- The development of a local and national prevention policy.
- A greater coherence in policy and practice concerning housing and care.
- More care for chronically ill elderly persons.
- Education as a condition for participation and prevention.
- Prevention of involuntary loss of work.
- Integration of policy goals of women's emancipation and policy for the elderly.
- Revaluation of old age.

These priorities are elaborated in sections on income, housing, health and participation. They lead to a lengthy programme of action. Some of the proposed actions are very concrete such as: more money for prevention, extra chairs for geriatrics at the universities, subsidies for projects which are meant to stimulate social integration of elderly women. A lot of the proposed action consists of more information, more research and experiments.

In the context of this chapter it is impossible to delve more deeply into the different recommendations (of which some have appeared earlier in other government papers, concerning health care, for instance). We do want to point out, however, that the 1990 White Paper takes a rather strong stand against age discrimination. It seems as if the pendulum is swinging back, from care and finances to revaluation of old age.

The first commentaries have now appeared. There is a certain degree of appreciation for the rather thorough job that has been done, but of course there is also criticism. Some of the main points so far are:

- There is little continuity with preceding White Papers.
- The consequences of the ageing of the population are not adequately assessed.
- The two age groups, 55-75 and 75 and over, are rather different and the question is raised whether they should be treated in the same way. Participation is a more realistic goal for the younger age group, whereas care is more important for the older age group.
- The government gives no concrete indications of how to achieve integration of the elderly.
- Too little is said about the financial situation of the elderly. The effects of living on the social minimum for years on end are underestimated. It means real poverty, which affects elderly women especially.
- Housing policy has so far done little for the elderly. As the government promotes home care instead of residential care, adequate housing needs to be provided. This will affect the budget of the Ministry of Housing. This effect of care policy on housing has not been recognised.
- Prevention is used as a medical concept. One should also look at the impact of policy measures in other sectors and their effect on the well-being of the elderly. Prevention should mean that elderly persons are not put at a disadvantage.
- There is no coordination of research on ageing.
- There are positive reactions to the paragraphs on age discrimination. It is also stated that the government, in spite of its good intentions, has recently taken several measures which are discriminatory.

One commentator goes so far as to say that a policy for the elderly in itself is discriminatory. In some other recent publications such as the Social and Cultural Report doubts are expressed about the necessity of a policy on special provisions for the elderly.

## Other Relevant Policies

As has been said, many sector policies are relevant for elderly persons. In this section we will discuss some policies related to care.

### Income policy and social security

Income policy and social security are important because a higher income makes elderly people less dependent. The financial situation of elderly persons depends in the first place on the amount they receive as a State Pension. The amount of the State Pension is linked to minimum wages. This linkage guarantees that the State Pension keeps up with increases in wages. Because many elderly have no other income than the State Pension it is important that it be sufficient to live on. This is a political issue at present. As we stated before, it is rather difficult to make ends meet with the State Pension only.

It is true that growing numbers of elderly persons also have work related pensions. Because of the low labor participation of women it is especially women who do not have an additional source of income in old age. It is clear that it will take decades before women's work related pensions will be at the same level as those men enjoy. It is a matter of employment policy to take sufficient measures to assure all workers of an adequate work related pension.

Social security provides income for the unemployed until the age of 65. Social security also provides additional financial means in certain circumstances as well as aids and adjustments for disabled persons. In 1986 47,000 households of elderly persons received social security money in addition to their State Pension. Social security is based on extensive and detailed legislation and is controlled by the Department of Social Affairs. Executive tasks have been delegated to the regional and municipal level. Some municipalities have in the recent past established funds for special expenses (for instance, for social participation by the elderly) because they felt that the State Pension was too low to meet such needs. There has been a debate as to whether this is within the competency of municipal government. Income policy is supposed to be a national, not a local, task.

## The social services

The story concerning the social services is a different one. Most social services started as private organisations set up by volunteers. Gradually they became professionalised. In the sixties and seventies the national government stepped in with subsidies. The financial support of the government has grown until it amounted to practically 100%. At the end of the eighties the social services were decentralised to the municipal level. This means that the national government, after having made important cuts in the budget for the social services, has transmitted the remaining amount to the Municipal Fund to be divided among the municipalities. Policy concerning the social services has since then been the competency of municipalities.

It is too early still to evaluate the results of municipal policies. It is likely that in due time there will be a great variety of local social services. Because of successive cuts in the national contribution to the Municipal Fund the prospects for the local social service organisations are not very promising.

Among the social services on the local level which are relevant for elderly people we find:
-   generic social work
-   information services
-   community centres
-   service centres
-   volunteer organisations
-   coordinating services for the elderly
-   services developed as part of support policy for the elderly (we will discuss this further in the next section).

Before decentralisation, home help was considered to be one of the core disciplines of the social services. We will next explain how home help made the transition to the medical sector.

## Health care policy

The Netherlands has a peculiar system of health care insurance. Until now the lower income groups (65% of the population) have been insured by Health Insurance Funds. This insurance is compulsory and the premiums are income related. The higher income groups are insured by private health insurance companies. They pay a flat rate, proportionate to the insurance coverage.

Medical expenses in the Netherlands, as in other countries, have soared. In the period 1975 to 1982 the costs almost doubled. From 1982 to 1987 the growth was comparable to the growth of the Gross National Product. The government tried to gain control through mechanisms such as planning and structuring, but was not very successful. Gradually the government has gained control by laying down the prices which producers are allowed to charge and the prices which consumers must pay. More effective measures to control volume have been introduced. Institutions like hospitals receive a predetermined budget from which production must be achieved. In 1990 the expenses for care amounted to Dfl. 47.8 billion or 9.5% of the Gross National Product (WVC, FOZ 1991).

The insurance system does not hold any incentives for cost awareness. Apart from that, the health care system is very complicated. It is governed by a variety of different laws such as the Health Insurance Funds Act, the Hospital Services Act, the Act on Tariffs in Health Care, the Extraordinary Medical Expenses Act (AWBZ), the Act on Residential Homes for the Elderly (WBO), several social security laws and the Act on Well-being. The diverse and detailed legislation hinders smooth cooperation between the many organisations which play a role in health care. Other complicating factors are the differences in catchment area between the various institutions and the fact that most of them developed as independent organisations or disciplines.

With a view to these problems the government set up a Commission under the chairmanship of Dekker to advise on ways of controlling volume, on revision of the health care insurance system and on deregulation. The Dekker Commission presented its report in March 1987. The Commission warned against only accepting parts of its recommendations. In order to work, the plan had to be implemented as a whole. Because the plan was very imaginative we will briefly sketch the basic ideas.

The Commission started from the following premisses. Health care and social care are closely related and need to be brought into the same system. Quality and accessibility need to be guaranteed by greater effectiveness. Providers and consumers have to be made more aware of the costs. Unnecessary care should be avoided. Flexibility should be built into the system. Through the introduction of "market elements" effectiveness and flexibility can be stimulated. At the same time the principles of solidarity and righteousness have to be maintained. The new system has to remove the obstacles to replacing expensive intramural care with less expensive institutional or home care.

On the basis of these premisses the Dekker Commission has proposed a basic insurance plan for the entire population, which includes approximately 85% of the "package" which Health Insurance Funds cover as well as the major part of the social care services. The 15% portion not included in the basic insurance comprises medicine, dental care for adults, physiotherapy and a few other provisions. For these items each individual will have to obtain separate optional insurance for a flat rate fee, according to Dekker. The premium for the basic insurance (85% of the "package") is for the most part income related (75%) but also has a flat rate portion (10%). For the use of several services (such as nursing homes and residential homes), patients also have to pay a contribution. Individuals can choose their own insurance company.

Insurance companies have no right to refuse "bad risks." The income related premiums and the income related contributions of users go into a central fund which is redistributed among the insurance companies according to the characteristics of their clients (e.g. an insurance company with many elderly persons will get more money from the central fund than one with mostly young clients). Competition between insurance companies is based on their flat rates. That is why the Commission finds it important that a considerable part of the total premium (namely the optional insurance which covers 15% of the services and another 10% included in the basic insurance) be a flat rate. The insurance companies contract care providers. The care providers will no longer be subsidised by the government.

The central government will state the amount of income related premium to be paid through the fiscal system. The insurance companies in turn have to make ends meet with the money from the central fund and their flat rates. The role of the government will be reduced to planning hospitals, controlling quality and guaranteeing patients' rights, according to the Dekker Commission.

Where are we now (in early 1991)? In the first instance the government accepted the plan with only slight amendments. As a very first phase it was decided to bring the home help services (until then part of the social services and about to be decentralised to the municipal level) under the Extraordinary Medical Expenses Act (AWBZ). This transfer brings home help into the medical sector and enhances the desired integration of medical and social care.

Then the government, a coalition of Christian Democrats and Conservatives, fell and was replaced by a coalition of Christian Democrats and Socialists. This government looked somewhat more critically at the plan, especially at the "market elements." Having made some more amendments the new government has decided to carry on with the plan. The amended Dekker plan is called the Simons plan (after the minister responsible for health care).

The main issues of the Simons plan are:

- The basic insurance will not comprise 85% of the currently insured services but approximately 96%. It is felt that the risk is too high that the lower income groups will not take the optional insurance and might therefore be deprived of such essentials as medicine and dental care. All essential elements of health care will be brought into the basic insurance. However, a precise description of what will be covered by the basic insurance and what by the optional insurance still has to be made. This task is not likely to be an easy one.

- 85% of the premium paid for the basic insurance will be income related and will be collected through the fiscal system. 15% will be a flat rate fee, to be paid directly to the insurance company.

- Insurance companies can compete on the basis of their flat rate fees, but also on the basis of their optional insurance. They are obliged to charge the same amount for the same services (i.e. higher fees for "bad risks" are forbidden), but they have the freedom to agree that clients take a certain financial risk in exchange for a lower flat rate fee.

- The services that must be paid for by the insurance companies will be described in terms of functions, not in terms of the organisations which deliver the services. For instance, "nursing" need not necessarily be provided by the nationally recognised District Nursing Organisation, but may also be contracted from a nursing home or from a different private organisation which complies with certain requirements concerning quality. It is expected that this will increase the flexibility of the system. At the same time this leaves the insurance companies a certain freedom to fill in these functions as they deem appropriate and at as low a price as possible. This will stimulate competition between insurance companies.

- Insurance companies will obtain budgets on the basis of certain norms. These norms will have to be established. This is one of the main problems to be solved before the system can be put into effect.
- There will be a law concerning the quality of medical and care services. Organisations which provide care must comply with this law.
- Clients will have more rights. They will have to be represented on the boards of recognised insurance companies and also in the new Council on Care Insurance.
- The Extraordinary Medical Expenses Act (AWBZ) will be changed so that the different medical and care services can gradually be brought under this law. When this operation is finished the AWBZ will be replaced by the Act on Care Insurance. This new law should be effective by 1995.

At this point it is difficult to predict whether all existing problems can be solved, and what effects these plans will have.

## Some Specific Concepts

In the preceding sections we have given an outline of some policies relevant to the subject of home care. In this section we will present certain concepts which have been used in one or more of the described policies and which have been or are likely to be influential for the development of care. Quite often such concepts are introduced, are discussed, may lead to experiments and research, and then become part of regular practice or are rejected.

At this particular moment many experiments and innovations are taking place based on notions that were developed in the first half of the eighties. These are the experiments we will discuss in the next section. In order to enable the reader to understand the purpose of these experiments and research we will first explain these concepts.

### Coordinating services for the elderly

These services were introduced in the seventies. They had several purposes: on the one hand they had to coordinate different existing services for the elderly which, at that time already, were many and often overlapping; on the other hand they had to organise educational and recreational activities for the elderly. They were also meant to help improve the image of elderly people in society.

The coordinating task has proved to be difficult because the new organisations did not have any powers over the others. They were more successful in organising educational and recreational activities for the elderly. In recent years they have been increasingly engaged in activities in the care sector such as meal services, alarm systems or day care. They have also supported groups and associations of the elderly in a process of emancipation. In doing so they have improved the image of the elderly. Volunteers play an important role in the activities of the coordinating services.

## Support policy for the elderly

Support policy was introduced in 1983 when the government had already realised that the ageing of the population would cause tremendous increases in the costs of care. Until then it was relatively easy to be admitted to a residential home for the elderly. At that point the government decided to make important budget cuts for residential homes. In order to counterbalance the effects of these cuts some extra money was made available for what was called "support policy." This extra money was not meant for new organisations but for the existing ones. With this extra money they were expected to develop new activities which would enable elderly persons to stay in their own homes longer. "Support policy" was supposed to fill in the gaps between organisations through cooperation and extended services. As it turned out, most of the money went to residential homes and to coordinating services. It was used for day care, alarm systems, meal services and a number of other facilities.

## Substitution

Substitution is a concept which has played a key role in the efforts of the government to contain care costs. Substitution means that care given by more expensive intramural services (like hospitals or nursing homes) should be replaced by less expensive services (like day care) and preferably by services in the community (home care). It was believed that through certain mechanisms in the health care system it was quite common that more care was given than really was needed. For instance, people often stay longer in hospital after medical treatment has ended than is strictly necessary because of the lack of sufficient care at home. Similarly, people move to residential homes prematurely for fear they will not be able to get sufficient support in their home when the need arises. If sufficient home care (tailored care) can be made available, the costs of care can be reduced, according to the government.

Later on we will discuss some experiments in which substitution has been tried out. Here we want to mention that there are serious obstacles to substitution outside the experimental setting. If expensive forms of care have to be replaced by less expensive ones, these less expensive forms of care have to be available. In many cases they are not. A reasonable substitute for hospital care is care in a nursing home. However, there is a dramatic shortage of places in nursing homes. If people are sent home earlier from hospital or from a nursing home and cannot enter a residential home (in which the number of places has been reduced considerably), one would expect that more home care facilities would be made available. However, the volume of home help has practically not increased since 1985 and that of district nursing only slightly. In addition, the working conditions in the care sector are not at all attractive and the nationally fixed salaries so low that it is very difficult to get vacancies filled.

## Case management or care management

As we have seen, many organisations provide different services for elderly people who need "tailored care." In most cases there are fixed rules (set by law or otherwise) that state who is entitled, how needs must be assessed, and how much should be provided and under which conditions.

This means that it is a rather complicated affair to contact the different agencies and to combine different elements of the care services so as to make an adequate arrangement for the individual person in need of care. In order to do so one must be able to make a good assessment of needs, one must be informed about the services and the conditions through which they are available, and one must have time and patience and an ability to negotiate. For many persons in need of care this task is rather complicated. It would be helpful to them if this task could be delegated to a professional to negotiate on their behalf. There are different names for such a person: care manager, case manager, care mediator or care coordinator. Their tasks and their powers may be defined differently as they are part of different organisations but the underlying idea is the same.

### Individual care budget

So far, persons in need of care receive services. The question has been raised whether it would not be more practical to give these persons a budget which they can use to buy the services they need. It is likely that this will induce more cost awareness and at the same time provide the client with more suitable services. Of course there are a number of problems to be solved: who is entitled, how shall the budget be fixed, will the client become the employer of the caregivers, how will social security and taxes of the caregivers be dealt with, etc. Sometimes the idea of the individual care budget is linked with that of care manager: it is then the care manager who decides together with the client what services will be purchased with the care budget and who actually makes the necessary arrangements.

### The caring society

This concept is, more so than the preceding ones, an ideological concept. It was launched in the early eighties by the Christian Democrats. The Minister of Social Welfare, Health and Cultural Affairs, himself a Christian Democrat, stated time and again that it was necessary for citizens to take a greater share in caring. According to his views too much was expected of the state. Right from the beginning this view has been criticised. It has been pointed out that the smaller size of families, geographical mobility and the increasing number of women at work are some of the factors which make it unrealistic to expect that more voluntary care can be produced than is actually being given. The concept of the caring society was later replaced by "responsible society." Since then a lot of research has been done on voluntary and informal care. After the change of government the caring society has disappeared from the political agenda.

### Limits of care

The ageing of the population, new medical technology and well informed patients who want the best of care are factors which are likely to increase the demand for health care. Even though the Simons plan is expected to contribute to cost containment, the time has come to ask ourselves if it really is desirable to provide all treatment which is technically possible. There have already been some discussions in Parliament on the limits of care.

The present government has invited a committee to advise on these matters. The official mandate of the committee consists of the following tasks:

- to develop strategies for handling the making of choices;
- to describe the problems involved on the national, institutional and individual levels;
- to launch public discussion on the question: "Should everything be done which is technically possible?" This third task is meant to make the general public aware of the fact that choices need to be made.

## EXPERIMENTS AND RESEARCH

In this part we will describe a number of experiments and new practices. Our description is based on research reports. We will start with two series of experiments which have been supported by, respectively, the Health Insurance Funds Council and the Ministry of Social Welfare, Health and Cultural Affairs. The advantage of experiments supported by influential organisations is that the latter can decide, if necessary, to suspend the effects of certain laws for the purpose of the experiment. Such experiments usually obtain adequate funding, are accompanied by research, receive a lot of publicity and have a relatively great impact. This does not necessarily mean that they are the best or the most imaginative experiments. For that reason we have also selected some other experiments which have been initiated on the local level and have been developed with less or no help from the national level.

We know that in very many places innovations have been introduced. Sometimes they are adequately described and evaluated, and sometimes they are not. At present there is no central point in the Netherlands where all information is collected and made available to the public. Nor is there coordination of research on these new developments. However, when one makes a number of searches it is surprising how much material can be found. Its quality and scope are very different. It is therefore difficult to establish criteria for the selection of experiments to be presented in this chapter. We have decided to look on the one hand at the expected impact of the experiments and on the other hand at the availability of research reports. We have also tried to show the diversity of ongoing innovations.

More care is given by informal carers and volunteers than by official agencies. The discussion on the caring society has generated a lot of research on informal care. Some important studies have appeared in the last few years. We will discuss the results of these in a separate section.

## Research on Substitution

### Experiments in intensive home care

There experiments have been initiated by the Health Insurance Funds Council. The experiments were developed because it was felt that there was insufficient home care available for those terminal patients who wished to spend their last days at home. In many cases these patients could not obtain the necessary care and attention in hospital either. Especially missing in the home situation was night care. At the same time the question was raised whether other patients staying in hospital or nursing homes could be cared for at home. The experiments were started in order to find out what goes into providing adequate home care. The experiments have been evaluated by ITS (Institute for Applied Social Sciences in Nijmegen).

The experiments were conducted in three regions (Amsterdam, the province of Groningen, and Breda and vicinity, regions with a varying degree of urbanisation). The aims of the experiments were formulated as follows:

- to derive an understanding of the quantitative and qualitative demands of home care;
- to assess the capacity of informal and formal care;
- to investigate the legal, financial and organisational obstacles in the present system;
- to find out how the necessary conditions for home care can be realised;
- to monitor the effects of substitution. Intensive home care has been given in those cases where the following conditions were met:
  - the patient wants to be cared for at home;
  - the patient has been assessed for care in a hospital or nursing home;
  - informal care is available;
  - the expected duration of the home care is no longer than three months;
  - the average costs of the home care do not exceed Dfl. 200 per day.

In the three regions the organisational set-up differs. All three locations have an agency which is responsible for coordination of care. Apart from regular care provided by the GP, the district nursing organisation and the home help organisation, there is a pool of other helpers either employed by the coordinating agency or by other subsidised organisations or contracted on a personal basis or from a non-subsidised organisation. The research is based on data collected in the three experiments and on journals written by formal and informal carers.

Approximately 800 patients have been included in the experimental phase. In some cases the patients have come home from hospital after medical treatment has been finished. In other cases intensive home care is supposed to prevent or postpone hospitalisation and to support informal carers. The average age of the patients is 70. More than half of the patients live in a two person household. There are more single women than single men in the experiment. Most patients come into the experiment through their GP, the district nurse or home help.

The need for care is usually assessed by the person who will later be the care coordinator. This is often a district nurse but it can also be a GP or somebody from the home help organisation. The most frequently felt needs are general care (described as nightwatch, washing and refreshing, and help with getting dressed and undressed and going to the toilet), household tasks such as shopping and cleaning, medical care and nursing. It is clear that in almost all experimental cases the patients would have gone into a hospital or nursing home if no intensive care had been available. It has been difficult to estimate how many "hospital days" have been saved. The researchers do not present figures.

Most participants in these experiments have a partner, relatives, neighbours or friends who are willing to provide some help. In some cases a volunteer organisation is mentioned. However, when the intensive home care starts the informal care is mostly given by a family member living in the same house. Other informal helpers give less assistance than was expected at the outset.

During the period of intensive care most patients have three or four visits per day from helpers. The average duration of a visit varies in the three regions between 4.4 and 5.3 hours. One third of these visits are made by a district nurse, and 7 to 9% of the visits are made by the GP. In spite of one of the criteria of the experiment, about half of the patients have no informal carer. In those cases where informal carers are available they account for 30% of the visits.

The average period during which intensive home care is given varies from 15 days in Amsterdam to 22 days in Groningen and 32 days in Breda. The most frequent reason for ending the intensive home care is the death of the patient.

Between 66 and 71% of the help for which patients apply is extra help (i.e. help which is additional to the regular home care services). The figures for help which has been allocated (GP care excluded) are, per week: Amsterdam: 16 hours regular help and 54 hours additional help; Groningen: 20 hours regular help and 47 hours additional help; Breda: 16 hours regular help and 37 hours additional help.

In a separate publication the experiences of helpers and informal carers have been recorded. This part of the research is based on 992 journals and on questionnaires which patients and/or informal helpers were asked to fill out when intensive home care was finished. In general, informal carers are satisfied. Only 6% mention that next time they would choose a different solution. This is predominantly in psycho-geriatric cases or cases in which the patient had to be hospitalised after all.

The main problems that have been mentioned by the informal carers are the number of different persons who come into the home as formal helpers and the loss of privacy in the households concerned. It is difficult for the informal carers to perform all the necessary tasks. One third of the informal carers say their tasks are too heavy. The formal helpers are satisfied with the cooperation among colleagues and among formal and informal helpers. The nightwatch is considered to be an important aspect of intensive home care, in the perception of both informal and formal carers.

Among the recommendations made on the basis of this part of the project we find a strong plea not to overburden the informal carers and to strengthen the coordination of care. Different models are possible: a special care manager who has no helping tasks or the creation of one single organisation which has all the different services available.

In these experiments the costs of the additional care have been calculated without the costs of regular care. The average additional costs are Dfl. 230 per day in Amsterdam, Dfl. 192 per day in Groningen, and Dfl. 136 per day in Breda. In this average some days on which no additional care has been given are included. When individual patients are compared it turns out that there are important differences in the amount of care received. The most expensive patient (in Amsterdam) received services costing more than Dfl. 750 per day.

On the basis of these experiments it is impossible to compare costs between intensive home care and intramural care because there are no data available on the costs of intramural care for the same group of patients. The costs vary with the intensity of care, in both home care and intramural care. However, it seems too simple to say that, as a general rule, home care is less costly than intramural care. Reality proves to be more complicated than that. Nevertheless, the Health Insurance Funds Council has decided on the basis of these experiments to make intensive home care available in the entire country.

## Demonstration projects on substitution

The Ministry of WVC (Social Welfare, Health and Cultural Affairs) selected some local projects as demonstration projects on substitution. These projects are supposed to run three years (1988-1991). They are evaluated by a team of researchers from three research institutes and four universities coordinated by ITS (Institute for Applied Social Sciences in Nijmegen). The researchers will describe how the projects work and their effects. At this moment a final evaluation is not yet available but there is an interim report which we have used for the following description (WVC 1990).

Four projects (two in rural regions and two in urbanised communities) deal with the full range of care for the elderly. Two other projects, one in The Hague and one in Rotterdam, deal with a specific aspect of care. The first four projects are aimed at all the elderly in the community, whereas the projects in The Hague and Rotterdam target elderly persons who need intramural or semimural care. The first four projects will try to change the relationships between organisations in such a way that elderly persons will use more care in the community and less intramural care. This means that new, integrated kinds of home care have to be provided and that procedures for the allocation of care need to be changed. The two projects in The Hague and Rotterdam will serve to find out if elderly people who have signed up for intramural care can get other, more effective services than the traditional intramural care.

In The Hague an attempt is made to integrate functions of intramural and extramural services in one new service. In Rotterdam care mediators and individual care budgets are made available to elderly persons. In these demonstration projects there are five areas in which interventions are possible. These are:

- the supply of services, i.e. more day care, home care and informal care and less intramural care;
- the allocation of care, i.e. integration of assessment systems and the creation of one central office for all the different kinds of professional home care and mediation of care;
- the coordination of care, i.e. integration of organisations involved in (specific parts of) home care and integration between intramural and extramural care;
- financing, i.e. channeling all the different kinds of subsidies into one central fund and creating uniformity of contributions by users of services;
- planning of care, i.e. integration of different organisations involved in planning.

What are the results so far? Five of the six projects seem to have fair to good results. One project has been stopped for lack of results. Some of the reported difficulties in this project are:

- a lack of clarity about responsibilities;
- the project team does not have any powers over the participating organisations;
- a lack of consensus;
- uncertainty about the future;
- differences in target groups (some organisations work for the entire population and not exclusively for the elderly);
- the complexity of the project: 31 organisations are involved, spread out over a large territory in this rural area.

In the other projects most of the intended interventions have taken place or are being developed. Different forms of integration have been tried out such as joint consultation or the introduction of a care manager. Organisations with different catchment areas have harmonised these. In some cases the capacity of home care services has been increased at the expense of (planned) intramural services. Financial integration has proved difficult. It has only been fully realised in one project.

The project in The Hague has realised sheltered housing for people with different degrees of need. Some of these receive services from the local home help and district nursing organisation, whereas others, in need of more care, obtain this from the adjacent nursing home. The idea that people can stay in their private but sheltered apartment, even if they need intensive care, has been realised for the most part. However, in the case of persons with serious psycho-geriatric problems who have no informal carers who can watch over them 24 hours a day, it has not been possible to keep them in their apartment.

The care mediators in Rotterdam serve 75 elderly persons. They have no formal coordinating power. Nevertheless, some coordination has been realised. The care budgets are used to purchase additional care on top of the home care services that are available for all elderly. It has been a surprise that only part of these budgets have been used. Although there are not yet any final results the impression so far is that the elderly in the experimental group stay in their homes longer than the control group (60% of the experimental group are still in their own homes versus 20% of the control group). The elderly in the experiment feel reassured that they will get the necessary care once they need it.

During the experimental period one more project has been recognised as a demonstration project: it is a project for elderly people in Hengelo. It functions much like the first four projects discussed here. What is special in this project is that there is a group of elderly who are given special attention. This group consists of persons who do not yet receive any help but who may need it at any moment. An agreement has been made with them that they will obtain help as soon as the need arises. It is expected that they will feel reassured and will therefore use less services. In Hengelo a demonstration centre has been established where technical and other adaptations to the house are shown which make it possible to remain at home for a longer time. Sponsors of this centre are the local health care insurance companies and industry.

These are the results of the demonstration projects as far as they are known at this moment (early 1991). It is too early still to be able to say what the effects of substitution have been. It seems, however, that in the course of these experiments there has been a shift in emphasis: quality of care has become a central theme.

## An experiment in Gouda

An experiment in the city of Gouda (60,000 inhabitants) is the subject of a

dissertation by Swinkels (Swinkels 1990). She has selected 30 surgical patients for early discharge from hospital and has studied the consequences. She has compared this experimental group with a matched control group. The patients vary in age. Those who are discharged early have given their permission beforehand. Apart from the patients the following categories of persons are involved in the experiment:
- surgeons and surgeons in training in one hospital
- nurses in the wards with surgical patients
- a team of GPs
- a unit of district nurses.

It is important that there be cooperation between all these categories and this has been assured before the start of the experiment. For this purpose bilateral protocols have been drawn up. During the period of home care GPs and district nurses can rely on the support of the hospital.

Swinkels finds the following: early discharge can be realised for most patients in the experiment but not for patients who have undergone cholecystectomies. The other patients are discharged 1.0 to 2.7 days sooner from hospital.

All early discharge patients but one receive informal care, mostly from members of the family. More employed partners in the experimental group take a few days off than in the control group. The experimental group has had more help from the GP than the control group. The activities of the GPs are described. These include both contacts with the patient and with the other professionals in the experiment. Only 10 out of the 30 experimental patients receive help from the district nurse. Early discharge patients resume their normal household tasks sooner after coming home than the control group. They also go back to work sooner. The experimental group does not show more anxiety after leaving the hospital than the control group. They take a positive view of the formal and informal care they have received.

Swinkels also makes a cost benefit analysis. She finds that there are additional costs for GPs (they spend 33 extra hours on the 30 early discharge patients) and also, but to a lesser extent, for the district nurses (they spend 14.5 extra hours). She also calculates how much money is saved in the hospital. She looks at the time spent by nurses and at the costs of medicine, food and laundry. Her conclusion is that the costs of home care are considerably higher than the costs of hospital care. She admits that the costs for the GPs can possibly be reduced by replacing them by nurses.

We can ask ourselves what these data mean in relation to care for the elderly. In the first place in this project home care was only a matter of days and most patients (23 out of 30) were under 55 years of age. They all had informal care. In the case of chronically ill or elderly people the needs are likely to be different. Although it is possible to raise some methodological questions about the figures presented by Swinkels, the study can serve to illustrate that home care is not necessarily less expensive than intramural care.

## Research on the Living Situation of the Elderly

In this section we will present some research and experiments that deal with the situation of the elderly living at home. We start with a research project in North Amsterdam which describes the situation of the elderly and the available services rather well. After that we will discuss a number of experiments.

### A survey in North Amsterdam

In many municipalities research is commissioned on the living situation of the elderly. One such survey was made in North Amsterdam with a view to policy making. It resulted in a report with the title: Housing and care for the elderly in North Amsterdam (Hofland 1988).

North Amsterdam is situated on the other side of the river IJ from the part of town which tourists know so well. Local government has been decentralised in Amsterdam and North Amsterdam is one of the regions that have recently obtained more powers. The research targets those elderly who are beginning to have difficulties in living by themselves. The central question is: what is the housing situation of these elderly and what care can be provided? What problems do they experience in their situation?

Hofland comes up with the following findings and recommendations. The house and the immediate environment of the house are important factors influencing the well-being of the elderly. According to the report, a suitable house is one which has no more than three rooms and contains a minimum of 32 square metres. The housing is situated on the ground floor or first floor or is accessible by elevator; it has a shower, it is reasonably well kept and the rent is not more than Dfl. 400 per month. An additional criterion is that the house is close to public transportation, shops, post office and the like (the distance is 600 metres at the most). Of all the houses that meet these criteria 58% are occupied by elderly persons. It is difficult for the elderly to find suitable housing by themselves, and they rely heavily on the municipal housing office. There are long waiting lists for these suitable houses; almost 400 households of elderly persons are on the waiting list.

Social networks are very important for the elderly; therefore the municipality often tries to adapt the houses of the elderly, rather than making them move to a different neighbourhood. The elderly prefer to live near age mates but they dislike large housing estates for the elderly. Alarm systems are helpful when the elderly remain in their own homes.

Hofland recommends preparing a housing plan for each neighbourhood together with the elderly concerned. More suitable housing should be made available through adaptations. New houses for the elderly should be built in small clusters. There should be possibilities for communal living. The formation of social networks in the neighbourhoods should be stimulated. The municipality should pay more attention to the elderly aged 75 and over. As far as the social services for this group are concerned, Hofland concludes that there is less informal care available than there used to be. In this respect the situation is better in older quarters than in recently built up areas. Volunteer services play an important role. The activities of community centres, churches and clubs are helpful in creating social contacts.

All the regular home care services are available. There is a long waiting list for home help. Some elderly persons have to wait two years. There is a growing number of what are called semi-commercial services. There is also a shortage of day care facilities for somatic and psycho-geriatric patients. There are 250 persons on the waiting list for a place in a residential home. The five residential homes in the area have an increasing number of facilities for elderly persons living at home, such as meals and day care. Other facilities in the area are: meals on wheels, an alarm system, telephone circles, a neighbourhood bus and a project for odd jobs.

An important finding is that many elderly persons feel lonely. Hofland states that old networks need to be reestablished and that activities in the community are needed to create new ones. He suggests that there should be friendly visiting, and support for informal carers. A better coordination of all the existing services seems desirable. The greatest obstacle for the vulnerable elderly in this area is the lack of home help.

## Experiments in communal living

Many younger elderly, seeing what difficulties the older generation encounters, are trying to find new solutions. One of these solutions is communal living. Although it is still a vanguard approach, it seems to be a growing movement. There is a National Association for Communal Living for the Elderly. This association supports existing groups and tries to bring people together who want to start a new group. Here we will discuss two studies on communal living for the elderly.

The first one is a descriptive study by Peeters and Woldringh (1989) in which they present data on four projects. They find that important motives for joining such a group are the desire to feel safely embedded in a social environment, to prevent loneliness, to remain active and to find ways of avoiding dependency on institutional housing and care.

The groups differ in the extent to which they share domestic tasks such as preparing meals, having coffee and tea, and cleaning the premises. Most groups have agreed on what to do in case of members' illness. If the illness is temporary some groups divide up tasks to help the ill person, whereas others have made arrangements with the regular home help and district nursing organisations. Two of the four groups have already decided on how to deal with permanent infirmity. In that case the decision whether the patient can stay or should leave the project will be placed in the hands of an external agency (an assessment committee or the GP). The two other groups have not yet come to an agreement regarding this matter. It is still too early for the researchers to draw any conclusions.

The second study, by Toneman (1990), attempts to evaluate eight projects involving communal living. In this study special reference is made to the premises where the group lives. There is great diversity between the groups. The smallest group has 11 apartments and the largest 87. Some are situated in a rural area, others in a large city or in a new quarter of a rapidly growing town. Some of the projects consist of apartments which were built for this purpose; others use existing buildings which have been adapted. In the rural projects most apartments are on the ground floor and have a garden. In two cities an old factory and an old school are used.

Some of the findings in this study are the following. The largest group has more activities than any of the others. In two groups the participants not only take their meals together but also run a farm. The other groups have a varying degree of communal activities except for the one in Rotterdam which has not worked out well. The three groups with the most positive results seem to have the following characteristics in common:

- the apartments and the common rooms are fairly spacious;
- there are quite a few communal activities;
- a large number of the present inhabitants are among the founders of the group.

The author hypothesises that this third factor is especially influential and is possibly related to the other two factors as well. The two groups with most communal activities find it difficult to recruit new members. This may mean that only relatively few elderly desire many communal activities. It is important that the members of the group have the right to select new participants. Inadequate quality of the building and of the individual apartments is likely to cause dissatisfaction. There is no relation between the size of the project and the degree of satisfaction. The author is moderately positive about the future of communal living, not only for Dutch people but also for elderly immigrants. He recommends that municipalities and housing corporations facilitate the construction of suitable premises.

### Visiting the elderly

We came across several reports on visiting the elderly. We will discuss three of them which have started from different approaches. They have in common a certain concern about the living situation of the elderly.

In Rotterdam it was a research project on poverty which led to the conclusion that relatively many households of elderly persons could hardly make ends meet. The associations of the elderly asked the municipality to take into account that many of the elderly are not well enough informed about subsidies, facilities and services and therefore do not receive all they are entitled to. Besides, the older generation does not like to ask. They therefore proposed not to ask the elderly to come and get the services but to take the services to the elderly.

With this purpose a project was set up in an inner city area where the elderly were visited with a view to finding out if they were in need and if they used what they were entitled to.

In September 1990 an interim report appeared (Kalfs, Doorgeest and Bout). Four home visitors went to see the elderly, using a questionnaire. In April 1990 they had contacted almost 400 elderly persons aged 80 years or older. They provided information on the subjects in the questionnaire and advised about financial and other facilities. Where necessary they helped the elderly person to gain access to these facilities. In some cases they paid a second visit in order to find out if their help had been effective.

This project not only provides the elderly with information but also provides the municipal policy makers with information about the situation of the elderly. The findings are that there are no persons in desperate need, but there are quite a few situations which are worrying because of a lack of housekeeping or hygiene or bad housing. Moreover, it has been found that there is far too much information which causes confusion. The quality of most of it leaves much to be desired.

In Apeldoorn an experiment is going on involving special contact persons for the elderly. These persons are volunteers who are available to the elderly for small tasks which cannot be taken up by professional helpers. For each (rather small) area there are two contact persons. They will take the initiative of visiting all the elderly in their area. The contact person on duty can be reached by telephone between 9:00 and 10:00 in the morning when the elderly have problems. The person arranges for such things as running an errand, going for a walk, accompanying someone to the hospital, or putting in a light bulb. These tasks are only performed if no one else is available and if these problems are incidental. The contact persons receive consultation and training. They are given a small allowance which is meant for reimbursement of costs and they are insured. The project has been evaluated after one year.

In the report (Kerstjens-Loeff 1990) it is explained that research is being done a little too early because many persons such as professional helpers have not yet seen enough of the contact persons to be able to assess their value.

The contact persons themselves state that it takes quite a bit of energy and courage to go and see all the elderly. As it turns out, 75% of the elderly appreciate the visit and this encourages the contact persons, who all happen to be women. In their experience, the elderly prefer that the contact person take the initiative to come and see them a second time. Many elderly do not want to ask for a visit. About 60% of the elderly like to stay in touch with the contact person, but many of them say they do this with a view to "later on" when they may be really in need of help. In most cases the elderly think that the contact person can help with practical tasks. A smaller group of elderly also want them to visit just for a chat. Less than 5% of the elderly refuse a visit by the contact persons.

In Amsterdam a project has developed out of two streams of research at the Free University. On the one hand there was a tradition of research on loneliness, and on the other hand there was research on the helping professions. The project was started when the university was consulted by social workers in one particular area in Amsterdam. These social workers found there was much loneliness among the very old in spite of their efforts to do something about it. After a survey had been made the researchers developed a course which was given to professional helpers and volunteers. The course was evaluated by the participants and the researchers. It turned out that participants, even though some had been sceptical at the beginning, found that the course had deepened their understanding of the phenomenon of loneliness and the stages people go through when they experience losses. They felt that this understanding as well as some practical skills helped them to be more effective in dealing with lonely older persons. Theory and a description of possible interventions have been set out in a text which can be used as a guideline in other areas as well. At the end of the text a precise description is given of the course contents (Linneman et al. 1990).

So far we have described some experiments that have been accompanied by research. We discovered many other interesting projects while searching for material for this chapter, for instance, small scale projects that fill in gaps, such as a laundry service for households with an incontinent person, or a "sitter" service. Several large scale projects deserve to be mentioned as well, such as "De Flesseman" in Amsterdam where intramural and extramural services cooperate in an inner city area and where the project is really part of the neighbourhood, using whatever forces are available, including commercial ones. Or the neighbourhood project in 's-Hertogenbosch where the health services are part of a broad community development project and health care is closely related to the daily living situation of the people. Or the development of support centres in the province of Brabant, where sheltered housing in small villages is built adjacent to a health care centre, which enables older people to stay in the village instead of having to go to a residential home in the next town.

This chapter would become too long if we were to describe these projects in more detail. We hope it has become clear that many innovations of a widely varying scope and nature are being developed.

## Research on the Caring Society

Under this heading we will discuss some of the research that has been done on informal helping and volunteering.

### Informal care

Since 1985 quite a few studies have appeared in which informal care is an issue. Doing research on informal care is not easy: it is very much part of people's private life. The concept has to be defined carefully. So far no standard definition is available and therefore the results of the various studies differ.

Buis (1990) quotes the outcomes of a life situation survey of persons aged 55 and older (in 1984). This survey shows that partners of older persons are the most important source of informal help. But there are other sources of help as well, such as that given by:

- children (30%)
- other relatives (9%)
- neighbours, friends and relations (15%)
- a cleaning lady (19%)
- a home helper (12%)
- a district nurse (4%).

Tjadens and Woldringh (1989) have done research on informal help in the personal sphere (help with washing, dressing, eating, getting in and out of bed and with household tasks). They find that 33% of persons aged 20 to 65 provide informal help as do 20% of persons aged 65 and over.

Van Daal (1990) uses a narrower definition: his research focuses on informal help given to persons who are not part of one's own household. This means that informal helping between partners and between parents and children who are part of the same household is excluded. In his survey the help is *not* given on an exchange basis. He finds that 4.8% of the population aged 18 and over provide informal help. The average amount of time spent on this is 4.2 hours a week. Twice as many women are involved in informal help as men. However, elderly men do not provide much less informal help than women.

Kwekkeboom (1990) has done a secondary analysis of the data from some large, national surveys and summarises the most important literature on the caring society. She tries to answer four questions:

- what ideas have developed on informal and formal care and what assumptions are they based on;
- what are the developments of informal care in practice over the last 10 to 15 years;
- what are the major problems with informal caring and what further problems are to be expected;
- what can the government do to solve existing problems?

The assumptions underlying the philosophy of the caring society are, according to Kwekkeboom, that there is less willingness among the population to give help to family members, relatives and friends, that professionals are the main helpers even in home care and that informal help is to be preferred over formal help. On the basis of her analysis she comes to the conclusion that the reality is quite different. Although there is a general belief that people nowadays are less ready than they used to be to give informal help, the figures show the opposite: there is an increase in the number of people who say they are ready to give informal help.

In 1985 a little over 20% of the respondents in a time budget survey said that they had given informal help to members of their household, a decrease of 5% compared to 1980 and 1975. Kwekkeboom relates this finding to the fact that a growing number of persons live in a single person household. The help given to relatives over the same period has not decreased. The average amount of time spent on this has remained the same: 5 hours per week. There are indications that the willingness of persons with higher education to provide informal care outside their own household is less than average. She estimates that the total amount of informal care is eight times as much as the care given by subsidised home help. She concludes that under certain conditions, but not always, informal care is to be preferred over formal care.

Kwekkeboom also looks at the informal care received. The need for care seems to be rather stable over the years. Long term care is especially needed by the group aged 75 and over. Those primarily in need of care are widowed persons with little education and a low income who live by themselves. The total amount of care received from persons not living in the same household has decreased over the years: in 1979 one third of those in need of care received informal help from persons outside their household; in 1987 the proportion was one quarter. At the same time there has been a decrease in the amount of care received from the home help organisations:

in 1979 most clients received 6 hours of home help a week; in 1983 the figure was 3 hours. There has been an increase in the use of services by private, paid helpers. This help was mostly received by highly educated persons with a high income. Social networks are an important source of help. On the whole, more informal than formal help is received.

Kwekkeboom concludes that specific groups lack the necessary formal and informal care. Informal carers are quite often overburdened. The discrepancy between desired and available informal care is likely to grow because of demographic and social developments. Therefore, she recommends that more support and special facilities be made available for informal carers.

Kwekkeboom is not the only one to make such recommendations. The Dutch Institute for Care and Well-being (NIZW), a recently established national institute for development work, has put the support of informal carers on its agenda, organised a conference and published a book with examples of good practices in the support of carers. Efforts are being made to start a Carers' National Association, following the British example.

## Volunteers

There is a generally accepted definition of volunteering. According to this definition, volunteer work is work which is done in an organisational setting, on a voluntary basis, without remuneration, and for the benefit of others or the community. Although this definition is seemingly clear, it is sometimes difficult to make a distinction between active participation in an organisation and voluntary work. In 1985 and 1986 several surveys were done in which questions were posed regarding voluntary work. These surveys found that approximately 45% of the population aged 18 years and older participated in voluntary work. It is likely that these surveys used a very broad definition which included active membership in sports' clubs and churches, for example.

Van Daal (1990), using the above definition in a strict sense, finds that 14.7% of the adult population perform voluntary work; 4.9% work in the social sector and half of these (about 2.5%) work with elderly, handicapped or sick persons. On average, volunteers spend 5.1 hours a week on this work. Volunteers have a better education and higher income and are more often churchgoers than the average Dutchman. 72% of volunteers are women. Middle-aged persons are overrepresented. The smaller the municipality, the greater is the percentage of volunteers, according to van Daal.

Van Overbeek (1987) has tried to find out if there have been changes in the characteristics of volunteers. She finds that the traditional volunteer organisations still work with the same kind of persons: predominantly middle-aged housewives. Their numbers have not decreased.

Participation in voluntary work by unemployed or disabled persons, which was originally low, has increased in the eighties to the same level as that of housewives. Van Overbeek comes to the conclusion that there are two streams of volunteers: the traditional type and a new type. The former work in the traditional volunteer organisations, whereas the latter mostly perform voluntary work in professionalised organisations. When they work in new types of services, which are not yet fully professionalised, their unpaid work comes close to a professional job.

The traditional volunteer organisations, according to van Overbeek, are confronted with increasing demands. Volunteers are more often asked to assist with home care. The cases in which their assistance is sought become more burdensome. Quite often volunteer organisations cooperate with professional organisations, although they are not equipped to share in the work on an equal footing.

Mandemaker and van Raak (1987), having researched voluntary work in health care including self-help initiatives, find that many local organisations have financial problems. Few organisations have a professional coordinator; about half of the organisations express a need for (more) paid staff. Half of them also have difficulty in recruiting enough volunteers. Several researchers find that the working conditions are not very favourable. More than half of the volunteers do not get any or receive only a partial reimbursement of costs, more than one third are not insured, and many would like to be coached by a professional or follow a course. In spite of these negative conditions many volunteers get a lot of satisfaction from their work.

Claassen and Ladage (1989) have done research among volunteers who work with elderly persons in the province of Gelderland. The main activities of these volunteers are visiting the elderly, taking them out, taking them shopping or to the doctor, and organising social meetings and transportation. The volunteers are also in charge of the delivery of meals. The authors find that the volunteers do not want to take on tasks that are the responsibility of professionals. They are only willing to do so in emergency cases. Volunteers and professionals in fact belong to different circuits which rarely overlap. The main problems in volunteer organisations are the recruitment of new volunteers and the ageing of the present group of voluntary workers. So far the associations of the elderly are doing little in the sphere of voluntary helping. Claassen and Ladage's conclusion is that voluntary work is an extra dimension in caring but it cannot replace professional care.

## The quality of the caring relationship

As we saw above, one of the underlying assumptions of the caring society is that informal help is to be preferred over formal help. Kwekkeboom therefore summarises what other studies say about this subject. She remarks that this qualitative aspect of caring has been researched even less than the quantitative aspects. In most studies on informal caring the central research question is a different one. Nevertheless, some studies, such as the study by van Daal, contain relevant material. Kwekkeboom hypothesises that the following conditions influence the quality of the caring relationship:

- the cause of the need for care
- the motivation for giving or asking for care
- the intensity of care
- the duration
- the quality of the relationship between caregiver and care recipient
- the number of caregivers per care recipient.

We present here some of the data as summarised by Kwekkeboom.

Van Daal distinguishes between those who help a relative (whom he calls "family helpers") and those who help a friend or an acquaintance (whom he calls "acquaintance helpers"). In the case of family helpers caregiving is most often a matter of course. Two thirds of the family helpers in his survey have themselves offered their help. The acquaintance helpers more often mention other reasons for giving care such as being asked to by the person in need of care or by an organisation, such as the church. When help is given to friends it is mostly on the basis of reciprocity.

Even though they consider it natural, this does not mean that all family helpers like their caring task. One fourth of them would rather not do it, compared to only 4% of the acquaintance helpers. It is supposed that the reason is that acquaintance helpers help more often on the basis of free choice. Negative feelings about caring are almost exclusively reported by family carers. They complain about the burden, the obligation to care, the ungratefulness of the care recipient, etc. Notwithstanding these negative feelings most carers also experience a certain degree of satisfaction. One third of the family helpers and one eighth of the acquaintance helpers report problems. These are mostly health problems, and conflicting duties with regard to their own family.

The degree to which the caring relationship causes problems is strongly influenced by the quality of the relationship between caregiver and care recipient. The worse the relationship, the heavier is the burden of caregiving. Acquaintance helpers mention considerably less often than family helpers that they find caring stressful.

Other research studies cited by Kwekkeboom all point in the same direction: the carers of a partner or a parent especially just step into caring and consider it the natural thing to do, even though it is a heavy task. Quite often they prefer informal care to formal care. A bad relationship between caregiver and care recipient tends to have a negative influence on the motivation of the caregiver. In some cases caregivers are known to set certain limits.

Kwekkeboom notes that even less research is available dealing with the experiences of the care recipients. One reason for this may be, of course, that some care recipients are not able to be interviewed.

Tjadens and Woldringh (1989) have recorded the opinions of 87 care recipients. Only 10 of them are dissatisfied with the help (both formal and informal) which they receive. Many care recipients are very appreciative. When criticism is voiced this has to do with tension in the relationship between caregiver and care recipient. It is painful to be dependent within a bad relationship. It is clear, however, that it is felt to be difficult to ask for help from relatives who are not part of one's own household or friends.

Kwekkeboom concludes on the basis of her study that in those cases where the relationship between caregiver and care recipient is good it can be said that informal care is preferable to formal care, but when the relationship is bad the individuals concerned have other preferences. If informal care is to be sustained, more support for informal carers is necessary, such as respite or allowances.

Since the publication of Kwekkeboom's work, two more studies have appeared in which the role of the central informal carer is discussed. Both of them are part of the research series on the demonstration projects on substitution mentioned earlier.

The first one (Hommel, Koedoot and Knipscheer 1990) describes the role of the central informal carer in the experiment with the individual care budget for elderly persons in Rotterdam. More than 80% of the central informal carers consider themselves to be the most likely person to provide care. Three quarters of them do so out of a sense of duty and two thirds say that they do it out of love or affection. More than 80% of the central carers find it a matter of course. Some informal carers (7.6%) find that they have to do too much as it is, 36.3% are not willing to give more help if this should prove necessary in the future, 22.3% are willing to do so and the rest say that it depends on the circumstances.

It turns out that those informal carers who are the partners of the person cared for report more complaints about their well-being than other central carers. Partners give more help and receive less support than other informal helpers. Many informal carers report that they never feel free. Not feeling free is one of the most taxing circumstances. They believe that the care recipients underestimate the burden of the carers.

Finally, we want to mention the study by Janssen and Woldringh (1991). They studied 91 central caregivers found in a nationally representative survey of the elderly. The survey was held in 1988 and was repeated in 1990 to compare the changes in the elderly population with the changes that will be found among the elderly in the demonstration projects. The data presented here were collected in 1988.

Although a very thorough analysis is made of the situation of the central caregivers, their tasks, the support received, their feelings about caring, and their motivation, the relationship between caregivers and care recipients is not specifically studied. We will not repeat those findings which are very similar to what has been mentioned above. It is interesting, however, that the authors differentiate between partners, children and children-in-law and compare them. They find that the first are most committed and the last least committed. They distinguish between four aspects of motivation:
- the wish to meet others' expectations (extrinsic motivation)
- avoidance of negative feelings
- intrinsic positive motivation
- a sense of duty.

The sense of duty and intrinsic positive motivation play the most important roles. Daughters-in-law have considerably lower intrinsic positive motivation than partners and children. The type of relationship between the caregiver and care recipient proves to be important for the caregiver's motivation. Only 20% of carers are ready to provide more care if needed, and 40% are not ready to provide any more help. Among these are all the daughters-in-law taking part in the survey.

Janssen and Woldringh also distinguish three kinds of stress:

- care stress (direct consequences of caring, such as lack of freedom, physical complaints);
- relation/context stress (dissatisfaction with the behaviour of the elderly person or problems in relations with others);
- network stress (disappointment with the help from others).

Care stress proves to be most prominent. Care stress is relatively high for partners whereas the other two kinds of stress are relatively low for partners; network stress is relatively prominent for children, and relation/context stress is found mostly among daughters-in-law.

Janssen and Woldringh conclude that the kind of motivation is a good predictor for the kind of stress caregivers will experience. When they are mostly extrinsically motivated or when they have the feeling that there is no way out, they are likely to experience a great deal of stress. This leads the authors to the conclusion that in the experimental situation attention should be paid to the motivation of informal carers and that a way must be found to guarantee to informal carers that they can give up when the burden becomes too heavy.

Finally, we want to mention a study by Hofstede and Nazarski (1988). They conducted a project on the experiences and desires of elderly people concerning help given by volunteers. They stress the importance of reciprocity in the relationship. Voluntary work should be arranged in such a manner that it has value both for the volunteer and for the elderly person. There should be an open relationship in which the elderly can say what their desires are and in which volunteers (or the organisation to which they belong) are free to set certain limits on what they will do. Such a relationship cannot exist when the elderly person is very dependent on the help of the volunteer. Elderly persons should be able to maintain their independence in their relationships with volunteers. In a good relationship volunteers derive satisfaction from their work. If this is the case both the elderly person and the volunteer profit. Ideally the volunteer and the elderly person have a great degree of freedom in setting out their relationship.

When there are problems the volunteer organisation has the task of serving as an intermediary. A precondition for effective voluntary helping is the availability of formal help when the need arises. Hofstede and Nazarski are very explicit about the fact that a government stating that more care has to be given by volunteers sets poor conditions for voluntary work.

## THE FUTURE OF CARE

In this part we will reflect on the data, policies and practices which have been described in the preceding sections. We will try to assess their effectiveness with a view to the growing needs for care. Are our present solutions adequate for the problems of the future or do we have to find new ways? If so, what alternatives are available? We will end this study by sketching some rather different approaches which may help us to define existing problems in new terms.

## A Critical Assessment of the Present Situation

The two main questions to be answered concerning care for the elderly are:
- how can we assure that care is available that suits the needs of the elderly;
- how can this care be financed, now and in the future?

These questions seem the more pressing when we look at the expected demographic changes: an increase in the elderly population from 12.8% to 23.4% and a corresponding decrease in younger age groups. Since the seventies policies and practices have been developed to attempt to provide some answers. In the following we will take a critical look at what has been achieved so far.

### Filling in the gaps between services

Ever since the idea of the closed circuit of services was introduced new initiatives have been taken to add to the existing services. After the shift to home care there has been a rapid growth in projects for the delivery of meals, alarm systems, telephone circles, "sitter" services, laundry services, transportation and the like.

Day care and respite care by residential homes and nursing homes have proved to be important additions to the existing services for home care. Because of the greater variety of services there are better possibilities of providing "tailored care" to the elderly in the community.

## Coordination of services

From the middle of the seventies coordination of existing services has been an issue. With this purpose in mind, coordinating services for the elderly were launched, as mentioned earlier. They were not really effective in their coordinating task because they lacked the necessary powers. Coordination was also one of the aims of support policy. Support policy was more successful in filling in the gaps than in coordinating. Now the care managers are supposed to bring about the necessary coordination. Knapen and Willems (1990) have shown that most care managers have insufficient powers to bring this about. The problem of coordination is an excellent example of what the Social and Cultural Planning Office has called overproduction of policy. Without taking into account the effectiveness of earlier attempts at coordination, new attempts have been introduced that do not succeed for the same reasons as their predecessors: a lack of powers. Nevertheless, all these coordinating agents remain in action and are in addition to the many existing organisations.

The lack of coordination remains a vital problem in care for the elderly. We will have to wait and see whether the Dekker/Simons plan can tackle it.

## Substitution

In the recent past substitution has been one of the cornerstones of care policy. The main reason for substitution was the expectation of a decrease in costs. Now that the results of experiments are beginning to come in it becomes doubtful whether substitution will make much difference from a financial point of view. The Social and Cultural Planning Office (SCP 1990) expects it will reduce costs by 5 to 15%. This estimate may be on the positive side. But even if the SCP is right this is not enough to compensate for the increasing demand for care. It seems as if the impact of substitution has been greatly overestimated.

## Upward pressure

With the increasing intensity of policy making and the many reorganisations taking place to make services more effective, growing numbers of policy makers and managers have become employed in this sector. The care sector is becoming top heavy. There is an increasing interest in the system instead of in the problems of the elderly.

## Shortages in care

We have already pointed out that the capacity of certain services is insufficient. The needs are most pressing in home help and in nursing homes. The capacity of nursing homes will be expanded. Nursing homes will obtain additional means to take part in home care. The capacity of home help has not increased. It is amazing that no measures are being taken to strengthen home help which has a key role to play in home care.

## The caring society

The concept of the caring society was meant to get more informal and voluntary helpers involved and to reduce the role of the state in caregiving. As we have seen earlier, the assumptions on which the concept was based were not valid. Because of the research that has been done it has become clear that a great deal of informal help is given. Informal carers are often overburdened and need support. New initiatives are being developed to this end.

Research on voluntary work has shown that there is a growing shortage of volunteers. It is not yet clear how the existing problems can be solved. A new development seems to be taking place: payment of volunteers. Will this be a solution for the future and help to get more people interested in volunteering or does it take away precisely those aspects of voluntary work which make it attractive? It is difficult to weigh the advantages against the disadvantages. The author of this chapter is involved in an attempt to spur some cross-national research on this issue. In order to maintain the present level of informal and voluntary care, new investments need to be made.

## Commercial care

In the discussion on the financial aspects of care one of the alternatives seems to be care on a commercial basis. In fact, many—mostly small scale—

commercial initiatives exist. Some of them, especially those involved in intensive home care, have gained recognition so that their services are now included in the package of the Health Insurance Funds and companies. However, when the costs of commercial organisations are not paid by an insurance scheme they are so high that only a small group of rather well-to-do elderly can afford them. Therefore, the commercial sector can only make a limited contribution to the solution of the care problem.

## Prevention

Prevention seems to be one of the new central issues of policy for the elderly. This is another concept which needs to be considered carefully. If we succeed in preventing certain illnesses, what will be the result? Does it mean that we will add extra and healthy years to our lives or does it mean that these illnesses will be replaced by others which are not lethal, such as rheumatism, worn-out joints or dementia? A recent research report, reviewed in *NRC Handelsblad* (Köhler 1990), states that the chances are that we are adding extra years of illness. This certainly will not help to solve the problems of care for the elderly.

## The Dekker/Simons plan

Much is expected of the Dekker/Simons plan. However, before it can be implemented some rather tricky problems have to be solved such as the definition of what will be provided as part of the basic insurance, the description of services in terms of functions, and the norms according to which the insurance companies will get their budget from the central fund. Not only do these problems have to be solved, but the resistance of some parties concerned also has to be overcome. Assuming that all these difficulties can be surmounted, certain questions arise about the effects of the plan:

- Will it really lead to a reduction of costs? The commercial elements in the plan may cause a greater demand for health care.
- Most of the premium will be collected as a tax. Will that make consumers sufficiently aware of costs?
- Will consumers have sufficient influence?
- Who is going to provide care? The definition of care in terms of functions may result in the strongest institutions such as hospitals and nursing homes taking over the work from less powerful and less

influential agencies such as district nursing and home help.

The Dekker/Simons plan is a very interesting proposal. But it is not at all clear what its consequences will be. It may be less cost effective than has been anticipated.

## Limits of care

We explained earlier how the limits of care have become part of public discussion. We feel this is a useful attempt to try to get a grip on the costs of care. It seems as if on the one hand there is growing pressure from patients and the medical profession for ever more medical treatment. On the other hand awareness seems to be growing that this does not necessarily have a positive influence on the quality of life. Moreover, in some cases the costs are disproportionate. Defining the limits means that we will have to make choices. Choices between who will be treated and who will not, choices between cure and care. These are difficult ethical dilemmas. Nevertheless, they need to be faced.

## Beyond care policy

There are other factors than care which are extremely important for the well-being of the elderly. One of them is an adequate income; another is good housing. Therefore, the basis for a good policy for the elderly does not lie within the realm of care but begins with education, employment, good work related pensions and a flexible housing policy. In other words, policy makers in other departments have an influence on the situation of the coming generations of the elderly.

Some people say that the most effective policy for the elderly is income policy. If all the elderly had a sufficient income there would be no need for a special policy for the elderly. We still have a very long way to go before all the elderly, especially women, have a good work related pension in addition to their State Pension.

## Care and the labor market

At this moment it is extremely difficult to find personnel to work in home help, district nursing or intramural care. The work is hard, the conditions are not very good and the pay is comparatively low. It is not at all attractive to work in the care sector. This problem can only be solved by improving working conditions and salaries. If not, it will become impossible to recruit personnel and to maintain good standards in the care sector. It is to be expected that care will become more expensive because of the mechanisms of the labor market.

## General wage increases

The present state of the economy is such that in many branches wage increases are occurring. This means that in due time the collective sector will have to follow the private sector. There seems to be little awareness especially among the trade unions that a general wage increase makes collective goods such as health care more expensive and therefore less accessible.

## Concluding remarks

To return to the two questions at the beginning of this section we can say that progress has been made in providing services that are better tailored to the needs of the elderly. In this respect it is important that a greater variety of services in home care has been developed, that in some experiments a certain degree of coordination has been realised and that experiments like communal living have been possible.

Are the needs of the elderly met? Gerritsen et al. (1989), studying the problems of care for the elderly, state that there is a definite lack of knowledge of the needs of the elderly. We do not entirely agree with this statement, because in many studies on care, information is given on the needs of the elderly as well. But it seems symptomatic of the present situation that the needs of the elderly are not the focal point in policy making.

On the basis of the many studies we have read, our hypothesis is that the most important needs are:

- more home help;
- a smaller number of professional helpers working with one client;
- more coordination between services and easier access to services;
- reassurance that intramural care will be available when it is really necessary.

However, when we look at policies we see that the first two needs especially seem to be ignored. Here a dilemma becomes apparent: more and better services will cost more money, but this is contrary to the policy of cost containment. It seems that cost containment gets priority over better services.

Looking at the financial problems we can say that considerable efforts have been made to solve these problems. In this section we have explained why we have our doubts about the effectiveness of these policies. If substitution, the Dekker/Simons plan and innovations such as communal living do not bring about important savings, it will be difficult to counterbalance the consequences of demographic changes and the mechanisms of the labor market.

## NEW VISTAS

In the course of time ideas have been launched that take an altogether different starting point. Some of these have hardly been discussed because they were so far removed from reality, whereas others are beginning to become part of public discussion. In this section we will outline four new approaches.

### The congregational system

The sociologist Abram de Swaan published a number of essays in a national newspaper, which later appeared as a book (de Swaan 1983). His idea was to form congregations of approximately 2,500 persons. The members should live within easy reach of each other, they should be ready to try to solve their problems together and they should be like-minded. The congregations would discuss the problems of the members and decide which problems they could solve themselves and for which problems they would need a professional, for instance, a GP. They would then apply for professionals. A National Council would handle the applications and allocate the money, provided by the state. The congregation would then be able to select and employ these professionals.

The great advantage would be, according to de Swaan, that the members of a congregation would have to talk about their problems. They would be stimulated to help each other and to learn from each other's experiences. If they wanted more care than could be given by the available professionals they would either have to raise the money or do the work themselves. If there were problems between the members of the congregation and professionals they would have to be solved by those concerned, instead of by umbrella organisations or bureaucracies. This idea seems rather revolutionary, but it has some very interesting aspects. It would make people less dependent on professionals, give them more responsibilities and make them more aware of costs. The members of the congregations themselves could decide where informal care should end and formal care should begin.

The congregations would also be a good way to create new social networks, which is important, as we saw earlier. This idea has not been taken very seriously. It does not seem altogether impossible to try it out under the auspices of an insurance company in the new Dekker/Simons system.

### Time to Care

Time to Care is the title of a rather elaborate study by the Swedish Secretariat for Future Studies (1984). The Swedes came to the conclusion that it will be impossible to pay for all the necessary care in the future. They did see, however, that growing numbers of people have more free time. They suggested that all citizens 18 years and older should be obliged to contribute some of their time to be spent on care. They should receive some additional training for their care jobs. The municipalities would be responsible for dividing up the care jobs. It seems that the idea was not picked up in Sweden. In the Netherlands this idea is now mentioned occasionally in the public debate. That does not mean that it has been accepted in the Netherlands; it seems, however, that it is beginning to be taken seriously as a possible solution when other policies fail.

### The collective bargaining scenario

The former PCMD (Programming Board for Research into the Social Services) organised a conference in 1989 for which three scenarios on the future of care were developed. Two of these seem to open some new vistas so that it is worthwhile to mention them here.

The collective bargaining scenario proposed that employers and trade unions should come to an agreement that in addition to such facilities as training and pension schemes the provision of care would be part of the employment contract. One of the problems in this scenario is that a rather large proportion of the Dutch population is not employed and would therefore be unable to obtain these rights. A trade union official who was asked to speak about this idea came to the conclusion that a better model would be a "tripartite" model in which the state would also participate. There are other examples in the country where such a model has been put to work.

### The insurance scenario

The second scenario developed by the former PCMD proposed that citizens should themselves obtain insurance for care. They should try to organise themselves to obtain insurance at the lowest possible cost. If enough people had such insurance the costs for the state would be reduced.

The speaker, who was asked to elaborate this idea, nevertheless saw many problems. How is care to be defined? Who is entitled to care? Why consider this solution when every citizen will obtain basic insurance under the Dekker plan? He made one interesting suggestion, however. It appears that people who retire spend a lot of money at first. This is when they are vital and want to do all those things they never could do before. After that there comes a period when they undertake less activities and stay at home more, but do not yet need care. This is a period when they spend considerably less. During their last years, when they need care, their expenses are very high. The speaker's suggestion was to vary the amounts of the pension according to the retirement phase.

Since then one Dutch insurance company, Centraal Beheer (CB), has started to consider a similar approach. CB has recently launched the idea of a flexible old age pension in which insured persons who need care can obtain this care from the insurance company. In that case part of the pension will not be paid in money but in services which have been contracted by the insurance company. CB believes that it will be able to provide qualitatively good care at a lower price than the present home help and district nursing organisations. CB administered a questionnaire to some of its clients and the response was quite positive.

These are some of the new approaches to the problems of care. They have not yet been worked out. It may prove impossible to implement them. Nevertheless, they are inspiring because they show that there are different ways of looking at these problems. We will need a lot of imagination to develop new concepts for care in the future.

# References

Buis, M. (1990). *Ondersteuning van mantelzorg. Een staalkaart van intitiatieven.* NIZW, Utrecht.

CBS (1990). *Statistisch vademedum ouderen 1990.* SDU, 's-Gravenhage.

Claassen, A.W.M., and J.P. Ladage (1989). *Tussen grenzen en mogelijkheden.Vrijwilligerswerk voor en door ouderen.* Stichting Gelderland, Arnhem.

Daal, Henk Jan van (1990). *Vrijwilligerswerk en informele hulp in Nederland.* NIMAWO, 's-Gravenhage.

Gerritsen, J.C., C.P. van Linschoten, L. Schaap, and E.W. Wolffensperger (1989). *Samenhang in de zorg voor ouderen. Overzicht van knelpunten in de zorg voor ouderen.* Raad voor het ouderenbeleid, Rijswijk.

Geus, M.J. (1990). *Pensioen vanuit toekomstperspectief. Relatiedagen 1990.* Centraal Beheer, Apeldoorn.

Hofland, Evert (1988). *Huisvesting en zorg voor ouderen in Amsterdam-Noord. Een probleemverkenning.* OSA, Amsterdam.

Hofstede, W.B.M., and E.A.M. Nazarski (1988). *Van waarde voor twee.* LSW, Utrecht.

Hommel, A.C.C., C.G. Koedoot, and C.P.M. Knipscheer (1990). *De centrale verzorg(st)er van de ouderen in het project individuele zorgsubsidie.* Rotterdam, deel 1, VU, Amsterdam.

Houben, Piet (1990). "Trendbreuk in de volkshuisvesting voor ouderen." Nota "Ouderen in tel." *RIW Nieuwsbrief,* December.

Janssen, Toos, and Claartje Woldringh (1991). *De centrale verzorg(st)er van ouderen.* ITS, Nijmegen.

Kalfs, Hanny, Karin Doorgeest, and Albert Bout (1990). *Project Huisbezoek Ouderen Crooswijk. De stand van zaken tot nu toe.* Rotterdam.

Kerstjens-Loeff, H. (1990). *Contactpersonen in de buurt- een experiment binnen de thuiszorg - nader bekeken.* Gemeente Apeldoorn Coördinatie Ouderenwerk, Apeldoorn.

Knapen, Mat, Jos Mensink, and Clarie Ramakers (1988). *Experimenten thuisverpleging. Eindrapportage over de proefperiode van september 1987 tot mei 1988.* ITS, Nijmegen.

Knapen, Mat, and Dries Willems (1990). "Zorg coördinatoren meestal zonder formele bevoegdheden." *Tijdschrift voor de sociale sector,* September, nr. 9.

Köhler, Wim (1990). "Preventieprogramma's en het probleem van de vervangende ziekten." *NRC Handelsblad,* 13 December.

Kwekkeboom, M.H. (1990). *Het licht onder de korenmaat. Informele zorgverlening in Nederland.* VUGA, 's-Gravenhage.

Linneman, M., G. Leene, K. Bettink, M. Schram, and J. Voermans (1990). *Uit eenzaamheid. Over hulpverlening bij ouderen, Bohn Stafleu Van Loghum.* Houten/Antwerpen.

Mandemaker, T., and A. van Raak (1987). *Vrijwilligerswerk in de gezondheidszorg.* IVA, Tilburg.

Overbeek, Riki van (1987). *Ontwikkelingen op het terrein van het vrijwilligerswerk in de hulpverlening sinds 1975.* NIMAWO, Den Haag.

Overbeek, Riki van (1988). *Gezocht: Vrijwilligers (M/V) voor de toekomst.* NIMAWO, Den Haag.

Peeters, José, and Claartje Woldringh (1989). *Groepswonen van ouderen.* ITS, Nijmegen.

Pommer, E.J. (1990). *Inkomens op leeftijd, Sociaal en Cultureel Planbureau.* Rijswijk.

SCP (1990) Sociaal en Cultureel Planbureau. *Sociaal en Cultureel Rapport 1990.* Rijswijk.

Swaan, A. de (1983). *Halverwege de heilstaat.* Essays. Meulenhoff, Amsterdam.

Swinkels, M.A.A. (1990). *Eerder thuis - beter af?* Proefschrift. Samsom, Alphen aan den Rijn.

Tjadens, F.L.J., and Cl. Woldringh (1989). *Informele zorg in Nederland. Zelfzorgproblemen, behoefte aan zorg en praktisch-instrumentele onderlinge hulp.* ITS, Nijmegen.

Toneman, H. (1990). *Woongemeenschappen van ouderen, Stuurgroep Experimenten Volkshuisvesting.* DELWEL b.v., 's-Gravenhage.

Verschuur, A., and Chiel Wollaert (1991). "Ouderensteunpunten schieten als paddestoelen uit de grond. Brabant biedt alternatief voor verzorgingstehuis." *Leeftijd*, January, nr. 1 (32).

Welling, Nardy, and Theo Miltenburg (1989). *Oordelen over thuisverpleging.* ITS, Nijmegen.

WVC, *Werken aan zorgvernieuwing.* SDU, 's-Gravenhage, 1990.

WVC, *Financieel Overzicht Zorg (FOZ), 1991.* SDU, 's-Gravenhage, 1990.

WVC, *Ouderen in tel, Ouderenbeleid 1990-1994.* SDU, 's-Gravenhage, 1990.
-   "Tussenrapportage demonstratieprojecten ouderenzorg." Deelnota 3 bij nota, *Ouderen in tel.* SDU, 's-Gravenhage, 1990.
-   "Gegevens voor ouderen." Deelnota 5 bij nota, *Ouderen in tel.* SDU, 's-Gravenhage, 1990.

# five

## Care of the Elderly in Sweden—Formal and Informal Support

*Lennarth Johansson*
and
*Mats Thorslund*

## THE SWEDISH SYSTEM AND ELDERLY POPULATIONS

### Population trends

In most modern welfare states increasing elderly populations are producing a growing number of elderly people who usually need both health and social supports. The Swedish situation is not different; indeed, there are a number of ways in which Sweden can claim to represent an extreme and an example of the development which can be expected elsewhere.

In January 1989 Sweden had a population of some 8.5 million. 17.8% of these were over 65 years of age. The life expectancy for a newborn girl is 80.1 years and for a boy 74.1 years.

Thus, Sweden's population has one of the highest proportions of elderly people anywhere in the world. And it has been estimated that between 1988 and the year 2000, for example, the group of those aged 80 and over (which in 1988 constituted 4.1% of the total population) will rise by 30% (SCB 1989).

On the other hand, we can look forward to a decrease in the number of elderly between 65 and 75 years. The number of people now aged 16 to 24 will also decrease, according to projections. The expectancies of these two groups are of interest to future care for the elderly. The younger elderly are the children of the older elderly. And the 16 to 24 year olds will be the source of the coming generation of health care personnel.

Another characteristic of the Swedish situation is the large number of women working outside the home (81% in 1989). This means that the future potential of informal care is to be questioned.

Even if international comparisons regarding the number of elderly living with their children are hard to conduct, we can state that Sweden represents an extremely low position in this regard. Migration, urbanization and increasing numbers of broken families will also limit the extent of informal support.

## Some facts about the Swedish system

Nearly all care of the elderly is publicly provided and financed, under public control and guided by legislation. Public control has always been great—but the system has moved further in this direction during the last decades (Anderson 1972, Heidenheimer and Elvander, eds. 1980).

The general aims of care for the elderly are to assure the elderly of a secure financial situation, good housing, and service and care according to needs (Thorslund 1989). The public help which the individual receives should contain an element of choice and influence on the part of the recipient and maintain high standards.

An explicit principle of equity further implies that the service and care provided by public agencies should be based only on "needs." All the elderly should have equal access to these welfare benefits regardless of where they live, regardless of purchasing power, etc.

## The responsible authorities

Overall responsibility for the various elements of care for the elderly rests with the state. Government and the parliament legislate and formulate guidelines as to how the elderly shall be cared for and who shall bear responsibility for the various services.

Sweden's municipalities (284 in all) are responsible for the social services and the county councils (26) for health care and medical services. The boards of both these bodies are locally elected, and they enjoy an internationally unique degree of autonomy (though the other Nordic countries are comparable). They levy taxes and spend money at their own discretion. Most services are provided locally, and it is difficult for the national government to monitor these authorities. To be sure, there is national legislation as to what shall be provided and how, but the legislation is of a framework kind and extremely vague for those who seek concrete guidance.

In the area of old age care, two main pieces of legislation apply, both of recent date. Thus, in 1982 the new Social Services Act (Socialtjänstlagen) came into effect. This framework legislation emphasizes the right of the individual to receive public sector service and help at all stages of life. Everyone who needs help to support themselves in their day-to-day existence has the right to claim assistance if their "needs cannot be met in any other way" (a stipulation of the Social Services Act that may be interpreted differently).

In 1983 a new Health and Medical Services Act (Hälso- och sjukvårdslagen) came into effect. According to this Act, health care and medical services aim to maintain a good standard of health among the entire population and to provide care on equal terms for all. Responsibility for the running and shaping of health and medical care rests mainly with the 23 county councils and the three metropolitan municipalities of Malmö, Gotland and Göteborg.

From these laws themselves and the extensive work that preceded the first law especially, one can extract a number of general aims for the care of the elderly, as mentioned initially (finances, housing, service and care).

Both laws stress that help shall be given in as "normalized" settings as possible. This means that old people should be helped to remain at home for as long as possible, and in principle no one can be forced to move to an institution due to extensive need for personal care. Most municipalities have one or more cases where they have to provide 24-hour homemaking services.

The autonomy of local administrations and the direct election of local politicians in conjunction with the "loftiness" of the legislation on services and on health and medical care allow the municipalities and the county councils very great freedom to plan and organize their own services.

The autonomy of these two levels of local government also means that services for and care of the elderly have to a certain extent come to be organized differently in different parts of the country. Thus, the number of institutional beds in relation to the size of the local population and the scope of home help services and home nursing care, for example, can vary considerably. There are variations between urban and rural areas especially, to the disadvantage of the former (Sundström and Thorslund 1991).

On the other hand, the general principles of the Swedish welfare state regarding the care of the elderly are the same nationwide: namely that care of and services for the elderly are primary public sector responsibilities and that care shall be given by trained and qualified staff.

## Informal care providers for the elderly

Research studies and policy debates concerning care of the elderly in Sweden have, for a number of reasons, focused mainly on the formal care system. Public policies and programs providing health and social services, as well as pensions and other forms of social insurance, are highly developed. The high percentage of women in the labour market presupposes a formal system of care for the elderly. There are no statutory requirements for children to provide care for the elderly. Thus, until recently, little public interest has been accorded to the role of the family and the informal care system.

The demographic trends, along with migration, urbanization and broken families, are firm evidence that Sweden is moving away from the traditional Western world concept of the nuclear family (Popenoe 1987). The consequences this will have on the care of the elderly are not yet known. Without doubt, it will put certain limits on the potential of the informal support system (Teeland 1978).

However, despite the assumption of a decline in the amount of informal care based on Sweden's labour participation rates for women, the reality appears to be that there are increased burdens on caregivers who have to both maintain a paid job and provide the necessary care. Only in those cases in which the dependent relative is incapacitated or otherwise demanding does it become a full-time role, but many caregivers are relatively old themselves and do not work full time anyway. Others work part time and find ways to combine work and caregiving.

The consequence of expanding public care of the aged, therefore, is that today many elderly seem to receive more overall care and support, from both their families and from public services. Another effect of expanded public care is that, increasingly, the housebound elderly manage on their own in their own homes, without having to take refuge with their families or move into an institution. Longitudinal studies clearly show that the aged initially rely on a spouse and other family members, and only later turn to public support, usually for home help services (Zappolo and Sundström 1989).

The willingness of women, and sometimes men, to continue to care for their elderly relatives in a society that stresses public sector responsibility is probably a reflection of enduring family ties. It is unlikely that changes in the family structure, especially rising divorce rates and ever more single parents, will affect the availability or willingness of family members to engage in informal care. The issue at stake, then, is how to implement support programs for family caregivers. This will be elaborated further later on in this chapter.

## ECONOMY

### Pensions and allowances

The Swedish system of national pensions and housing allowances is designed to give elderly people financial security (Hokenstad 1988).

The national pensions scheme covers a basic pension (folkpension), payable to everyone regardless of previous working income, and a supplementary pension (ATP) based on income from gainful employment. A special partial pension makes it possible for employees and self-employed persons aged 60-64 to combine part-time work with a pension.

To be eligible for the ATP pension, one must have had an income higher than the base rate for at least three years. The size of this pension is calculated on the basis of average pensionable income during a person's 15 best-paid years.

A recipient of the basic pension may be entitled to a municipal housing allowance. This is a means-tested benefit and the rules for eligibility are determined by the municipality. In 1988, 31% of old-age pensioners received this type of benefit. The housing allowance is only one of a wide range of main and supplementary benefits which can be combined with the basic and ATP pensions.

Pension amounts are set by the government each year and are calculated according to a base amount which is related to the consumer price index. Sweden leads the OECD countries in terms of net replacement level. The net replacement rate exceeds 70% for an average Swedish production worker; the economic importance of private pension schemes is consequently only marginal for the majority of recipients. Recently, however, the number of private personal pension insurance policies has increased. The reasons for this new development are at least partly due to the fact that private personal pensions have been treated favourably in terms of taxation and have thus constituted an advantageous form of saving. It must also be admitted, however, that some people are questioning the likelihood of the national pension scheme being able in the future to continue to pay out pensions of the same size as hitherto (Thorslund 1991).

### Subsidized services and care

Both the health care and medical services provided by the county councils and the social services provided by the municipalities are strongly subsidized, with the recipient usually paying only a fraction of the actual cost. Table 5.1 demonstrates the relation between the real costs and the charges made to the recipient. Charges can vary between the various county councils and municipalities. One precondition for receipt of care and service is that a need is assessed to exist.

The total public cost of care and services for the elderly is estimated at some SEK 74,000 million. Most of this (65%) goes to various kinds of institutions, such as hospitals, long-term care and old-age homes (Governmental Committee Report 1987).

At the present, the fees (out-of-pocket costs) for health care and social services are successively increasing. But, to limit the cost for the recipient, there exists a "high-cost-coverage," which means that no one has to pay more than a total of SEK 1,500 per year for health care, regardless of the type and amount of care received.

Resources for health care and care of the elderly in Sweden have been steadily increasing since the middle of the 1950s—in a similar pattern as that shown for the majority of welfare states (Calltorp 1989b). Since the beginning of the 1980s the amount of total health care spending in relation to the Gross National Product (GNP) has been between 9 and 10 percent.

## CARE OF THE ELDERLY—PAST DEVELOPMENT AND CURRENT SITUATION

For many years, care of the elderly in Sweden was virtually synonymous with institutional care. Even in comparison with the other Scandinavian countries, Sweden leads the way in this respect (Statskontoret 1987).

**Table 5.1    Costs of services and care**

| Type of service/care | Running costs (gross, 1991) | Costs for recipient (1991) |
|---|---|---|
| Hospital care | approx. SEK 1,800/day | max. SEK 70/day |
| Geriatric dept. | approx. SEK 1,200/day | max. SEK 70/day |
| Nursing home | approx. SEK 1,000/day | |
| Old-age home | approx. SEK 380/day | means-tested, max. 70% of pension |
| To visit the doctor at<br>- hospital<br>- the health care centre | <br>varies<br>varies | varies<br>av. SEK 100<br>av. SEK 90 |
| Home visits:<br>- district doctor<br>- home nursing | <br>approx. SEK 400/hour<br>approx. SEK 150/hour | <br>max. SEK 90/visit<br>free |
| Home help | approx. SEK 150/hour | means/needs-tested |
| Day centre | approx. SEK 100/day | free |
| Day care | approx. SEK 100/day | SEK 35/day |
| Security alarms | approx. SEK 35/pers. | varies, usually free |
| Transport services | approx. SEK 90/trip | varies greatly, heavily subsidized |
| Home adaptions | varies | free up to SEK 30,000 |
| Technical aids | varies | free |
| Medicines | varies | max. SEK 90 per prescription |

Institutional care accounts for around two thirds of all resources allocated to service and care for the elderly population.

During the postwar period, the number of places in old-age homes and long-term care institutions steadily increased until the beginning of the 1980s. During the 1960s and 1970s the number of old-age homes and long-term care institutions increased dramatically. The total number of institutional beds was doubled and in that regard kept pace with the increase in the population aged 80 years and over. This increase in institutional beds has now halted, however, and for the last decade the number of institutional beds has remained largely unchanged. At the same time, the number of the very elderly in the population is continuing to rise. This means that, given the unchanged number of institutional beds, a relative decrease in the number of beds is actually occurring (Berg et al. 1988).

In 1988, around 6% of those aged 65 or over were resident or being nursed in old-age homes, long-term care institutions (geriatric departments and nursing homes), or within the psychiatric sector. To these must be added the patients receiving general in-patient care. Even though there are no corresponding figures for the number of elderly receiving general in-patient care at any one time, we do know that the group aged 65 or over accounted for 55% of all days of general somatic in-patient care in 1985 (Landstingsförbundet 1988).

However, by far the majority of elderly people, including the very old, live in their own homes. Among those aged 85-89, for example, less than one fourth are cared for permanently in institutions of the types mentioned above. Even in the small group of persons aged 90 and over less than half are being cared for more or less permanently in institutions (Thorslund 1991).

Given the fact that by far the majority of elderly people live at home, the home nursing and home help services have to be expanded to take into account the increase in the numbers of the elderly and the fact that the number of institutional beds is no longer increasing. The number of people receiving social home help services has also more than tripled since 1964, when the first statistics appeared. The numbers of elderly and handicapped persons receiving help increased particularly during the late 1960s and the 1970s. During the 1980s, on the other hand, the number of recipients of help decreased somewhat. A closer scrutiny of the situation reveals that it is younger pensioners (under 80 years of age) and persons under 65 who now receive less help than previously.

On the other hand, the number of working hours within the home help services has steadily increased since 1969. In that year, around 35 million hours of home help were given, compared with 93 million hours in 1988.

A recently published research report, however, has pointed out that in the city of Stockholm, the number of help hours that have actually been provided to the elderly has decreased (Szebehely and Eliasson 1991). In earlier days, the home helpers were mainly housewives. They had no professional training or formal education and usually were part-time contracted workers. Today, working in the home help services is a full-time profession, in which certain working hours are spent on training and education and conferences. Every morning there is a meeting to decide on how the working day should be scheduled. Meetings, training and time to travel around to the care receivers could explain—at least partly—why a growing proportion of the working hours in the home help services are spent on non-client work. This development could of course also be seen as an ineffective use of public resources. On the other hand, it is hard to argue that in a modern welfare society, the home helpers should not be given the same working conditions that most other professionals take for granted.

The number of staff working in the social home help services clearly dropped somewhat during the 1970s and the early 1980s, only to increase again over the past few years—reaching in 1986 almost the same level as in 1970. At the beginning of the 1970s, hourly-paid staff were in the majority. Since then the number of hourly-paid staff has steadily fallen, while the number of part-time staff has been on the increase. The number of full-time staff has also risen, especially during the 1980s.

Together with the home help services and the work carried out by families, home nursing is seen as the most important element of home-based care of the elderly. The number of district nurses has more than tripled since 1974 and the number of general practitioners has also risen over the last few years.

Data on the development of the primary health care services have not been collected on a routine basis so far. However, in 1989, the first nationwide study was carried out to obtain some basic information on the scope of the primary health care services (i.e. home nursing, staffing, etc.). The results indicate that roughly 100,000 persons aged 65 and over were receiving home nursing care (i.e. almost 7% of the total elderly population) at the time of the study (PVU 89 - 1990). How many of these persons were at the same time receiving home help services is not known.

Furthermore, there are no reliable estimates of the proportion of their time district nurses and general practitioners devote to elderly persons living at home. The extent to which the increase in the number of staff has meant an increase in the medical care that can be offered to elderly people in their own homes is therefore unclear. In Sweden today, for example, it is unusual for general practitioners to make home visits; they normally see their patients at their offices and at health centres. District nurses make more home visits than doctors, but nevertheless more elderly people see a district nurse at the clinic than in their own homes.

In general it can be concluded that "traditional" institutions as well as home services and home health care have not kept up with the increasing numbers of older elderly in the population. However, there has been an increase in alternative living arrangements and other forms of service and health care.

## INSTITUTIONAL HOUSING AND CARE

### Sheltered accommodation

In 1989 almost 40,000 people lived in sheltered accommodation—service houses (servicehus)—owned and managed by the municipality. Such accommodation takes the form of apartments in buildings containing 20 to 100 housing units, most of which were built during the 1970s and 1980s. The availability of sheltered accommodation, allocation policies, and thus the age and fitness range of the tenants vary from municipality to municipality. The tenants are for the most part pensioners who have ordinary rent contracts with the local authority. The apartments consist of 1 to 3 rooms plus kitchen and bathroom. Subsidized municipal home help services are available to residents (according to assessed needs) in the same way as they are available to those living in their own homes. There is usually a restaurant in the building and a day centre, as well as activity rooms, chiropody services, etc.

The number of apartments in sheltered accommodation increased by some 3,000 yearly in the 1980s, which means that this is the most important contribution to the Swedish system of care for the elderly in recent years. However, the object of sheltered accommodation has not been—in our opinion—thoroughly discussed. For example, who should be eligible for a place in sheltered accommodation? The rather independent elderly who primarily need modern housing? This was the original idea when this housing concept emerged in the 1970s. Or should this housing and care opportunity serve the most needy and dependent elderly? Today there is a confounding mix of eligibility criteria. In many service houses the majority of residents are independent, but the number of persons needing daily assistance is increasing. The question is whether these more frail and dependent elderly should be moved and, if so, where? There are increasing problems in finding vacant beds in, for example, nursing homes. This development will probably mean that in the long run the service houses will become more like nursing homes.

## Group dwellings

During recent years, group dwellings (gruppboende) have also become an alternative to institutions for persons with great need of care and supervision. There are group dwellings for, among others, physically handicapped or mentally retarded persons. Most common, however, are group dwellings for persons with senile dementia. "Group dwelling" as a concept and form of housing has no standard definition, but it usually means a small housing collective for 6 to 8 persons, in which each resident has their own apartment, shares communal areas and has access to service and care provided by resident staff around the clock.

In 1989 there were around 2,500 persons living in group dwellings. Previously in Sweden there was no suitable form of housing or care for persons with senile dementia. The ideas behind the group dwellings have many similarities with those underlying service houses, that is, to offer home-like housing with high standards and service and care according to needs. Experiences with group dwellings have been favourable to date and all municipalities and county councils running such units are planning an expansion of group dwelling capacity during the coming years.

The experiences with group dwellings thus far have been mainly positive in that the quality of care and standard of housing are viewed as superior to traditional institutional care. A higher degree of work satisfaction among care personnel in group dwellings is reported than for those employed in institutional care. Residents and families, in general, feel very positive about the group dwelling as a care alternative for their family member.

There are also problems. A critical question is what to do with a resident as the illness progresses. Should the resident remain in the dwelling? Is it possible to manage the care of a deteriorated bedridden person in this kind of unit? What about persons with extensive psychiatric symptoms?

These questions still remain largely unanswered, but it is obvious that permanent residence requires increased staffing. Yet many people question whether even increased staffing would permit permanent residence.

There is also some criticism of the physical milieu. In several units, care of frail and dependent residents has become very burdensome because of shortcomings in the physical environment. Another problem is the risk of "burnout" among care personnel. While many experience their job as stimulating, many also report feelings of exhaustion (Johansson 1990).

## Old-age homes

In 1989 there were some 900 municipal old-age homes (ålderdomshem) where around 39,000 elderly people, unable to cope at home even with the aid of the home help and home nursing services, were living. With increasing numbers of people remaining in their own homes, the building of old-age homes started to decline during the 1970s and almost completely ceased during the following decade. In the 1980s the number of places decreased by some 3,000 yearly.

Most residents of old-age homes live in small single rooms (approximately 10 to 15 square metres) with their own toilets. Residents may bring their own furniture with them. Meals are served communally at set times. Various types of facilities and activities are available. Care is provided around the clock by regular staff. The monthly fees charged by old-age homes are income related.

The small rooms and the low overall standard of housing are beneath what is usually regarded as proper housing in Sweden today. During the 1970s and the beginning of the 1980s the general policy favoured replacing old-age homes with service houses. However, the residents, their families, the staff and the general public loudly opposed the closing down of the old-age homes. This resulted in a shift of policy, confirmed by the parliament, which decided on new funding for modernization of the old-age homes in 1988. Therefore, the trend today is to rebuild or even build new old-age homes. This is of course a lengthy process, and in the older old-age homes, there are reports of increasing difficulties in caring for the elderly.

## Long-term care

In 1988 there were 49,000 beds for somatic long-term care in Sweden (geriatric departments and nursing homes). Geriatric departments (långvårdskliniker) are often linked to general hospitals. Here the aim is to rehabilitate and allow the elderly patient to return home as soon as possible. Such departments also offer the opportunity for so-called relief care, whereby the patient is admitted for a certain time to allow the family taking care of the patient at home to have some relief. They also provide respite care, when patients spend certain regular fixed periods in the department.

Nursing homes (sjukhem) provide care for longer periods under more home-like conditions. In Sweden, three general types of nursing homes have developed. Central nursing homes are usually attached to a geriatric department and function essentially as an annex. These seem to be diminishing in importance. Local nursing homes are usually independent of hospitals and come under the organizational auspices of the primary care system, with the district physician usually having referral authority. At present the number of beds in such local nursing homes is being increased. Finally, 4% of all beds in long-term care are to be found in private nursing homes.

During the 1980s both the total number of beds and the number of days of somatic short-term care have decreased, the number of beds being around 36,000 in 1988. On the other hand, the proportion of days of hospital care consumed by the elderly has risen continuously. In 1985, 54.6% of all days of care within the somatic short-term care sector were accounted for by persons in the 75 and over age group (6.3% of the total population). There are many factors behind this trend. One is the rise in the numbers of the elderly. Another is the fact that geriatric medicine has become more advanced, with larger numbers of old people being able to benefit from new forms of treatment. It is, furthermore, often difficult to discharge elderly patients whose medical treatment has been completed if they cannot be cared for at home and if there is a shortage of beds in long-term care institutions to which they should otherwise be transferred for more appropriate care. Such elderly patients—"bed blockers"—could remain in somatic short-term wards for a long time. This has been one of the most debated problems in care of the elderly in Sweden during recent years.

## TECHNOLOGIES TO SUPPORT HOME-BASED CARE

Most municipalities provide a wide variety of services and programs to enable the elderly to go on living in their own homes as long as possible. These programs could partly be seen as an effort to increase the general welfare of the elderly, for example, improved housing and public transportation, etc. There are also special programs which target people with special needs.

Most elderly people in Sweden (92%) live in ordinary homes and around half of them are owner-occupiers. The general standard of housing is high, with most elderly people living in modern, warm homes with well-equipped kitchens, hot and cold running water and an indoor toilet. Nevertheless, the policy that as many as possible should remain at home often creates the demand for ordinary dwellings to be adapted to special needs and for there to be sufficient care and help available when the elderly person can no longer manage on their own at home. Municipalities therefore carry out home adaptions in order to minimize such difficulties as stairs and thresholds. The cost of such services is heavily subsidized or free (Brink 1988).

Other forms of service are often given in combination with home help. Most municipalities offer chiropody, haircare, food services (meals on wheels), help with bathing, snow clearing, etc. A number of these services are run and offered at day centres, which are either free-standing units in the community or incorporated into sheltered accommodation or old-age homes. Day centres function as meeting places where the elderly in the area can get together for meals, group activities and sometimes occupational therapy.

The number of day centres is increasing at present. All were originally run by the municipalities but this is no longer the case. It is becoming increasingly common for the elderly themselves to take over the running of the day centre after it has been set up by the municipality, the idea being that the direction and shape of the activities should be determined by the users' own needs and interests.

More recently, special day care units have been established for elderly persons with senile dementia. Many senile elderly still live at home and are looked after by their families, often constituting a heavy burden for the latter. The day care units for the senile can therefore play an important role in giving the elderly the supervision and care they need and—especially—in offering the family necessary relief. The number of patients in these units at any one time is limited and the care is given by specially chosen staff. These day care units are at present undergoing a rapid expansion. Vital for the functioning of the day centres are the municipal transport services (färdtjänsten), which are described in detail below.

Postal services for the elderly may supplement home help in rural areas. After consultation with the municipal home help service, rural postal workers provide certain services to elderly people who live alone and far from neighbours.

## Transport service

The transport service supplements the public transportation system, and is aimed at increasing the mobility of handicapped persons who have considerable difficulty in using public transportation or in getting around on their own.

The transport service may be used for various purposes, namely, travel to and from work, travel for treatment, and other trips such as shopping, obtaining haircare and chiropody services, visiting relatives and friends, going to the movies, theatre or church, or participating in organized activities.

The transport service is generally provided by regular taxicabs, but specially equipped vehicles are also often used, for example, for transporting wheelchair-bound persons. In some areas, the transport service must be ordered days ahead. In others there is almost immediate access to the service. Although the fee for the transport service varies in different geographical areas, it is usually heavily subsidized.

The transport service has been expanded since the mid-1960s and is provided today in every municipality. In 1987, 14% of the 65-79 age group and 53% of the 80 and over age group were entitled to use the service. Even though many entitled persons never use this service, the average number of journeys per entitled person per year was 41 in 1987.

There is evidence of quite considerable differences among municipalities regarding the organization and availability of transport services. In most municipalities—but not all—the service is available around the clock. In many municipalities there are restrictions on the number of permitted trips, the number of miles or the cost of travel per transport service permit. However, the number of entitled persons is still increasing and generally this kind of service is regarded almost as a "citizens' right" for older people.

## Security alarms

Almost all Swedish households have a telephone. For persons with functional impediments it may be necessary to add technical aids to the ordinary telephone in order to facilitate its use. For example, pressing a button attached to a bracelet or band around the neck will automatically alert the alarm reception office in the nearest service house or the night patrol on duty. At the same time the telephone activates a loudspeaker function so that the care personnel can communicate with the person without the individual holding the receiver.

In the 1970s and early 1980s other alarm systems were installed in newly-built flats and service houses. Some of these systems were based on the principle that an alarm is given if a normally occurring activity, e.g. use of the toilet, does not take place by a certain time (so-called "passive alarms"). These kinds of system are seldom if ever installed today.

Security alarms are installed in every Swedish municipality. The provision of alarms to the single recipient is based on assessed needs. It is not possible to estimate the total number of persons supplied with an alarm system. However, there has been a shortage of available alarm systems fitted by municipalities and it is today possible in some places to subscribe to systems run by private security companies.

These systems are already rather widespread in Sweden. The current development concerns their technical performance and improving target efficiency. In spite of the fact that security alarms are widespread, no serious evaluations have been carried out. The benefits are not questioned, and it is often seen as a citizens' right for the elderly to have this kind of security alarm.

## Technical aids

Disabled persons in Sweden are supposed to have access to technical aids regardless of their age, economic means or place of residence. Virtually all technical aids in Sweden today are issued free of charge through a national system of provision. One disadvantage of this system is that decisions about who receives which aids are made solely by health care personnel. Users are not always informed of the choice of aids available. Another disadvantage is that information about aids is seldom available to the general public. People with mild disabilities or frailties do not know that aids exist which could make their lives easier. Only recently have aids been available on the free market, and only in certain areas of the country (Parker and Thorslund 1991).

In order to obtain a technical aid, a person must go to a doctor, occupational therapist, physical therapist or district nurse employed by the county. Sometimes this involves a waiting period due to a lack of qualified personnel. The therapist, or other prescriber, assesses the person's needs and issues the appropriate aids. This is usually done in close consultation with the disabled person, and sometimes involves a home visit.

Simple aids, such as canes or reachers, are usually issued through outpatient clinics or hospitals. More complex aids, such as wheelchairs, may involve a visit to the technical aid centre for evaluation, fitting and training. Technical aid centres are located in every county and are staffed by occupational therapists. Simple adaptions in the home, such as the installation of grab bars near the bathtub, can be ordered during the home visit. More extensive alterations require a complicated process of approval. There are also sight and hearing centres that are responsible for aids for these impairments, as well as separate orthopedic workshops for prostheses and ortheses.

There is no organized system of follow-up after prescription. Those persons with continual contact with the prescriber, for example, those receiving therapy or nurse's visits on a regular basis, thereby receive an informal follow-up. But many people are evaluated and issued aids on a one-time basis. Nor is there an organized system for collection and "recycling" of aids no longer used, with the exception of some expensive aids such as electric wheelchairs. It is usually up to the individual to return those aids which can be reused.

## IMPROVEMENTS IN MANAGEMENT OF CARE FOR THE ELDERLY

### Care planning teams

Care for the elderly in Sweden is highly decentralized. Viewed from an international perspective, the authorities in both the county councils and the municipalities are very autonomous. Also within these organizations, the decision making about service provision is highly decentralized. In many municipalities, for example, a single untrained home help supervisor (case manager) has the authority to decide if an elderly person will be permitted a place in an old-age home.

This highly decentralized system has advantages as well as disadvantages. In order to decrease some of the disadvantages when single decisionmakers have to make difficult and complicated choices, care planning teams have been organized. These teams may have different compositions. The main core consists of the district nurse and the home help supervisor, responsible for the home nursing and home help services respectively in the same district. Sometimes other professionals with responsibilities in that district are included as regular members of the team. In other teams, these professionals (physicians, occupational therapists, geriatricians, managers of old-age homes, social workers, etc.) will be called upon when the district nurse and the home help supervisor find it necessary.

The team is responsible—within existing resources—for covering the needs for housing, service and care for the elderly within the team's catchment area. This includes case finding, outreach activities, needs assessments and monitoring the services. The home help supervisor has the authority to decide on home help services and different forms of municipal housing for the elderly. The nurse decides on home nursing care and (together with the physician) admittance to nursing homes. Although the care planning teams assess and discuss each case, the responsibility and duty to make adequate decisions rest with different single case managers.

The establishment of care planning teams started in the early 1980s. There are now teams in all municipalities and almost all districts. Since no data exist about these teams, there are no available figures on the number of teams, how they are composed, how regularly they meet or how many cases they assess and discuss.

There is much evidence that discussions within care planning teams have made it easier for case managers to make adequate decisions. There is also an increased awareness that different parts of the system of care for the elderly often have to face the same problems and that there is a need to cooperate to solve these problems. In districts where the teams are working well, the probabilities of a better use of the total resources and of elderly persons obtaining the proper care should increase.

No serious evaluations have been carried out. However, several local reports indicate improved quality (especially in targeting and follow-up) in case management.

## Discharge planning

A major problem in hospital care occurs when patients whose medical treatment has been completed cannot be discharged from the hospital. This is often the case with older patients who cannot manage on their own at home. In some departments of internal medicine the number of patients whose treatment has been completed can sometimes account for nearly one quarter of hospitalized patients. Quite apart from the fact that patients whose treatment has been completed are now receiving care at the wrong level and run the risk of becoming "hospitalized," this constitutes a poor utilization of expensive institutional resources.

The effort has therefore been to reduce the length of time between completion of medical treatment and discharge from hospital by means of various administrative measures. Members of both the primary health care and hospital systems have been given the task of drafting a program to run a collaborative activity. For example, each hospital department choses one person responsible for ensuring that the primary care district (and the municipality) will be informed as soon as possible whenever a hospital patient in their area has completed medical treatment. Similarly, each primary care district must select staff who are always available by phone so as to start planning for the patient's return home.

While people are well aware of the problems connected with discharging elderly patients, there are few documented local cases of systematic attempts to review and improve routines and standards among different types of caregivers. Up to now (1990), four counties have tried to implement this type of systematic discharge planning system.

In one case it was possible to reduce the average number of days from completion of medical treatment to discharge from hospital from 13 to 11 days. From the same project it is estimated that another 3 days could be cut by avoiding the use of the postal service and by further trimming administrative systems.

It is thus apparently possible to reduce the number of care days in many institutions. However, it is still doubtful how much this reduction in the number of days spent in hospital represents any great reduction in total institutional care. Many of the patients who can now be discharged earlier from hospital are transferred to other institutions, for example, nursing homes.

On the other hand, the experiences from the discharge planning projects have been incorporated into the forthcoming reform in care for the elderly in Sweden. The idea is to add an economic incentive to the discharge process. If the municipality cannot offer the patient home care (and/or residential care, etc.), and the patient has to stay in the hospital after treatment is completed, the municipality will have to pay the full cost of the hospital care according to certain criteria. The intention is that this economic incentive will promote a more rapid development of home-based care alternatives and, on the whole, reduce "unnecessary" institutional care.

## INFORMAL CARE OF THE ELDERLY

New eldercare policy in Sweden reflects a newfound interest in and commitment to family caregiving. Recent research has confirmed that informal care is still the largest source of support for old people (Hokenstad and Johansson 1990a). While the formal service system has been an important component of policy designed to help the elderly manage at home, there has been increasing awareness that most families provide some informal care and many prefer informal care.

The new interest in informal caregiving should be viewed against the information presented earlier. The experiences in providing home-based care of the elderly have highlighted the role of the family as care provider. At the same time, increasing needs in the population and the problems of the formal system in meeting these needs have underscored the obvious risk that families will have to carry an increasing care burden in the future.

Research on informal caregiving is still only beginning in Sweden. There is a lack of theories, concepts and empirical data. But what is known may be briefly summarized as follows:

The first important study to consider the role of informal caregiving for the elderly was performed in 1979. On the basis of interview data from a representative sample of almost one thousand elderly people, it was found that the elderly received almost three times as much informal as formal help (counted in number of hours). This data was not correlated with any data on assessed needs, but it at least gave an idea of the quantity of informal caregiving (Lagergren et al. 1984).

A more detailed and localized study of family caregiving was carried out in Tierp, a rural municipality of about 20,000 inhabitants. 2,000 persons, 75 years or older, were surveyed in different ways on their health status, activities of daily living (ADLs), social contacts, living conditions, etc. The major purpose of the study was to supplement registered data on the provision of social service and health care with information on the need for service and the amount and type of informal and formal care given (Johansson et al. 1991).

The results showed that the elderly living in their own homes were quite independent, and actually a "healthy elite." Those who required help needed to be assisted primarily with chores, bathing/showering and walking outdoors. A comparison of formal and informal support given to these elderly documented the fact that most of the care was given by the families. Family caregivers functioned as prime caregivers in 68% of all cases, and the formal system in 32% of cases.

These local data have recently been confirmed by preliminary findings in a study of a nationwide sample of elderly people, aged 65 years or older, living in their own homes. Self-reported data on the elderly's ability to manage basic and instrumental ADLs and use of informal and formal support were gathered in a representative sample of 1,600 elderly, projected to a total population of roughly 1,400,000 elderly. The results showed that informal caregiving exceeded formal support in every single task. It was only among the very old that formal support reached the level of informal caregiving. These data have been used for a quantitative comparison of the amount of informal and formal care given to the elderly on the national level. Once again, the results showed informal support to be more than twice the extent of formal support.

Other Swedish studies have also revealed that family caregiving is often connected with personal sacrifice and emotional strain. Berg and Holmgren (1984) found, in a study of family caregivers in two different municipalities, that they often experienced caregiving as a heavy burden. Almost 60% reported that they had to curtail social contacts due to the caregiving task. 55% experienced mental strain and 40% found themselves "tied to" the care situation. Caring for an older relative suffering from dementia compounds the caregiver's task. Data from several studies document different problems. Adolfsson et al. (1981) reported on psychosomatic illness among caregivers. Tornefelt and Johansson (1988) found emotional strain, and Winquist (1984) found symptoms of depression, anxiety and remorse.

As part of the Tierp research, a case study was also carried out with a group of 39 family caregivers (primarily spouses and daughters) functioning as the "brunt bearers" in caring for frail elderly. In the cases selected, the elderly would probably have had to move to an institution if intensive family caregiving had not been available (Johansson 1991).

The results of this study revealed that caregiving for a dependent family member was clearly connected to proximity with the person in need of help. The findings also exposed the overburdened nature of women's role as caregivers. Family caregivers needed support, but were often poorly informed about available services. There was an urgent need for respite services, psychological support, counseling and help in coping with everyday caregiving problems. Families were strongly committed to caregiving, but at the same time they expressed a need to share the responsibility for the care of the elderly with society and the formal care system.

Several local studies have then reaffirmed the well-known fact, found in other countries, that informal care plays a dominant role in care for the elderly. It is conclusive that this care for the elderly could not function without the help provided by the informal care system. Formal care should be seen as a complement to informal care and not vice versa. So far, there is no evidence to show that the development of an extensive formal care system, as in Sweden, will cause a decrease in informal caregiving (Sundström 1986).

One obvious problem, though, stressed by both researchers and the general public, is that formal care very seldom functions as a direct support for carers. So, despite the fact that there exists a rather comprehensive system of formal care for the elderly, these resources are not used as a strategic support for the provision of informal support. Instead, the two systems seem to function rather independently of each other.

## Caregiver support policy

The Swedish government's Care of the Elderly Bill for the 1990s has made support for caregiving relatives one of the key objectives of eldercare policy for the coming decade (Hokenstad and Johansson 1990b). Caregiver support is one of several components of the new legislation. The proposed policy reaffirms the commitment that government has the statutory obligation to take care of older people in Sweden. Local government is mandated to have a major role in care for the elderly. At the same time, the bill highlights the burdens of caregivers and the need to support their efforts as part of a comprehensive eldercare policy.

Policy initiatives to support caregiving families and caregiver relatives provide both more economic assistance and better focused service support. Perhaps the most innovative of these initiatives is the incorporation of a care leave policy into the Swedish social insurance system. This policy has already been enacted and went into effect on July 1, 1989.

The care leave policy entitles employed persons to take time off from work and be paid an insurance allowance for up to 30 days to care for an elderly family member. This new policy has been incorporated into the health and sickness insurance program which is a major component of the Swedish social insurance system. It is similar to the parental insurance program which is available for the temporary care of sick children. Although more limited in duration than the parental insurance benefits, the caregiver insurance benefits serve an equivalent function. The allowance corresponds to the sick allowance reimbursement for the person providing the care.

This paid leave is limited to a total of 30 days in the lifetime of the individual receiving the care. Thus, it is intended to be used for emergency care and terminal care situations and not for ongoing caregiving which is more appropriately handled through caregiver salary and other economic support programs (as described below). It is possible for the caregiving relative to take this leave at different times for a day or less as well as for longer periods. A written application along with a doctor's statement of need for care are necessary to receive care leave insurance benefits. The elderly person receiving care must consent to the arrangement.

Support of family caregivers through social insurance is a major innovation in care of the elderly. This policy will alleviate emotional stress since family members now know that they will lose neither income nor jobs in the event of an emergency or terminal care situation which requires their presence in the home. It will also lighten the caregiving burden by enabling family members to relieve each other in times of acute need. The primary caregiver can receive a respite from this responsibility now that temporary care can be provided by an insured relative. While the amount of paid leave time is quite limited, the new policy provides a balance between labour market employment requirements and family caregiving needs.

Direct cash payments by local government are available if need for in-home care is established and if the family is willing to serve as care provider. The payment goes to the older person and is used as compensation for the cost of care to the family. The level of economic support is based on the assessed need for care and the number of hours of help needed by the elderly person. Certification of need is most often done by a district nurse with a doctor's approval. An economic means test is not required. The subsidies may come from either the county or the municipality, but the latter is now assuming primary responsibility for this type of support. Cash allowances are financed through local income taxes. They are not subject to taxation.

About 20,000 Swedish families are receiving cash allowances for caregiving. Many more are entitled to this type of support but, for various reasons, do not claim it. One explanation is lack of knowledge about the availability of the cash allowances. Another is the use of differing eligibility criteria in different parts of the country (this is also a local government program). There are also families that, for ideological reasons, do not want to depend on this type of public support. Still, the home care allowance is an important form of support for many Swedish families.

When the elderly person needs more constant care and attention, a family member can be employed by the municipality or the county as a paid caregiver. Caregiver salaries have been available in Sweden for a number of years now. Relatives of elderly people who provide care for at least twenty (20) hours each week are eligible to apply for this support as an alternative to seeking employment in the labour market. Their salaries are paid by local government and provide taxable income with benefits, including vacations and pensions. The salaries are equivalent to those paid to the home helps who are employed by the Swedish municipalities to provide care in the home. There are over 10,000 salaried family caregivers in Sweden at the present time.

Labour market training for salaried family caregivers is an additional support to be expanded as a result of the new policy. Local government will become responsible for helping salaried relatives enter the labour market when there is no longer a need for paid family caregiving service. Whatever the reason, family caregivers will be targeted to receive job training, job placement and other labour market services in making the transition to other employment. Thus, the current policy is expanded to support the caregiver through outreach services in addition to employment assistance.

Service supports for caregivers will also be emphasized as part of the new policy. In this case, the policy initiative does not mandate increased services. Rather, it calls for an increased focus on family caregivers. The municipalities are mandated to complement informal care with their services. Services delivered by local government will be targeted to assist caregivers in addition to the elderly themselves. For example, day care and respite care are to be delivered strategically to support caregivers and relieve caregiving burdens. Home nursing and home help services are also to be organized and to provide caregiver support as one major objective. The planning and provision of these services will emphasize the reinforcement of care already being provided by relatives.

This new emphasis on caregiver support also makes local government health care and social service agencies responsible for funding caregivers. The home care program of the municipality will have the task of identifying family caregivers and involving them in the care planning process. This includes informing them of the services available and of the rights of their elderly relatives to these services. In this way, family caregiving is recognized as an essential component of eldercare and the complementary relationship of formal and informal care is emphasized.

## CHARACTERISTICS OF THE SITUATION TODAY—IS THERE A CRISIS?

"Crisis" is a relative concept. People compare today's conditions with those in the past which they have "got used to"; they draw comparisons between the situation at home and that in other countries, and look to see whether goals set in the past have been achieved, etc.

During the 1980s, development in the care of the elderly in Sweden came to a halt, or even went into reverse, when viewed against the ever-increasing numbers of elderly people. It is clear that throughout the 1980s the chances of someone in the group aged 65-79 getting home help or a place in a service house or any type of institution have been radically diminished.

The picture is not quite as clear for the oldest age groups. The number of those living in sheltered accommodations has more than doubled, and the proportion receiving home help has increased somewhat. On the other hand, the proportion of those living in various types of institutions has, taken together, also dropped for the oldest age group.

The proportion of elderly people in institutions has fallen in Sweden and many other countries since the early 1980s. There has been a widespread belief that by reducing institutional residence in favour of remaining at home, both humanitarian and economic benefits can be reaped (Thorslund and Johansson 1987).

Even if social home help has greatly expanded in terms of working hours of help given, the proportion of elderly people receiving help did not increase during the course of the 1980s. Thus, the relative decrease in the number of those being cared for in institutions has not been met by any corresponding rise in the amount of home help provided. If we assume that care resources in 1982 were allocated in the best possible way, i.e. that they were always genuinely needed, and that the service and care needs of the elderly were unchanged, then we may speak of a crisis in care of the elderly today. However, these assumptions, and particularly the first, are of course unrealistic.

The main conclusion, however, is that Sweden still has, in international comparisons, a very comprehensive system of old age care, with extensive coverage. Even the cutbacks described above cannot change this basic fact. Furthermore, there is legislation to support demands for these services and to provide equally well to everyone according to need.

Yet, in reality, there are differences. These are mainly "geographic" rather than of a social or class nature. The large variations—and hence inequalities—are hard to explain rationally and therefore may in a sense be more palatable than if they were the result of class injustice, etc. At the same time there are great local variations even within administrative units. Taken together, this suggests that welfare bureaucracies have less than perfect control over the services they provide (Sundström and Thorslund 1991). In a situation where needs grow drastically and funds are restricted, this becomes politically unacceptable and appears to be a sign of inefficient use of resources.

Other differences in the provision of services and care have also been mentioned. In particular, social and medical services cater to those weak in social resources, especially those who live alone. Only with those moved to institutions are there indications that social class influences use, though it might be misleading to see this as segregation. Parts of the population may— as surveys indicate—instead see institutional care as a component of welfare (although, of course, they prefer not to have to use it).

## What about tomorrow?

Demographic development and cost containment in public services will mean that greater needs have to be met with relatively fewer resources. The government's strategy regarding current and forthcoming problems in care for the elderly emanates from two lines of action. First, a further expansion of general welfare—better housing, indexed pensions, improved public services—is supposed to lead to less need for service and care for the elderly. Second, by transferring the main responsibility—politically, economically and administratively—to one responsible element (the municipality), it is expected that considerable advantages in terms of coordination will be achieved.

In December 1990, the parliament decided on a new eldercare policy, containing guidelines for the future organization and responsibilities regarding care of the elderly. In short, this means that:

- the municipalities will be given the statutory responsibility for all types of institutional housing and care facilities for the elderly, that is, long-term care hospitals (excluding geriatric clinics), central and local nursing homes, old-age homes, service houses, group dwellings and day care facilities.

- the municipalities will also be given the statutory responsibility to provide health care to elderly residents needing help, within the institutional housing and care facilities mentioned above. By agreement with the county, municipalities could also take over the responsibility for home nursing care. However, the responsibility to provide health care does not include care provided by physicians.

- the municipalities will be financially responsible for all other types of long-term institutional care not operated by themselves. The responsibility also includes patients in acute somatic hospital care ("bed blockers") and in geriatric clinics. By agreement with the county, municipalities could also take over the same financial responsibility for patients in long-term psychiatric care.

The main aspects of this decision are in line with what has been suggested before. Details are still being discussed and the final suggestion as to how the proposal should be financed will be presented to the parliament in spring 1991. The new eldercare policy is to be implemented by January 1, 1992 (Socialutskottets betänkande 1990). Of course, at this time, it is too early to have a definitive opinion about whether the new eldercare policy will be successful or not.

Considering the previous discussion, securing service, care and welfare for the elderly population will certainly be an arduous challenge during the 1990s in Sweden. For example, if one assumes that care consumption in the various age groups will remain constant, that the state of health of the various age groups will remain unchanged, and that no great changes will occur in the field of medical technology, etc., then it is clear that resources for all forms of care will have to increase. A summary of the calculated increases in all forms of care shows a total required increase of 18% of resources between 1989 and the year 2000 to keep up with 1989 standards (Thorslund 1990).

In Sweden there are at present no plans for an expansion of resources for old-age homes, long-term care, nursing homes, psychiatric care or general somatic hospital care. This means that even if the same proportion of elderly people in the population are receiving services and care from the public sector in the year 2000, a massive expansion of the social home help services and of service flats would be necessary—an expansion at a rate which would considerably exceed, for example, the impressive increase that occurred during the 1970s.

An increase of such magnitude is hardly realistic, for various reasons. Costs would rise dramatically, and since these costs are financed more or less entirely from taxation, income taxes would therefore have to rise. One cannot, of course, exclude the possibility that taxes might be raised even further in Sweden. Certain surveys, for example, indicate that many Swedes would be prepared to pay more tax if they knew that the money was going to a better health care service. However, it is also the case that there is at present a political consensus that taxes cannot be raised further.

Resources can be obtained by carrying out rationalization and efficiency improving measures. The development during the 1980s could be interpreted as a sign of improved service effectiveness. For example, it has been possible to reduce the amount of expensive institutional care available in spite of the rise in the number and proportion of elderly people. Between 1970 and 1987, the number of general hospital beds fell by nearly 20%. In spite of this reduction, shorter hospital stays have meant that the number of those receiving care has actually continued to rise.

There are alternative explanations as to why it has been possible to reduce the relative number of different kinds of institutional beds. Firstly, there has been an increased emphasis on home-based care. Secondly, during the 1970s and much of the 1980s organizations and care services were actually in need of trimming back. Now, however, even if there is still scope for some rationalization and efficiency improving in care of the elderly, it is naive to believe that the "gains" which have been achieved to date can be repeated (Thorslund 1988).

More staff will be needed in future, irrespective of the variety of care forms available. The governmental report from 1987 has calculated what predicted trends will mean in terms of staffing needs. The example is based on the assumption that the absolute number of institutional beds will be reduced through closures and/or that institutions will be converted to provide a greater number of single and double rooms. Increased resources would instead be put into social home help and home nursing. The estimates reveal that in the social home help services alone, staffing levels would have to rise by between 80% and 100%. These figures necessarily prompt the question—is this possible? Even if we in Sweden should opt for higher taxes or secure the necessary financial resources from some other source—how do we obtain the staff?

According to various estimates based on population changes and decisions already taken, the care and nursing sector will need just over 200,000 further staff during the period 1985-1995, an increase which would account for some 96% of the total estimated increase in the workforce. If one further aimed to tackle the backlog in such areas as eye, hip replacement and cataract surgery and to keep up with continuing developments in medical technology, the health care sector during the same period would have to take on a number of new staff greater than the entire predicted increase on the labour market (Lagergren 1988). Therefore, even if we allowed ourselves to consider the idea of the health care and nursing sector absorbing the entire estimated increase on the labour market, this would still not be sufficient. This projection is based on the assumption that the annual number of immigrants coming to Sweden will remain approximately constant.

Within the care of the elderly in Sweden, as in health care in general, no clearly formulated principles for priority setting exist at either the central or local level. In the past there have been scope and opportunity for the expansion which has taken place, and care has received a steadily growing share of the available public resources (Calltorp 1989a).

In practice, of course, decisions about priorities have to be made all the time. The fact that the total number of people receiving home help has not increased is one example of decisions made by local home help administrators to allocate restricted resources to certain consumers of help, leaving those who previously received the odd hour or so per week to manage without. Above all, it is the younger old-age pensioners who now receive less help than previously.

The development of the public care system which has taken place during the 20th century in Sweden bears the stamp of strong socio-political ambitions which were realizable because of a favourable economic situation. This led to a shifting of responsibility for care of the elderly from the individual and the family to the public sector.

Even though there are no figures at all on trends over time and the extent of various types of informal care, there are nevertheless several local studies which demonstrate that above all, in the care of the elderly, the involvement of relatives is extremely extensive—so extensive indeed that if the social home help services were obliged to take over the role at present played by the relatives, they would need to more than double their number of staff.

The amount of help given by secondary caregivers and various voluntary organizations, cooperatives, self-help groups, etc. in Sweden is not known. It is reasonable to believe that it is less extensive in Sweden than in most other countries, even though it is certainly not inconsiderable in many areas. If one looks at the situation in other countries, it is clear that this area represents an unexploited potential in Sweden (see, for example, Wells and Freer, eds. 1988). However, the tradition of the public sector assuming the main responsibility for services and care is well established in Sweden. The trade unions have also put up a strong resistance to voluntary work (Lagergren et al. 1984).

Quite apart from the fact that the services and care provided by the public sector will probably not be able to increase in pace with rising needs, there is also in Sweden, as in many other countries, the social endeavour for more and more elderly people to have their care and service needs met in the home rather than having to move to various kinds of institutions (see, for example, Bulmer 1987). One prerequisite for—or effect of—this, even if it is not officially acknowledged, is that relatives take greater responsibility for the help needs of their elderly. Is it realistic to assume that families will contribute as much in the future as they do today? Is it realistic to count on greater numbers of families being able to help? Given the fact that the informal care system is in regular use in Sweden, it is quite doubtful whether a heavier burden could be put on it (Tornstam 1989).

To conclude, the overall system of care for the elderly will certainly change in the future. We will probably have a more mixed system which is both operated and financed by a combination of public, private and voluntary efforts. In the city of Stockholm there are already examples of privately operated and financed home help services, home nursing and service houses, etc. This developmental trend is becoming more and more evident (Johansson and Thorslund 1991). At the same time it represents a significant shift in eldercare policy in Sweden, which states that service and care should be provided to all citizens on equal terms, financed, organized and operated by the public sector.

## References

Adolfsson, R., G. Kajsajuntti, A. Myrstener, L. Nyström, B. Olofsson, and P.O.J. Sandman (1981). "Anhörigas synpunkter på omhändertagandet av åldersdementa." *Läkartidningen* 28-29: 2519-2521.

Anderson, O.W. (1972). *Can there be equity? The United States, Sweden and England*. New York: John Wiley.

Berg, S., and A.L. Holmgren (1984). *Sjukvård i hemmet. En studie bland patienter, anhöriga och personal*. Jönköping: Institutet för Gerontologi (56).

Berg, S., L.G. Branch, A.D. Doyle, and G. Sundström (1988). "Institutional and home based long-term care alternatives: The 1965-1985 Swedish experience." *The Gerontologist* 28: 825-829.

Brink, S. (1988). *Housing policies in the context of social welfare goals in periods of economic restraint: A comparison of housing policies for the elderly in Canada and in Sweden*. Gävle: The Institute for Building Research. Research Report, SB: 12.

Bulmer, M. (1987). *The social basis of community care*. London: Allen & Unwin.

Calltorp, J. (1989a). *Prioritering och beslutsprocess i sjukvårdsfrågor. Några drag i de senaste decenniernas svenska hälsopolitik*. Dissertation, Department of Social Medicine, Uppsala.

Calltorp, J. (1989b). "The 'Swedish model' under pressure—how to maintain equity and develop quality?" *Quality Assurance in Health Care* 1: 13-22.

Governmental Committee Report (1987). *Äldreomsorg i utveckling. Betänkande av Äldreberedningen*. Stockholm: SOU 1987: 21.

Heidenheimer, A.J., and N.J. Elvander, eds. (1980). *The making of the Swedish health care system*. London: Croom Helm.

Hokenstad, M.C. (1988). "Cross national trends and issues in social service provision and social work practice for the elderly." In M.C. Hokenstad and K. Kendall, eds., *Gerontological social work: International perspectives.* New York: The Hayworth Press.

Hokenstad, M.C., and L. Johansson (1990a). "Caregiving for the elderly in Sweden: Program challenges and policy initiatives." In D. Biegel and A. Blum, eds., *Ageing and Caregiving. Theory, Research and Policy.* Newbury Park: Sage.

Hokenstad, M.C., and L. Johansson (1990b). "Swedish policy initiatives to support family caregiving for the elderly." *Ageing International* XVI (1): 33-35.

Johansson, L. (1990). "Group dwellings for the senile—A new care alternative." *Ageing International* XVI (1): 35-37.

Johansson, L. (1991). "Informal care of dependent elderly at home—Some Swedish experiences." *Ageing and Society* 11: 1-18.

Johansson, L., and M. Thorslund (1991). "The national context of social innovation—Policy framework and major reforms in care for the elderly." In R. Kraan et al., eds., *Care for the Elderly. Significant Innovations in Three European Countries.* Boulder, Colorado: Westview Press.

Johansson, L., M. Thorslund, B. Smedby, and K. Wernberg (1991). *Formal and informal support among elderly in a rural setting in Sweden.* Submitted.

Kangas, O., and J. Palme (1990). "The private-public mix in pension provision." In J.E. Kolberg, ed., *The study of welfare state regimes.* New York: Sharpe.

Lagergren, M. (1988). *Folkhemmets framtider.* Institutet för framtidsstudier. Stockholm.

Lagergren, M., L. Lundh, M. Orkan, and C. Sanne (1984). *Time to care.* New York: Pergamon Press.

Landstingsförbundet (1988). *Vårddagar per åldersintervall samt diagnos- och operationsstatistik per landsting och kommun 1985 med jämförelse bakåt i tiden.* Stockholm.

OECD (1988). *Ageing populations. The social policy implications.* Paris: OECD.

Parker, M., and M. Thorslund (1991). "The use of technical aids among community-based elderly." *American Journal of Occupational Therapy.* In press.

Popenoe, D. (1987). "Beyond the nuclear family: A statistical portrait of the changing family in Sweden." *Journal of Marriage and the Family* 49: 173-178.

PVU 89. *Primärvårdsuppföljningen 1989* (1990). Stockholm: Socialstyrelsen, SOS-rapport 1990: 35.

SCB (1989). *The future population of Sweden. Projection for the years 1989-2025.* Statistics Sweden, Stockholm.

Socialutskottets betänkande (1990). *Ändrad ansvarsfördelning inom äldreomsorgen m m.* Stockholm: SOU 1990/91: 9.

Statskontoret (1987). *Äldreomsorg i Norden - kostnader, kvalitet, styrning. KRON-projektet.* Stockholm: Rapport 1987: 34.

Sundström, G. (1986). "Family and state: Recent trends in care of the aged in Sweden." *Ageing and Society* 6: 169-196.

Sundström, G., and M. Thorslund (1991). *Ideals and realities of old age care in the welfare state.* Submitted.

Szebehely, M., and R. Eliasson (1991). "Hemtjänsten i Sverige - myter och statistik." *Nordisk Socialt Arbeid* 1: 15-31.

Teeland, L. (1978). *Keeping in touch. The relation between old people and their adult children*. Göteborg: Sociologiska Institutionen. Doctoral dissertation.

Thorslund, M. (1988). "The de-institutionalization of care of the elderly; some notes about implementation and outcome of a Swedish case-study." *Health Policy* 10: 44-56.

Thorslund, M. (1989). *Care of the elderly in Sweden*. Fact sheet. Swedish Institute, Stockholm.

Thorslund, M. (1990). *Kostnader för de äldres service och vård*. Stockholm: SOU 1990: 77, Bilaga G.

Thorslund, M. (1991). "The increasing number of very old people will change the Swedish model of the welfare state." *Social Science and Medicine*. In press.

Thorslund, M., and L. Johansson (1987). "The elderly in Sweden, current realities and future plans." *Ageing and Society* 7: 345-355.

Tornefelt, E., and L. Johansson (1988). "Anhöriga till senildementa i dagsjukvården blir ofta helt utarbetade." *Läkartidningen* 4: 207-208.

Tornstam, L. (1989). "Formal and informal support for the elderly. An analysis of present patterns and future options in Sweden." *Impact of Science on Society* 153: 57-63.

Wells, N., and C. Freer, eds. (1988). *The ageing population. Burden or challenge?* London: Macmillan.

Winquist, M. (1984). *SOS-syndromet: sorg, oro och samvetsförbråelser hos anhöriga till personer med åldersdement beteende*. Uppsala: Sociologiska institutionen (24).

Zappolo, A.A., and G. Sundström (1989). "Long-term care for the elderly in Sweden." In T. Schwab, ed., *Caring for an aging world: International models for long-term care, financing, and delivery*. New York: McGraw-Hill.

#  six

## Domestic Healthcare Production and Alternatives to Hospitalization in France: The Family's Role and Involvement in Home Care

*Martine Bungener*


In 1978, sociologist Agnès Pitrou published *Vivre sans famille ?*, an essay on family support in the contemporary world which challenged the hasty but oft-repeated assertion that "there is no more family support; everyone lives for themselves" (Pitrou 1978: 7 - introduction). She then noted that social policies of the welfare state had been following such a logic for several decades: social support was seen as having to "replace ties which were viewed as natural, but deemed impossible to revive" (Pitrou 1978: 9), without considering the realities of actual practices. Indeed, closer observation confirmed the vitality and strength of family relationships, as revealed, for example, despite certain stated dysfunctioning and deficiencies, in the role of caring for the elderly.

Ten years later, there had been no progression in generally accepted views in this area, and a former minister of health, in office for two years before falling "victim" to the socialist changeover, could still write in a book on his ministerial involvement: "If there is one word to aptly qualify the situation of the aged, that word is solitude" (Barzach 1989: 255).... The "disappearance" of intergenerational cohabitation without "the creation of other forms of nearby support" (Barzach 1989: 257) requires that "the diminishing role of the family be offset by State care for the elderly" (Barzach 1989: 257).... "Such a solution exhibits the paradox already noted regarding the mentally ill, that is, calling upon national support to finance costly solutions which had for centuries been the basic and natural expression of group and family support" (Barzach 1989: 260). Inadequate knowledge of the reality on the minister's part or use of electoral arguments seen as effective? The facts are completely otherwise, as recent census data show that more families than ever are caring for their elderly (cf. Joel and Bungener 1990). Population growth alone, moreover, is a sufficient explanation for this phenomenon. One is then entitled to wonder why such perfunctory and biased ideas on the role of family self-help persist, unaffected by the limited number of studies and research performed in this field over several years. However, a reversal of this trend has begun to occur in the past four or five years, which we would like to examine by presenting some significant research results.

Two sources may be found for the renewal of interest within social policies and social science research regarding the question of concrete expression of family and kinship support: the development of home care practices for the elderly, coupled with a simultaneous denunciation of the increased isolation of the aged, and the more recent desire to find solutions to the inevitable rise in medical expenditures, especially hospital costs. Yet it should be noted that in both cases, although the range of concrete measures implemented cannot be compared, political and administrative decisions were made (on home care for dependent individuals and home hospitalization), and procedures set up for providing care, without regard for their impact on the family group. An ideological line of reasoning which was at times erroneous (lack of family or community support), often peremptory (it is always best to remain in the family setting), and never questioned or verified, served as the ultimate justification. Thus, not only was there no accurate knowledge on the current status of needs—the number of individuals being cared for at home, the extent of their dependence and the difficulties encountered by their families—but there was also a failure to recognize the existence of possible obstacles to the approach chosen.

Due to the continuing pressure of financial constraints, demographic growth, and an acknowledgement of deficiencies and poorly functioning approaches (cf. Henrard et al. 1991), the requisite conditions are now being sought to enhance the cost-effectiveness of resources allocated to the medical, social and medico-social sectors. To the extent that early treatment and home care on the one hand and on the other a more general appeal to family and community support are seen as appropriate solutions to be pursued and indeed encouraged, it becomes essential to grasp how these approaches operate and where they break down, to determine what is needed to foster them and the support required to maintain them. A new research topic has thus emerged, in this country and elsewhere, for professionals in various disciplines: gerontologists, sociologists and economists in particular. Although as yet little studied, the results of empirical work in this area over the last five years make it possible to set out the terms of an original and documented line of reflection.

We can speak of a new area of study since domestic and family activity has long been neglected by researchers and economists. It is true that sociologists never really abandoned the topic, but as we pointed out at the start, reiterating Agnès Pitrou's criticism (Pitrou 1978), they have at times been too quick to note the disappearance of family support and too hesitant in acknowledging its persistence. Economists on the other hand have long exhibited their disinterest in activities outside the market, which economic theory excluded from their area of specialization, and have only very recently admitted domestic production, including services deriving from community support, into their sphere of concern. Similarly, the logic underlying development of the medical system, marked by three major trends—centralization, professionalization linked to a heightened technical component, and public financing—has helped diminish the status of domestic care production emanating from the family circle or lay volunteers to the point of completely overshadowing it. Family caregiving activity has then been set aside from the concerns of both economists and those involved in the healthcare system. There is thus a profound current of lack of understanding, even rejection, which recent studies must confront in order to bring to the fore work accomplished by, and the vital contribution of, the family.

## LACK OF UNDERSTANDING AND DISINTEREST IN FAMILY AND LAY CARE[1]

If sociologists must combat an erroneous assessment of family support, economists and medical practitioners must recognize a new professional area.

Activity which generates goods and services finds its economic justification in the realm of market exchange. Domestic production, the original form of the production process, was thus shunted aside from the sphere of economic analysis when the separation of housing and production areas occurred, and was marked by a generalized lack of interest for several decades during the rise of industrialization. But everyday observation testifies to the significance of "extra-market" or "non-market" production which, from the perspective of rationalizing and streamlining public sector activity, is becoming increasingly harder to ignore. Domestic production is thus achieving renewed legitimacy within various currents of social science research. In economics, the family is no longer restricted to the role of consumer (cf., among others, Soffer 1985) but is also recognized for its productive function, although there are major methodological difficulties in this approach, since the timeworn tools of economic analysis centre on the use of prices, without which it is harder to immediately assess or measure the products of family activity (cf. Bungener 1986).

Such conceptual obstacles are heightened when services produced by the family involve the area of health. For the setting aside of family care production not only results from disinterest in family production in general but also from the trend to professionalize care of the ill, which displaced families and individuals from care management. Prior to the emergence of conditions fostering a healthcare market, care and help for the sick was primarily a family matter. Such care was only relegated or replaced in cases of family incapacity, inadequacy or non-existence, so that any failings or limitations (cf. Pitrou 1978) in traditional kinship support became the concern of religious or charitable organizations. When made possible by scientific and technical conditions, therapeutics became the subject of a virtually exclusive professional market, closely regulated by the medical profession, a market rendered accessible to the majority by social legislation. As the habitual use of medical care grew, traditional family care was increasingly displaced, encouraged by a permissive financial context which long allowed lay care to be ignored. The professional view of healthcare and therapeutic practices thus came to focus solely on the institutional model of care production.

This trend has burgeoned in the second half of the twentieth century to the point of being criticized for its corruption into an excessive[2] and costly (Levy et al. 1982) medicalization of all the activities and events of daily life (birth, child care, professional reorientation, death, etc.). Such growth has also resulted in a movement described today as hospital-centred care. The immediate outcome of this has been a diminishment of family competencies not only in promoting recovery from illness but also in the most trivial and non-technical activities of day-to-day hygiene. Essential healthcare aspects have thus been displaced from the context of domestic tasks to fall under the supervision of the health specialists.

## The Forces and Pressures Involved in an Emerging Approach

Significant development of institutionalization and residential care for the sick and elderly and the rise in related financial costs were fostered by an as yet unmatched degree of economic growth. This second aspect is one reason for the current, favourable view of family care production arising from the discussion on hospitalization alternatives and various forms of home care. Family responsibility for the elderly, the sick and certain forms of care at home is today postulated as a way to reduce hospitalization costs. This argument was developed in an official report commissioned by the government in 1982 (Caquet and Karsenty 1983). There would be a "saving" of costs for residential services, monitoring and care. Criticism of hospital-centred care together with financial constraints made it possible for the essential and, hopefully, economic role of family support to re-emerge.

There is evidence of a return to past tendencies and re-establishment of caregiving privileges previously supplanted in family activities. Such phenomena are being closely observed in several fields of research connected with medical or family sociology, gerontology, economics and management science.

Since the early sixties, French public policy on the elderly, regularly reaffirmed in a series of reports,[3] has advocated, in addition to material enhancement of the conditions of residential care and medicalization in retirement homes, determined approaches to home care centring on planning of housing and establishment of specific services. Such approaches must respond both to the recognized desires of some elderly people to stay at home and to crowding associated with the lack of places in residential care facilities for highly dependent individuals, as well as to the rising public financial burden of institutionalization. From this point of view, home care is not only seen as an objective in itself but also as a way to make medical therapy more effective by forcing elderly people to maintain a stimulating, although admittedly partial, form of autonomy. And what is the situation today?

In France, residential care is a reality for only a very small minority of the elderly, even those over age 85. The percentage of the population in residential care is 6% for those over 65 and 16% for those over 80. There were 450,000 places in residential care facilities in France in 1989 and 121,000 places in residential centres.[4] These places can be divided into three major categories with varying degrees of medicalization. Within each category, lodging costs are assumed by the individual, or by default, by social welfare; medical costs are assumed by healthcare insurance within the limits of fixed rates and independently established according to the level of care:

- Beds with the highest degree of medical care are located in long-stay hospital service facilities which are gradually replacing medical wards in hospices for the elderly, representing 60,376 beds, in addition to psychiatric hospital beds at times unnecessarily occupied by senile individuals.
- Retirement homes with medical services offer two levels of care at rates set by healthcare insurance funds: 81,000 specialized beds in medical treatment wards and 221,000 general care beds.
- In addition, a total of 217,000 beds without medical care exist in retirement homes[5] and residential centres.

The average age of those in institutions has risen over the past decade, currently reaching age 81; the age of entry has declined significantly; and there has been a marked increase in the female population.

In 1990, there were nearly 2 million elderly in France over age 80, 20% of whom were dependent and 40% semi-dependent. The percentage in residential care was estimated at 25% for the most dependent, that is, those who were bedridden or confined to their rooms. The majority of the aged therefore reside in private dwellings, in their homes or with a relative. Three quarters of the most extreme cases of dependence are thus cared for at home and, as we will see, primarily by the family. There are also, however, home help services of two kinds: homemaker services and home nursing care services. Such help increased considerably in the eighties, and the territory served was expanded in all regions of the country. There are now only some one thousand municipalities without available homemaker services for the aged. In 1989 such homemaker services were provided to 500,000 individuals over age 65 (i.e. 7%). However, these services tend to increase the number of beneficiaries with a resulting decrease in the number of hours provided to each, which are being reduced on average on an annual basis. The costs of such care are adjusted to the resources of the elderly served. The remaining financial burden is assumed by pension funds or social welfare. There also exists a broader type of aid than homemaker services in the form of everyday life helpers such as those who assist the handicapped, but their number remains marginal. There are 850 nursing care institutions with a capacity of 32,000 places, financed at rates fixed by healthcare insurance. But it should also be noted that the clientele of private nurses whose services are prescribed by private consulting physicians mainly comprises an elderly population for whom the number of nursing services reimbursed by healthcare insurance has been consistently growing for several years now.

This observation, backed by statistical data,[6] shows that despite a significant increase, services offered to the elderly and, all the more so, to the most dependent among them are not providing for all their care needs, which have chiefly fallen to the families. This clearly contradicts the widespread view in society of the elderly's isolation, but still does not automatically challenge the simultaneously mentioned necessity to increase the number of places in residential facilities as a way to offset the current needs of the aged, especially the dependent. Evidence of such needs can be found by examining waiting lists, which can be seen to provide irrefutable proof, susceptible however of manipulation. Absence of such lists does not in itself imply that estimated needs have been exaggerated, but merely that other types of solutions have been found, whether or not they are more productive or economically more effective. What are the costs involved in the various potential solutions? What are the negative consequences of limiting possible choices? These are some of the questions arising from current research on the elderly, to which numerous scientific disciplines are contributing.

One field of sociological research is also concerned with family involvement in the provision of care, in an approach focussing on chronic illness. Technological change has made ambulatory and home treatment possible for a number of conditions such as renal or respiratory insufficiency. Such studies are primarily interested in how such treatment becomes part of the daily life of patients and their families.

Another area of study deriving from economics or management science looks at the family and the network of lay support as potential contributors to therapeutic approaches. The effect of their work in supplementing or substituting for professional services is seen as increasing efficiency or reducing costs from the viewpoint of hospitalization alternatives for example.

The most longstanding and most numerous studies concern elderly people for whom the home care approach precedes work in this area with the sick by some twenty years. We will follow this chronology herein and consider the current results of such work by first examining family involvement with the elderly before looking at lay care for the sick.

## THE ELDERLY AT HOME: THE VITAL CONTRIBUTION OF THE FAMILY

The current situation of the elderly in France regarding home care and residential care calls for multidisciplinary reflection, independent in its approach and subject matter, and requires a fresh outlook due to both the number of individuals concerned and the new scope of the problems involved. For example, as stressed by Françoise Cribier, a researcher with the Centre national de la recherche scientifique (CNRS), if parent-child relationships are a preferred topic in the sociology of the family, "work involving parents whose children are adults is still quite rare" as is research on "the role these children play in the lives of their parents in their later years" (Cribier 1989: 35). Yet it is a question of the essential and primary aspect of family support for the elderly. To remedy such shortcomings, the team of sociologists and geographers she heads has been observing a group of retired Parisians[7] since the beginning of their retirement in 1972.

## Existence or Absence of a Family Circle: The Critical Factor

The description of the elderly's solitude, the assumed magnitude of which is part of that set of generally accepted ideas which must be denounced, is based on an ambiguity. Are the elderly alone because they no longer have any living relatives, particularly children, or because they no longer have emotional or supportive contact with them? This aspect can be quantitatively verified with the proper tools of study. Françoise Cribier's examination of the Parisian group provides valuable statistical data in this area and also makes an observation on the state of relations between the elderly and their families: we will summarize the main conclusions of her study in this section. The raw data are themselves illuminating: in this sample of retired Parisians, 27% (23% of the men and 31% of the women) are childless. If we restrict ourselves to women aged 75 to 80, one quarter of the sample have neither husband nor children. Among those with children, 89% also have grandchildren; for the total sample population, the corresponding percentages are 73% of men and 63% of women. Since assistance to the elderly is primarily provided by women, and by daughters rather than daughters-in-law, as we will show later, it is also important to see how many of these retired individuals had at least one daughter. This is the case for barely half the population examined (30% have one daughter, 11% two and 6% three or more).

This initial observation needs to be supplemented by an attempt to gauge the physical proximity of the children, measured by geographic distance and time required to cover that distance. For many of the retirees, the draw of the sunny Mediterranean area of France, like the understandable desire to end their days in their native region after their working years in Paris, has contributed to geographic remoteness from succeeding generations in Paris. But the impact of this phenomenon appears to be limited, according to the study results, since for those in the Parisian sample who retired to the provinces, 10% live with one of their children and 31% overall are less than a half-hour from at least one child. In the metropolitan Parisian area, these percentages are higher: 12% live with one of their children and 63% live a half-hour at most from their closest child. The authors view this limited travelling time as resulting from both conscious decisions, seen in all social classes, and the rules for access to housing coupled with the specific nature of the housing market in Paris and the surrounding region. 11.4% of retirees examined in this group share a dwelling with one of their children, 15.4% live in the same building or a nearby one and 38.3% live in the same urban area or district. This desire to maintain geographic closeness is highlighted in Agnès Pitrou's work as proof of the tenacious survival of the family network (Pitrou 1978: 34) and has been observed in recent studies on professional mobility. The wish to remain close to one's parents, even to parents who are still relatively young, has been found to be one of the strongest obstacles to professional mobility related to geographic transfers (Bungener et al. 1988a and Bungener et al. 1987). Such distancing from the family, when unavoidable and unresolved, can engender a process of illness which is fairly easy to point to as one of the factors associated with job loss (Bungener et al. 1988b). It would appear that distancing from the family, and more specifically between generations, creates a particular state of vulnerability in certain family members; proximity, on the other hand, provides social support and reinforces the capacity to cope with pathogenic events, according to a recent epidemiological exposition (Bungener and Joel 1988).

This group study allows us to observe the cohabitation conditions of the elderly. This phenomenon is the situation for 16% of the aged overall, but in four out of five cases (11.4% out of 16%), it involves an elderly person living with one of their children. However, the process is a progressive one: when the parent's retirement begins, there is often a child still living at home (the youngest, pursuing their studies or awaiting their first job); later, children may return to the parent's home due to divorce or unemployment problems; and later still, the elderly parent will go to live with one of their adult children (Cribier 1989: 38). Cohabitation is linked to the number of children, but poor health on the part of parents (or children) can also be a significant incentive. Finally, there is greater cohabitation in the surrounding region than in the city of Paris proper. The authors believe this difference to be due to the size of houses in the suburbs, which are generally larger than Parisian dwellings.

## A reciprocal flow of support ...

Examination of this group has also made it possible to observe the nature of the elderly's relationships with their children. The latter play a large part in the lives of the aged who receive material assistance in many different forms from their children (but rarely money) as well as moral support. Parents in turn help their children and support them in the difficulties they encounter. Such mutual assistance continues for a very long time on both sides, virtually right up to the end of the parents' lives. While acknowledging its importance in terms of domestic production, we will not be concerned with the aid provided to children in this text, but instead focus on how adult children help their aging parents as observed in this group.

In its most common definition, dependence is synonymous with incapacity to perform basic daily life activities on one's own. Dependence often visibly begins with a need for help with previously easily accomplished household tasks. This socially recognized need has been the subject of an institutional response viewed as one of the essential aspects of home care policies. Home help services, despite their unquestionable expansion, have often been criticized for their notorious inadequacy. What is the situation regarding help provided by families in this context? Is it a symptom of that inadequacy? To what extent does it lead to such a need? Before attempting to answer these questions, what kind of help do the retired Parisians obtain from their children with respect to household chores? The results show a strong correlation with age: among 75- to 80-year-olds in this group, 57% had no help and said they did not need it, whereas 12% had no help and did require it. Of the 31% with help: 7% mainly had the help of a housekeeper, 11% had home help, 9% were aided by one of their children (i.e. 12% of those who had at least one child) with no other assistance provided, and 4% were helped by someone else (Cribier 1989: 46). In many cases, the child's assistance was in addition to that provided by paid help. Such a context can also be examined based on the characteristics of the individual helped—aid is more frequent when the elderly person is in poor health and has a low income (Cribier 1989: 47)—and those of the helper: daughters provide more help than sons, except if there are no female children, and single children or those living alone help more than married children. As we will see in all the other studies we look at, this last point is a constant and apparently irrefutable one.

In terms of home help needs or help in daily activities, the degree of representativeness of this sample is limited by the relatively low age of the study participants. Other quantitative data must be added. We will restrict ourselves here to data which attempt to estimate the total number of dependent elderly: 200,000 are confined to a bed or chair (Colvez, Buquet et al. 1990), 233,000 need daily assistance, and 900,000 no longer go out alone. It is instructive to place these figures next to the corresponding data on those living in residential care facilities in order to predict home help needs. The rates for the latter are 24.7% for the most dependent, 19.7% for the second group and 7% for the third (Joel and Bungener 1990: 13). Three quarters of dependents today are therefore cared for at home, giving a basic idea of the extent of family involvement for, as we will see later, in such cases home care is only possible with a considerable degree of effort on the family's part.

If there is statistical proof of family help for the elderly, we still cannot necessarily assume that everything is going well. As Françoise Cribier and her colleagues emphasize, we cannot ignore the fact that in such studies the elderly tend to say little about conflicts and bad feeling.... At heart, they know that helping exchanges are fostered more by the supply provided by children than the demand on the part of elderly parents (Cribier 1989: 44). 5% of those surveyed say that they never or almost never see their children.

The authors go on to say that we know little about the extent of the children's feelings of obligation and duty. What is expressed by those who help their parents the most shows, not only the at times enormous burden of their responsibilities and their feelings of guilt and unfairness, but also the positive side of this human experience (Cribier 1989: 48). The elderly expect and receive a great deal of help but do not like to ask for it. They cannot risk not getting along with their children. Thus, they are all, and have been for some time, engaged in very delicate negotiations (Cribier 1989: 49). Nor do we know much about the emotional nature of parent-child exchanges. This aspect, which Geneviève Favrot attempted to investigate in her work on factors influencing the acceptance or rejection of caregiving activity in the system of family activities,[8] will be examined in a later section. But we would first like to offer a more specific description of domestic and family aid provided to the elderly at home, and attempt to assess the economic and financial costs before looking at the emotional costs, which are much harder to evaluate. We will base our examination on the results of public studies financed by the Mission Interministérielle Recherche et Expérimentation (MIRE), bringing together both practitioners and researchers: *Recherche sur les itinéraires de vieux : raisons et déraisons des filières* (5e secteur géronto-psychiatrique de l'Essonne 1989) and *Travail familial, solidarité de voisinage et maintien à domicile des personnes âgées* (Frossard et al. 1987).

## ... despite the difficulties frequently encountered in providing help

The observations of practitioners working in geriatric psychiatry in area five of the Essonne region may be summarized as follows: France has suitable homes for the ablebodied elderly and an appropriate level of hospital care for old people who are ill, but our system ignores the intermediary situation of the elderly who require regular and often daily assistance but do not possess the income to provide for themselves. They are at the mercy of the generosity of their families or local community help networks. When there are mental problems in addition to physical handicaps, since these are even harder to cope with in the family setting, support which is already tenuous is further reduced. This state of affairs, seen in these practitioners' day-to-day professional activities, has led them to debate the limits of home care and the relevant thresholds regarding institutionalization, and to question economic cost-effectiveness criteria for the use of public funds in the light of criteria based on the individual's welfare, particularly in terms of the ambivalent risks and benefits of remaining at home. This notion of a "threshold" situation, which includes a whole range of factors, is also central to the second study we would like to highlight. It is a way of discerning the multiplicity of factors involved in caring for a dependent elderly person at home, and also provides more relevant and less monolithic judgemental criteria.

The results of the study on the difficulties of home care in one area in Essonne can be outlined using a typical portrait: this is most often (in 43% of cases) a man between the ages of 80 and 90 who is not receiving help from his children (whether or not he has any or if he only has one child). Such a portrait confirms the vital role of children and the number of children, since these difficulties are only the case for one quarter of individuals with at least two children. The results also show that 28% of the patients taken on by the geriatric psychiatry team had previously been in a highly-specialized hospital setting as a result of their family's inability to cope, which reinforces (and permits measurement of) the professionals' perception of hospital use as an "emergency" solution for the elderly. This leads to reiteration of the oft-asked and as yet unanswered question: are mental problems linked to being alone or do they help to turn loved ones away?

Alternatively, there is a high rate of cohabitation with a family member (23.3%) for elderly people who are receiving home care services, which emphasizes both the necessity of family aid for home care and the need for support services for these families. This notion is contrary to the idea of replacing or excluding one or the other form of aid. The family's aid is primordial in 60.5% of cases; institutions are less in evidence and only serve as the principal caregiver for one in five individuals (20%); and the rate of help on the part of friends remains low (8.5%). Such family assistance is potentially even more important in that, in addition to current help provided, 36.5% of the individuals surveyed said that they could count on another family member if they had to, as opposed to 44.5% who felt that they could not. And it is known that families rally in times of need.

This diagnosis of a local reality is joined by a dynamic observation of where patients go when they are discharged from a stay in a general hospital. Up to age 70, very few encounter difficulties in returning home, whereas between the ages of 70 and 84, one third experience problems, as do nearly one half in the next age bracket. On average, for two thirds of cases, there is a possibility of returning home. However, the actual solutions vary in that half of those for whom home care is difficult return home nonetheless. Among those who could have gone back home with help, only two thirds are in fact cared for in this way; so that a third, without the necessary help, do not return home. On the other hand, of those not experiencing such difficulties, one third do not return directly to their homes.

A secondary benefit of such studies by professionals in the field is that they allow issues to come to light and permit a critical examination of the professional practice and its underlying generally accepted notions. In this study, the team has described what they learned in their case studies: on the one hand, the positive effect of a properly structured hospitalization approach in resocializing the elderly, and conversely, the isolating "ghettoizing" effect or process of gradual deterioration observed with home care, in certain cases! Another study benefit was to clarify to the team the vital role of a coordinated approach, allowing each participant in the home care process to recognize and comprehend their functioning within an overall perspective, and understand the necessary play of forces between the collective needs the system targets and the particularities of each individual situation. It is also a question of each being better equipped to face the multiple and sometimes contradictory set of individual needs, since the objective is to help the elderly while maintaining their autonomy. Such needs can obviously be effectively approached by a carefully formulated and rationalized form of help, and yet needs are also continually evolving over time, to be eventually replaced by other imperatives.

## A Dependent Person at Home: Multiple Tasks and Limited Help

Once the decision is made to care for the dependent person at home, how does this affect the family and what kind of help will they have to provide? This is the focus of the second text we will look at: *Travail familial, solidarité de voisinage et maintien à domicile des personnes âgées* (Frossard et al. 1987).

The aim of this study was to examine dependent elderly persons who had remained at home and had family to care for them, without, however, ignoring the fact that, as the authors point out, 25% to 30% of people over age 65 do not or no longer have any living children. The main aspects considered centre on three objectives:

- to measure the help provided by the family in terms of quantity (duration, frequency) and quality (types of tasks performed);
- to identify factors determining the effective level of help: recognition of the need, formulation of the request by the patient, geographic proximity, family availability, quality of the emotional relationship, existence or absence of professional help;
- to determine the thresholds of acceptability or breakdown of the family's contribution.

This was based on a set of original hypotheses which had to be verified:

1. Help is mainly provided by women according to degree of family closeness.
2. The amount of family help is based on the extent of the elderly person's dependence.
3. With equal dependence, there is a link between level of tolerance of the patient within the family circle, quality of help provided and quality of prior relationships.
4. The potential breakdown point in home care activities is more closely related to the family's feelings of distress or guilt and resulting social isolation than to the actual burden of the care provided.
5. Families have a greater tolerance for physical than mental dependence.

The methodology chosen involved the use of two similar questionnaires, one for the elderly person and the other for the family member determined to be the principal caregiver. The amount of help provided was assessed by means of a dependence grid which set out the main daily activities in typical daily order, combined with a second grid to determine the helpers' characteristics and time spent on each activity. In general, help given to the elderly persons studied approximated 76 to 90 hours weekly (as stated by the helpee or helper) and was primarily supplied by the family (85%), with 14% provided by professionals and about 2% by friends and the community. Three groups were distinguished based on the amount of help received: less than 30 hours of help weekly (51-32%);[9] 30 to 68 hours (28-33%); and 68 hours or more, representing permanent help (21-35%). Included in this last group are situations of cohabitation, which, in terms of the amount of help required, seems to be the necessary condition for home care. As for the number of hours spent helping the dependent person, it should be noted that the responses are not consistent: helpers estimate a significantly higher number of hours for their work than do helpees. One might expect this gap to narrow with greater dependence, where more measurable tasks are required, but this is not the case. The responses given by the elderly imply that their children's help does not vary with the degree of dependence, whereas helpers state that it does increase accordingly. This distortion is related to the fact that the children's help is mentioned less by the elderly person than the helper in cases of extreme dependence, with the opposite being true where there is little dependence. The family's perception of their involvement in the help required also varies according to the level of dependence, being underestimated where dependence is low and often overestimated when dependence is average or high.

There were 18 items in the helping activities grid. For 12 of these, the spouse or children were the primary caregivers, but there is evidence of some allocation of tasks between the family and professional workers. Professional services mainly involve helping the patient get up or go to bed, as well as housework, errands, medical care, etc.—all tasks for which there has been professional recognition. But it is important to note that even professional care (medical or nursing care) is to a significant degree shared and performed by family members. Washing and dressing and housework are less often taken on by the family. Such sharing is necessary due to the inadequacy of regular help on weekends and especially holidays. Yet the way professional and lay help is organized differs according to the participants' status. Involvement on the part of spouses and children is associated with professional help such as nursing care and housekeeping services. For individuals on their own, we see that lack of family support is in part replaced mainly by the use of homemaker services and home care attendants. However, it should be noted that individuals who are not alone are more dependent than those on their own, which can lead to greater mobilization of all types of help for the latter. For families with higher incomes, there is more extensive use of housekeeper services and less help provided by the family.

The questionnaire responses also provide a subjective assessment of the extent of the burden assumed by the principal caregiver: 3 out of 60 consider it unbearable, 24 perceive it as heavy and 23 as tolerable. The duration of time help has been given obviously has a wearing effect, as those viewing their burden as heavy have, on average, been looking after an elderly parent 50% longer than the others. The breakdown points for family help as shown in this study underscore the fatigue and discouragement of the principal carers and the restrictions placed on their social activities, in relation to which help provided by outside services is seen as a form of relief and a safety valve. These aspects, central to Geneviève Favrot's work, will be more closely examined in the next section.

Children, spouses and associated family members are naturally those most involved in helping the dependent individual at home. Children who provide a significant degree of help show characteristics which strongly differentiate them from non-helpers: they are mainly women, individuals living in the same dwelling (without it being established whether this is a cause or a consequence) or children who live nearby (remoteness being a major factor in non-provision of help). Professional activities have less impact than one would have assumed, although retired people are more often helpers than those who are working. The existence of a handicap is also a factor contributing to the provision of aid. Although diminished professional activity on the part of the handicapped can serve as an explanation for this last point, it is only a partial one, and one can agree with the authors that it seems as though there is a sort of duality at play: ablebodied individuals associating with each other and handicapped persons mutually helping one another out. Aside from children, other types of helpers are older, more alone (often single), more handicapped and farther away geographically than the children. Here again, the authors suggest an association of two precarious conditions, which leads to questions about the permanence of the support and its potential fragility. These results confirm what was previously known in a less formal way: that family help for dependent kin is a significant reality whose quantitative volume far exceeds assistance provided by professionals. But its limits are exhibited in excessive mental fatigue and/or financial problems. Even if a positive affective relationship with the helpee is frequently observed, can cohabitation or virtually permanent help for a high-need individual continue without major conflicts in the home setting? For the authors, this aspect in particular clearly requires a study on the family's role in home care, targeting a search for means to encourage and preserve this role in coordination with outside services. And such coordination is not without its problems, as shown in the following study.

## A Dependent Elderly Person at Home: An Often Extremely Heavy Mental and Physical Burden, Inevitably Assumed by Women

Geneviève Favrot has also focussed on care situations for elderly who are highly dependent due to advanced age or illness, favouring, unlike the previous study, a monographic approach centring on a dozen families. Her initial observation concerns the inadequate examination of family groups faced with home care for a dependent relative. Neither general studies nor analyses produced by professionals ever consider the workload or stresses that constant proximity with death or senile dementia can generate within a family. "And yet," for this author, "the impacts on the family's mental and physical health and equilibrium are far from negligible" (Favrot 1988: 20). Moreover, families' mental and emotional capabilities to face such a burden often vary as widely as their material and financial resources, and the two aspects can have a cumulative effect.

The author prefaces her study by emphasizing the ideological, economic and financial context in France today of home care for the dependent elderly. The purpose of such care is to allow the autonomous resources of the person and those of the family and lay support network to develop and continue, in order to avoid the costs of home help and volunteer services, which can lead to a progressive and subtle wavering between encouragement and blame for family failures. Such a choice appears questionable to the extent that innovative home care organizations have estimated these costs to be high, as we will see later, especially in view of the costs of all the services which seem necessary if families and the support network are not to be penalized relative to residential placement. It can be mentioned in passing that listing and properly assessing these services have their specific problems to which there are no easy solutions. In addition, families are not always left to assume such care on their own. Although there is recognition of the positive role families play, in some cases it is felt that they could perform it better with proper coordination. Thus, certain types of care transferred to the home continue to be associated with institutions (for example, home hospitalization, which we will examine in a later section). Such a context, not without ambiguity, leads the author to the crucial question of the respective status of professionals and lay people in home care: can professionals accept being replaced by lay people without repercussions concerning their professional identity? Are professionals there to provide help and support in the family setting or, conversely, do family support networks complement professional help?

In the field, due to budgetary limitations and inadequacy of existing services, this issue is spontaneously resolved as the family group adapts to what professionals can or cannot accomplish. Such empirical adaptation to concrete necessities is a fundamental aspect of family care. It is also a major characteristic of domestic production, explaining the latter's regulatory economic role regarding financial constraints, to which we will return. In fact, in many instances of home care, there is no outside help. In other cases, families generate the support they need by themselves mobilizing local institutional or private resources. Such an observation is instructive in that it counters the initial supposition: professional support does not supplement failing family help, but rather family involvement occurs where professional services do not exist or are unavailable.

As shown throughout this study, in cases of scarcity, the ability to obtain outside help is not equally provided to all. It is necessary to know the institutions and, at times, how to exert pressure on them, how to negotiate with them and not be subject to their dictates, and how to call upon one's own resourcefulness and support networks. In some instances, this may seem a clear case of a mutual exchange of services; in other cases, more is involved. The author shows that, aside from daily physical domestic tasks, a complete range of immaterial patient care management functions must be performed, and families do not possess equal capacities in this respect. In our healthcare system, caring for a family member also means managing the administrative aspects of the illness in order to most effectively benefit from social support and financial assistance for this illness. Inherent social inequalities in this respect reduce the help certain families can obtain in this connection. Such inequalities also influence diagnostic-type activities in the home management of illness, including knowing when to call in a doctor or specialist or when to perform specific acts. This type of activity, often associated with patient monitoring, must be recognized and separately examined to the extent that it affects the treatment undertaken. And monitoring an invalid means increasing interruption of domestic tasks, resulting in a real mental burden which must be considered. The level of supervision provided may not objectively or technically meet the subjective expectations of the family, whose perception of the dependent person's needs is often heightened by the distress and pain of waiting for death, despite their "denial" (it is never mentioned). Thus, a dual emotional and mental burden is added to an often considerable physical burden, resulting in postural fatigue (most frequently expressed in terms of backache) for many helpers who are themselves advanced in age.

Finally, there are inequalities with regard to families' differing capacities to foresee and anticipate future situations, to dissociate the various care aspects of these and delegate some while retaining others for themselves. For families, the work of caring for a dependent family member is never fully defined or limited; it constitutes an overall role whose various aspects are never completely distinguished. Maintaining the dependent individual's social life is based on numerous activities, including stressing cleanliness, keeping up mobility—or at least the appearance of mobility—by moving the person from bed to chair each day, and constantly stimulating their mental functioning. This last type of activity assumes various forms, from bringing the person back to the present when they are lost in the past, to preserving or reiterating some of their past knowledge (the husband of a former teacher tried to get her to relearn La Fontaine's fables and poetry or the multiplication tables). But such actions rarely appear in lists of tasks performed by the family as described to others. They are only mentioned in contrast to the presumed shortcomings of professional services or institutional care. But these activities are central to the work families accomplish, and for them justify their choice of home care.

In all the families observed, the author noted the adaptability of family activity with the introduction of this new constraint. Caring for the dependent individual competes with other domestic activities, so that choices have to be made: either using services offered by the outside market and/or redefining family roles and tasks. And the balance achieved is never established or definitive. As dependence increases, there is a constant readjustment to a generally heavier workload. Competition with other activities intensifies to the extent that external constraints are numerous and inflexible. Since social and leisure activities are by nature more flexible, they tend to increasingly centre on the home. Retirees, by contrast, also show the greatest degree of flexibility in time management. When, as often occurs, home care for a dependent individual leads to total isolation of the family unit, this becomes even more difficult from a social point of view in that the situation is seen as "abnormal" by everyone concerned. This is the most visible and most easily described hardship.

In the face of such physical and mental responsibilities, professional help obtained by the families observed shows unequal distribution between the sexes. Women receive less help than men, and only in the form of relief help when they themselves are unavailable. This discriminatory allocation of home help reveals how notions of the primary responsibility of families have been interiorized regarding non-qualified home care tasks. "Rallying the primary support of the family and community" means first calling upon available women, then early retirees and unemployed people and, in periods of economic recession, the latent feelings of guilt of non-working individuals (Favrot 1988: 59). We are again seeing a reiteration of the earlier observation concerning the primary involvement of women, especially daughters. Men's knowledge and skills are only called upon for a limited set of tasks, such as odd jobs and renovation of living quarters. As a corollary to the "natural" obligations of daughters towards their elders, particularly their mothers, many women look to the future from the viewpoint of their own daughters: they hope they will not become a burden to their daughters to the degree that they are presently facing such responsibilities in their own lives, or conversely, aware of the behavioural model they are transmitting to their daughters, they hope to themselves benefit from such help if they require it.

In the statements and attitudes of the families observed, there is still reference, to varying degrees, to a more or less flourishing tradition we might summarize as "aging at home." This is often linked to past experience or unquestioned family traditions. The situation for spouses, even more than children, is one of a duty to provide support. A cultural norm on which to base the use of institutionalized help does not seem to truly exist for these families. Home care is often seen not as a choice but rather as an emotional and social inevitability.

While these families sometimes describe institutional care as a current practice (although this is not very often the case if we look at the data mentioned earlier), it is not a commonplace situation for them. "Aging or dying at home remains a deeply rooted social norm, which the family support network cannot contravene unless there are 'objective,' i.e. socially acceptable, reasons for this, such as a double workload or too small a dwelling" (Favrot 1988: 104).... And yet these families also consider it an "abnormal" situation to live with an extremely dependent individual. The fact that they opt for a particular solution does not prevent feelings of regret about the other possibility. Nor is the choice of possibilities equally open to all; the family's decision is often an obligatory one as long as they can provide the required support. These families have an extremely negative view of institutions, which they see as synonymous with being shut away, to the extent that they have experienced problems in the past, and relate numerous stories of having to go back and forth between hospital and home. Although the need for hospital care in acute cases is not questioned, the consequences of this are seen as nefarious. Many hold out the hope of a "good" retirement home, even though there is no objective agreement on what "good" means! But residential care facilities are considered so harmful to patients' health—and doctors sometimes reinforce such views—that (in these families) the balance must inevitably swing towards home care. Although this basic choice is rarely questioned, there is a desire for material support: but what family members looking after a dependent individual at home ask for, more often than permanent help, is partial or momentary relief (a few hours off during the week or the possibility of taking a vacation). For it is the helper's social life which is affected first and foremost by the reorganization of household tasks involved in caring for a dependent person at home.

In the families Geneviève Favrot selected, the dependent elderly person could apparently not be cared for elsewhere or otherwise. There is no recognition of the possibility of making other choices. The question of choice is crucial since, theoretically, it would appear impossible to decide in practice in that such a decision seems to imply a host of lesser decisions none of which are a priori irreversible, but which nevertheless constitute a rigid and restrictive series of procedures leading to an inevitable conclusion (home or institutional care). We have seen how these procedures operate in the field work study in Essonne. Families' limited capacity for choice when faced with the situation of a dependent elderly person seems further reduced in cases of acute or chronic illness.

## CARING FOR THE ILL AT HOME: SUBSTITUTE THERAPIES AND ALTERNATIVES TO HOSPITALIZATION—FAMILY INVOLVEMENT, WILLINGLY OR OTHERWISE!

The patient's return to the home in the context of a home hospitalization program allows the treatment begun in the hospital to continue in the home setting. There is thus a transfer to the family of hospital services, patient monitoring responsibilities and care provided up till then by specialized hospital staff. Home hospitalization is therefore a particularly appropriate example of family care production in that there is a specific institutional equivalent for comparison purposes. Official documents often present home hospitalization as an alternative to traditional hospitalization. But actual observation of its functioning shows that home hospitalization is more often viewed by practitioners who use it as a treatment phase subsequent to standard hospitalization, serving as one way, among others, to discharge patients. Moreover, the term alternative suggests a process of choice allowing patients and their families to opt for either home or hospital treatment. But this is not the case. The decision process is exclusively medical, and it is rare for the patient or family to be able to do otherwise than agree to the home hospitalization proposal. According to hospital staff and social workers in this area, cases of refusing the home hospitalization proposal are the exception, with no more than one or two refusals per year in each department. Besides the fact that it is apparently hard for patients to disagree with a medical decision presented as the most suitable care procedure for them, there are few possible alternatives. There is no way for patients to unnecessarily prolong their stay in the hospital when they have been informed that their state of health allows them to be discharged. The prospects are then placement in an aftercare facility, convalescent home or medium- or long-stay institution, but the scarcity of available places makes this a rather chancy proposition. It may also be that home hospitalization was suggested because of previously unsuccessful attempts at such placement. Some patients may hope to organize their aftercare themselves through the use of private medical care, but other than those who emphatically reject hospital restrictions and any aftercare prolongation of such, this is rare for most patients faced with the suggestion of a more coordinated approach. Thus, the family organizes in view of the decision of which they have been informed.

There is no organized source of data on daily procedures at the patient's home. The available data only indicate home hospitalization service activities such as number of days of care provided, number of patients cared for daily and yearly, combined with patient demographic, geographic and pathological data, and number of nursing and paramedical staff involved. To learn more, one must gather more specific data. And this is precisely what was done in the case of another study (Bungener and Horellou-Lafarge 1987), also financed by MIRE. The data used come from a retrospective analysis of 1,151 patient files on individuals hospitalized at home under the Paris Health Authority (Assistance Publique de Paris) in 1984, and a two-part interview survey based on questionnaires given to a representative sample of 100 patients hospitalized at home and a control group of 60 patients in standard hospital care with similar diagnoses during the same period.

We were particularly interested in family involvement in response to the transfer of responsibilities occasioned by this treatment procedure: both the scope of involvement and the characteristics of the individuals concerned. We also wanted to see if there were significant differences in the two populations with or without home hospitalization, in terms of their needs and the ability of those around them to deal with these needs.

## Home Hospitalization: Diverse Needs and Varied Family Responses

The results obtained (see Bungener and Horellou-Lafarge 1987 and Bungener 1988: 27-37) initially reveal the extreme diversity of situations covered by the term home hospitalization as used by the Paris Health Authority.[10] There are no hospitals, "major suppliers" of services or patients especially predisposed to such treatment or delivery of services. Hospital departments sending patients for home treatment include all types of specialization, surgical and medical, and the diagnoses are varied, although malignant tumours and cancers preponderate (28%). Other types of diagnoses are represented considerably less often: trauma, wounds and post-surgical care (10%), high-risk pregnancies (8.4%), cerebro-vascular illness (8.0%), skin diseases (7.9%), endocrinal illnesses (7.0%) and nervous or sensory system illnesses (7%). The percentage of the chronically ill in home hospitalization is 57%. Such wide-ranging diagnoses cover extreme variations in the seriousness of the illness and extent of dependence. One quarter of patients are completely mobile and autonomous, 17% are bedridden, one third need daily assistance, and the remaining quarter. only require help three or four times a week for specific tasks.

It should be noted that the average age of patients in home hospitalization is higher than for standard hospital patients: 51% of home care patients are over 65, whereas the corresponding proportion drops to one third in non-university hospitals and is even lower in university hospitals. 70- to 85-year-olds represent the largest age group for this type of care (30%), which involves an additional 7% of individuals over 85.

Analysis of the files shows an overrepresentation of women (54.7%) in the home hospitalization population, similar to that observed in hospitals overall. One finds the same discrepancies as elsewhere related to morbidity and specific care provided during pregnancy and childbirth. However, despite their slight numerical superiority, women in home hospitalization are less often bedridden than men; they are also less frequently represented among the totally mobile, and are thus most often seen in the two intermediate categories of those requiring daily or weekly help.

A widely varying range of medical and non-medical care needs obviously result from conditions of advanced age, chronic illness, disability and handicaps due to illness. Technical medical services are provided by nurses and other professionals employed by the home hospitalization service or, where necessary, passed on to private individuals remunerated by the institution on a per-task basis. Purely medical supervision is transferred to the family doctor or failing this, specially arranged with a private consulting physician, in addition to periodic consultation visits to the hospital department concerned. Only 13% of families view this approach as unsatisfactory in terms of what they expected when this type of care was suggested to them. Conversely, 24% say that they were pleasantly surprised by the extent of professional care provided, and the remainder merely express their satisfaction.

Non-medical care of the sick person is generally the concern of the family since home hospitalization rarely provides for paid homemaker help. The files studied do not give a reliable picture of this type of data, which is probably underestimated. Only 15.2% mention the use of homemaker help, which is a fairly low proportion considering the restricted autonomy experienced by over half of these home patients. It is true that some had already been using paid housekeeping services: this was the case for 19% of patients in the survey. But 21% of the families were paying an outside individual to look after the patient at home, and in some cases these services went beyond housekeeping tasks and were provided by visiting nurses or medical students.[11] In 7% of cases, the patient's return to the home led to increased use of personnel the family knew and had previously employed. 14% of families stated that they had called upon paid help for the duration of the home hospitalization, although there is no way of telling if this referred to individuals they had found and paid for themselves or obtained through social services.

In more than half the cases, this paid work is in addition to simultaneous help provided by family and friends. One can imagine that in these situations, the workload involved when the hospitalized person returns home is considerable. But this is not always verified. For patients' non-medical needs met at home are extremely varied. Care for sick persons and their "objective" needs are first of all a function of their actual level of dependence. The extent to which help is called upon, whether or not provided by a family member, depends on the patient's degree of autonomy in performing necessary daily activities, either alone or with help. Among the patients questioned, 23% did not require any particular form of help. For the remaining 76%, the most frequently cited needs involved additional household tasks (extra laundry due to incontinence or other factors) for nearly two thirds of patients (44%), or more specific jobs: washing and dressing (35%), eating, including meals taken in bed (31%) and/or special diets (26%), and help in getting around (28%) or in performing essential bodily functions such as elimination (26%). These tasks are obviously cumulative in many cases, with only one of these helping activities being required in 28% of cases, two in 16% of cases and at least three for another

32%; 13% of patients need at least four of the five types of help enumerated.

The person or persons caring for the patient must thus take on tasks previously assumed by the hospital. Such tasks, added on to daily household chores and both complicating and increasing such work, are at times seen by the family as tedious and repetitious, with a high cost, both psychologically and in terms of time spent. In other instances, they appear to be viewed as routine when daily activities had earlier been rearranged around the sick person in cases of aging or chronic illness, and where a process of learning to cope with the illness had been initiated. The way these tasks are perceived and their objective costs also depend on the number, availability, age and work situation of family members.

Added to this is the specific aspect of the need to monitor patients, the question of whether or not they can be left alone and the time thus taken up. This aspect is a critical one, involving 88% of patients, but does not appear to be a real problem for half of them (45%). Arrangements in this respect are found to be tolerable for 35% of families, whereas the situation is intolerable for 8% of them. What is involved here is not only the individual characteristics of the patient—age, severity of illness and extent of dependence—but also, here again, the number of family members actually taking part in such supervision and their work situation. The reason for the high percentage of families with retired people in cases of home hospitalization becomes clear. The heterogeneity of needs is in fact matched by a similar diversity in the types of family support available to home hospitalization patients. Some patients are alone and have only occasional help in specific tasks, whereas others have large families. But there is no necessary relation between the two aspects, accentuating the disparities observed. In some cases, the use of paid help, at a considerable financial cost, reduces the gap between needs and unpaid help.

## Calling On an Extended Family Network, Predominantly Made Up of Women

The family situation is, in principle, one aspect of the data used to make the home hospitalization decision and consequently appears on the patient's file. It may thus be observed that most of the home hospitalization patients (68.3%) live in a home where there are at least two adults and 55% are married. Others may live with a brother or sister or one of their children.

However, homes where there is only one adult represent a by no means insignificant percentage of such patient file notations: 22.8%. This situation is of particular interest to our concerns here in that, depending on their needs, such patients must either face their home hospitalization alone or call upon a family or social help network outside their homes. These proportions are similar in the families surveyed, with 68% of them involving couples and 14% persons effectively living on their own. This data significantly differentiates this group of patients from those remaining in traditional hospital care, since 42% of the control group comprises individuals living alone.

According to the files, patient care is most often undertaken by the spouse (55%), and this is confirmed in the survey. Both research approaches also show similar data to the effect that 15% of patients are being cared for by one of their adult children, or conversely, a sick adult is being looked after by an ablebodied parent (11.7%). It is rare that help is requested from a more distant member of the family (4.2%) or a friend (5.5%) as either the principal or sole means of assistance. But in more than half the cases in the survey, such help may be called upon for additional, specific or occasional aid, with frequent requests for such help in some families, involving a number of different individuals. This is also in addition to paid help, as mentioned earlier.

Who provides such help? When it is the spouse, there is an inverse distribution of the sexes relative to the patient population, but in all other cases, a large majority of helpers are women. Analysis of the files shows a proportion of two women (65.9%) to every man (34.0%). The home care survey indicates that this percentage varies according to the degree of responsibility and extent of patient dependence. In the 32% of extreme disability situations, the responsibilities are taken on by women in 25% of cases and men in 7% of cases, with the latter, in all cases, also having a considerable degree of outside help, which is only obtained by a few of the women with similar responsibilities. Regarding their work situation, two thirds of helpers are not employed, being either without a professional occupation or retired; almost half are over 65. This aspect clearly attests to the real nature of the transfer of the burden to the family involved in home hospitalization. But all the studies confirm that there is no quantifiable link between extent of the workload and actual availability of the patient's family; some observations show a difficult and even problematic situation when care is prolonged over an extended period of time.

Home hospitalization therefore makes a variety of demands on those close to the patient, sometimes calling on a sizeable network of family and friends, who in some cases must assume a heavy and very constraining physical burden. Yet it is rare to find such constraints expressed in terms of costs. The financial costs are poorly accounted for and, according to the families involved, only slightly exceed remuneration for home help or loss of income, which in any case remains infrequent. The psychological costs and costs in time are perceived and expressed in different ways. These are important in younger households where there is less acceptance of illness and patient care, but they appear to be less significant in most families for two main reasons: the relatively advanced age of the patients and their immediate families, situating them within the non-working population; and the high proportion of the chronically ill. Daily activities follow a rhythm restricted by age or illness, or both. Any additional responsibilities tend to be attributed to the illness rather than home hospitalization, which has its advantages, especially in reducing the need to go back and forth to the hospital. There is also the emotional satisfaction of having the patient return to the home setting.

If we compare this to when the patient was in traditional hospital care, home hospitalization seems preferable to 40% of families, who say that time pressures are less; worse in one third of cases; and the same for one fifth. It can be noted that this assessment is affected, at least in extreme cases, by the patient's level of dependence:

- For autonomous patients, their present situation seems preferable to 65% and worse to 16%.
- For dependent patients, the respective percentages include 25% who view their situation as improved and 59% who say that they are worse off. Duration of care often influences this negative assessment. Although all the families say that they are willing to undergo the experience again if necessary, the constraints are being measured without the possibility of real choice at the outset. Faced with a substitute ambulatory therapy, the possibilities for choice are limited, with similar consequences for families, as shown in a 1988 study by Jean-Louis Pédinielli (Pédinielli et al. 1988).

## Family Behaviour and Symbolic Representations Regarding Substitute Therapies: Necessary and Often Vital Assistance in Patient Care

Studies on "family participation" in substitute therapies are rare, even if some therapies require such participation. This study attempts to determine the actual impact of the use of substitute techniques and the symbolic consequences for families, by using two specific sample groups involving chronic respiratory insufficiency treated by home oxygen therapy (62 families) and insulin-dependent diabetes (59 families).

The authors' presuppositions take them beyond a purely "reactive" view of illness (a coping process): they suggest that "the family group's confrontation with a loved one's illness and/or therapy can generate behaviour which induces a healing process and a will to fight the psychological effects produced by the illness and/or therapy" (Pédinielli et al. 1988: 6). The dual objective of analyzing both family practices and symbolic representations led the authors to choose a data gathering approach using a pre-established list of all possible types of care likely to be assumed in the family setting and then asking families to indicate how such care is provided. There is thus a simultaneous listing of activities and the ensuing comments generated. The study results are extremely rich in information and comprise more than simply an evaluation of family care activities, which we have selected here.

The therapy for insulin-dependent diabetes strictly regulates the patient's day due to the daily portioning of the glucose intake and the hypodermic injection of insulin (except where an insulin pump is employed), combined with daily urine and blood checks. This degree of regulation leads to a highly restricted lifestyle for the patient, as well as considerable acquisition of medical knowledge. But for most diabetics, there are no major handicaps creating a significant need for help, except where there are complications resulting in blindness or amputation. The technical medical aid the family must provide is limited to injecting the patient in the arm. For blind patients, this requires the daily assistance of another person, frequently a family member or, in other cases, someone from a home care service. The risk of glycemic coma means that the family has to be ready to act quickly and effectively at unpredictable moments. Finally, it appears essential for the family to strictly adhere to the patient's special diet, through the use of either a restricted diet for everyone or two types of diet, which creates extra work for the household.

For patients without complications, aside from the indispensable moral support (which is difficult to account for) that the family provides—for one's family can become the reason patients accept such care—the family's work is not extensive, and is sometimes limited to the non-physical task of supervision, i.e. vigilance. In fact, when a diabetic person (man or woman) is obliged to stop working, they often take on a considerable portion of the household chores. Family involvement is obviously greater in cases of blindness or amputation, and centres on hygiene and care relative to bodily needs as well as helping the patient to get around and take part in recreational activities. This kind of help is often described as a specific type of learning in order to re-establish the maximum level of autonomy.

The authors conclude that in 76% of the cases examined, there is a good degree of family cooperation and in 46%, patients view the family support as essential. However, this does not mean that there are no real or imaginary conflicts in cases where families try to prevent deviations from the regimen. 12% of patients speak of their problems with their families and the restrictions they must deal with. And 10% complain about their family's indifference or lack of understanding. It is significant that those diabetic patients who do not feel they are getting adequate family support are also those experiencing difficulty in carrying out their treatment, which is indirect proof of the extent of family influence.

The home treatment of respiratory insufficiency differs from the previous example in that it is a caregiving procedure where family involvement appears essential. Daily activities for these patients are often extremely limited. Their treatment is very restricting and requires considerable observation. Family members play the indispensable role of helping the patient to deal with daily life (failing this, paid help is required), but they are less often involved in the practical provision of treatment. "It appears that the more tasks require bodily care, the more difficult they are to perform" (Pédinielli et al. 1988: 165). Daily management of equipment is often carried out by the patient (in 76% of cases), with the spouse only becoming involved fairly rarely (16%), and children or an outside person in exceptional cases. However, it is frequently the family who looks after the administrative paperwork as well as the purchase and supply of medication and oxygen. "Roles are to some extent allocated by help function: treatment in the case of the patient, and care in the case of the family" (Pédinielli et al. 1988: 165). The family constantly refers to its caregiving status and sees its function as "close to that of nursing help," as one patient's wife put it (Pédinielli et al. 1988: 166). Patients speak about their families positively despite some disparity between what they say spontaneously and the specific listing of daily tasks. However, for the authors, the family's caring role largely revolves around their social relationship with the person they are helping (Pédinielli et al. 1988: 150 et seq.). Patients with respiratory insufficiency clearly expect a lot from their families, in terms of not only their physical requirements but also their emotional needs. The social restrictions involved in this illness cause the patient to fall back upon the family circle, and require from the family a substitutive role it cannot always fulfill.

This type of demand and the severity of the illness are likely to generate in the loved one (especially the spouse) "both an intense emotional effort and a considerable degree of psychological suffering, which is sometimes masked by the intensity of the activities developed to help the patient" (Pédinielli et al. 1988: 185). This represents one of the limits to the effectiveness of family involvement, requiring the creation of some specific form of help or at least recognition for the family itself. For, as the authors repeatedly emphasize (Pédinielli et al. 1988: 242 in particular), such *intense* activity is seen by the families as performing a caring function implicitly required by the situation, which is not in response to any form of medical *negotiation* or *supply* and thus does not require any medical or social recognition.

## CONCLUSION: A FUNDAMENTAL DEGREE OF FLEXIBILITY AND VULNERABILITY IN FAMILY INVOLVEMENT

The paradoxical element of significant family involvement generally obtaining little recognition, the social aspect of which was mentioned in our introduction, takes on a specific dimension here in being viewed as particularly problematic by the families of patients with respiratory insufficiency. This element is also found in what is said by those who face the restricting and conflicting realities involved in dependence or home hospitalization. In all cases, such a paradox seems likely to aggravate the difficulties and increase the risk of a breakdown in family unity when the burden becomes too great or emotionally difficult, and justify a refusal of such responsibilities, which are then passed on to the professionals. For when the poorly-acknowledged work done by families fails, the patient is often sent to a hospital or institutional care facility. Family activity thus, by default, assumes a great deal of economic and financial visibility which, moreover, helps to mask its real nature by leading decision-makers and public opinion to solely emphasize its shortcomings, as is still too often the case today. This is why it is important that there be a specific trend of research to foster the relevant visibility of and recognition for such work. This step is indispensable in order to subsequently establish support measures to help these families, if their role as producers of lay care is seen as socially useful and economically justifiable.

One of the particular characteristics of domestic production, which we observed in the studies examined in the specific case of the domestic production of care and hygiene, is its flexibility. It is in fact capable of accepting or rejecting a wide spectrum of tasks—depending on whether the family responds to perceived needs on its own or consumes a market good or service—and correspondingly adapting its use of professional production. In this way, domestic activity can have a significant influence as an economic and financial regulator, which is part of the reason for the increased interest it is enjoying. And the family is in fact intentionally given the role of a shock absorber or brake on public social expenditures when we promote home hospitalization as an alternative to hospital care, or home care for the elderly. Nor can we help observing the varied and practical capabilities of family services in the light of the frequent inflexibility, inadequacy and costliness, as Agnès Pitrou termed it (Pitrou 1978), of what is offered in the commercial or public sector.

Calling upon this domestic flexibility seems an easy matter, as all the studies attest to the continued vigour of family support and families' willingness to face every sort of difficulty and all the additional physical and emotional effort required by a family member's condition. Nor has this tendency been challenged by HIV pathology, contrary to what the public may have been led to believe in the early stages of this epidemic. The majority of AIDS patients today receive considerable material and moral support from loved ones, regardless of how they acquired their illness, for this disease has sometimes allowed families to become closer in ways they would not have thought possible earlier.[12] There is verbal testimony to a tradition of family support on the part of those who practise it. It is true that in France, dealing with highly centralized, hierarchical and bureaucratized public organizations is at times dissuasive, as many descriptions of the itineraries taken by the elderly have shown. However, it is important to point out the material and psychological limitations of family involvement and not minimize the constraints families must face in connection with various social and political options, in order to simultaneously call for essential measures to help families. The possibility of choice, for families and individuals, is primordial. This influences the social and institutional recognition of the family's contribution and determines the acceptability and permanency of the help provided. The family can become a recognized and reliable part of the therapeutic process as long as its work is not taken for granted nor underestimated in relation to professional activity.

The family's contribution must therefore be investigated, measured and recognized, despite the undeniable methodological difficulties (Bungener 1987). Attempts in this respect show, regarding the dependent elderly, for example, that home care in extreme cases can end up costing significantly more than institutional care when we no longer systematically neglect to assess services provided by the family (Frossard et al. 1990). It is also important to ensure that the most closely involved family caregivers enjoy similar advantages to those created for professionals. Aside from the fact that many lay workers do not even have relief in the form of legally authorized weekly and annual time off, there is today recognition of the need for psychological support for professional care workers faced with extreme illness situations (AIDS, cancer, etc.), and this need is clearly comparable to the case of those experiencing the same situation at home on a daily basis with a person emotionally close to them. To fail to adequately recognize the role and vulnerability of family caregivers is to risk that they may be caught in a vicious circle of having to refuse to continue their involvement while, at the same time, being abusively criticized for lack of involvement.

## Notes

1    The term "lay" is used in opposition to "professional" and covers acts performed by individuals whose competence has not been recognized or institutionalized.

2    The reader should refer to the frequently cited ideas developed by Ivan Illich during the seventies.

3    The first and most well known among these was the Laroque report published in 1962, subsequently followed by the Massé report in 1973, the Arrecks report in 1979 and the Legrand report in 1991.

4    In these centres, individual dwellings are located in a setting providing group services such as medical supervision or meal preparation.

5    In these homes, there are still beds for the disabled or partially disabled (approximately 7.5%) which are to be replaced by medical treatment wards.

6    All the data presented here derive from the previously cited report prepared by Joel and Bungener (1990) for the Social Affairs Department.

7    Caisse nationale d'assurance vieillesse des travailleurs salariés.

8    Research report prepared by Favrot (1988) for the Social Affairs Department's MIRE (Mission Interministérielle Recherche et Expérimentation).

9    Within this double percentage, the first figure corresponds to the responses obtained in the questionnaire given to the dependent person and the second to the responses of the principal caregiver.

10   L'Assistance Publique de Paris groups all the public hospitals in Paris and the surrounding region (41 hospital organizations) and represents the largest university hospital group in France.

11   These students perform paid monitoring activities for sick individuals as a means to earn their living during their studies and even finance such studies.

12   Martine Bungener and Marie-Christine Zuber. Research in progress for Agence Nationale de Recherche sur le SIDA (ANRS) and Agence Française de Lutte contre le SIDA (AFLS).

## References

Barzach, Michèle (1989). *Le paravent des égoismes*. Paris: éd. Odile Jacob, February.

Bungener, Martine (1986). "Malades à domicile : ce qu'il en coûte aux familles." *Informations Sociales*, special issue "Famille et Santé," No. 4, November.

Bungener, M. (1987). "Alternatives à l'hospitalisation : bilan du débat économique." *Prévenir*, No. XIV.

Bungener, M. (1988). "L'hospitalisation à domicile : réseaux d'entraide et implication familiale." *Revue Française des Affaires Sociales*, No. 3, July-September.

Bungener, M., and C. Horellou-Lafarge (1987). "La production familiale de santé : le cas de l'hospitalisation à domicile," *Approche économique* and *Approche sociologique*. Publications du CTNERHI.

Bungener, M., and M.-E. Joel (1988). "Activité économique et demande de santé." In *La demande en économie de la santé, Revue d'Économie Politique*, 98th year, No. 4.

Bungener, M. et al. (1987). "Mobilité et Santé : de la sociologie à l'épidémiologie ?" *Sciences Sociales et Santé*, Vol. V, No. 3-4, November.

Bungener, M. et al. (1988a). *Mobilité géographique et santé à Électricité-Gaz de France*.

Bungener, M. et al. (1988b). *Ruptures professionnelles et santé*. MIRE research report.

Caquet, R., and S. Karsenty (1983). *Rapport sur les alternatives à l'hospitalisation*. La Documentation française, January.

5e secteur géronto-psychiatrique de l'Essonne (1989). *Recherche sur les itinéraires de vieux : raisons et déraisons des filières*. MIRE report.

Colvez, M., Bucquet et al. (1990). *Approches épidémiologiques des besoins en services pour les personnes âgées dépendantes*. INSERM U 240 report, Montpellier.

Cribier, Françoise (1989). "Les vieux parents et leurs enfants." *Gérontologie et Société*, No. 48, March-April.

Favrot, Geneviève (1988). *Travail sur les facteurs d'insertion et de rejet de l'activité de soins dans le système d'activité familial*. MIRE research report, Ministère des Affaires Sociales et de la Solidarité, Paris.

Frossard, M., A. Jourdain, B. Ennuyer, M.-C. Léonard, M.-J. Guisset, and C. Roos (1987). *Travail familial, solidarité de voisinage et maintien à domicile des personnes âgées*. Cahiers de L'École Nationale de la Santé Publique, Rennes.

Frossard, Michel et al. (1990). *Le prix de la dépendance*. Paris: La Documentation française.

Henrard, J.-C. et al. (1991). "Soins et aide aux personnes âgées. Effets des caractéristiques structurelles du système sur la mise en oeuvre de la politique et le fonctionnement des services." *Sciences Sociales et Santé*, Vol. IX, No. 1, March.

Joel, Marie-Eve, and Martine Bungener (1990). *Le financement de la prise en charge de la dépendance des personnes âgées*. Rapport pour le Ministère des Affaires Sociales. Paris: Legos-Cermes, October.

Levy, E., M. Bungener, G. Duménil, and F. Fagnani (1982). *La Croissance des dépenses de santé*. Paris: éd. Économica.

Pédinielli, Jean-Louis, Pascale Bertagne, and Colette Campoli (1988). *Conduites et représentations des familles de patients atteints de maladies chroniques graves et soumis à des thérapeutiques de suppléance*. MIRE report.

Pitrou, Agnès (1978). *Vivre sans famille ?* Paris: éd. Privat, collection "époque."

Soffer, Catherine (1985). *La division du travail entre hommes et femmes*. Paris: éd. Économica.

# seven
## Home Care Services for the Elderly in Italy

*Carla Facchini*
and
*Renzo Scortegagna*

## THE DEBATE ON HOME CARE

The issue of home care acquired relative importance in Italy in the late sixties, a time of major social and cultural transformations. It is difficult, if not impossible, to identify a particular reason for the interest in this area. It is probably more accurate to consider home care, and the significance such care achieved, as one of the many effects of the social and cultural trends of this period.

Instead of listing all the aspects which shaped trends in this decade or describing the ensuing cultural and political debates, we will limit ourselves here to pointing out a few significant elements helping to explain the evolution of this specific problem.

Among the characteristic themes of discussion during those years, three in particular would appear to be essential to the issues involved in home care:

a) The crisis in residential care institutions, viewed as places with sets of rules where the individuals concerned tend to fall under an all-encompassing if not totalitarian approach, or an approach where they are excluded and segregated in the sense that such rules prevent any form of exchange with other components of the social structure. A significant indication of the interest in these issues is the translation, and great success, of a few "classic" texts by Goffman and Foucault: the translation of *Asylums* into Italian dates from 1968, that of *l'Histoire de la folie* from 1967 and that of *Naissance de la clinique* from 1969. The publication of *L'istituzione negata* by Franco Basaglia, the leading psychiatrist among those criticizing psychiatric institutions, dates from 1968.

b) The crisis in the family, seen either as a crisis of authority, especially in intergenerational relations, or as an internal institutional crisis in the social system, chiefly regarding the function of social and cultural reproduction. Here again, one can identify a strong link between the political and cultural debate and the publication of such texts as *The Divided Self* by Laing, *The Death of the Family* by Cooper and certain works by Adorno and Horkheimer, all of which were translated into Italian between 1967 and 1969.

c) Awareness of the discrepancy between the cited objectives of such institutions and the functions actually effected. In reality, if the objectives targeted were to provide care and rehabilitation, the functions in fact achieved were far more diverse: rehabilitation institutions for juvenile delinquents, rather than rehabilitating their charges, seemed to be themselves producing deviant individuals tending to form unstable families whose children would in turn become users of such institutions; and psychiatric hospitals seemed poorly equipped to perform a real therapeutic role for the mentally ill. Admission to such institutions was more often seen as a final rather than temporary solution.

Where criticism of these institutions resulted from a realization of the discrepancy between institutional objectives (rehabilitation and readjustment) and functions actually performed (merely containing the problems if not actually reproducing such problems in a real vicious circle), the social debate focussed in particular, on the one hand, on psychiatric hospitals, highlighted not only by Goffman's analysis but also by the critique on the part of those working in such institutions (a movement which produced the group "Psichiatria democratica"), and on the other hand, on institutions caring for orphans, abandoned children, juvenile delinquents, etc., which became the subject of efforts on the part of various religious and lay movements and groups, supported to a significant degree by youth court judges.

Institutions for the elderly were not the focus of such criticism, either because the effects of the provision of services and care were not at odds with those institutionally prescribed, or because the elderly are "quiet" users who do not raise problems. The only real criticism concerned the poor quality of services provided—a criticism common, moreover, to all institutions—which led to various protest campaigns during this period.

But the main reason for the limited interest in the elderly's situation involves the different temporal basis of their institutionalization. Indeed, for children and young minors, the institutional function of care and education occurs within a temporal perspective with a known limit, in that, regardless of the results achieved, the young person will be discharged from the institution upon reaching the age of majority. The process is in some ways similar for the mentally ill: in this case, the institutional function of care and rehabilitation is secondary to that of custody and public security. And although at that time the patient's stay was most often for an indeterminate period, there was nonetheless the possibility of releasing patients, at least temporarily.

For minors and the mentally ill, the objectives, in short, involved education and treatment and thus, despite acknowledged limitations and inadequacies, focussed on a "healing" approach, on positive solutions to recognized problems. In other words, the official objective was in fact to be able to discharge users. The situation of institutions for the elderly is quite different: their traditional role is one of care and help, with no orientation toward the future. Admission into such institutions has thus always taken on a permanent quality.

Such a view of institutions for the elderly would seem, moreover, to be strongly influenced by the very conception of the aging process. Aging has long been seen as a process which is immutable, predetermined and inevitable. If this is the dominant analysis of aging, services will only be aimed at maintaining an established situation over time. With no positive results anticipated, not only in terms of a cure but even in terms of improvement, services provided will not focus on results and will thus be essentially seen as a "no-return" investment. This is why services for the elderly have been, for a very long time, lacking any prescribed objectives, and consequently requiring no value attributed to the work, and no efficiency or effectiveness.

If services offered to young people in difficulty, the mentally ill and the elderly responded to partially differing rationales, they nonetheless had in common the fact that they were addressed to individuals incapable of fully exercising their responsibilities and, in the case of psychiatric hospital patients, seen as a danger to society. These services were, moreover, organized so as to offer a full range of help within the institution, and so as not to require any contact with the outside world. To the point of, in the case of institutions for juvenile delinquents, for example, setting up schools and even occupational training workshops within their confines.

The avowed objective of political approaches during the sixties and seventies was to eliminate these institutions and instead assign to the "*territory*" (territorio), that is, society and the series of social relationships which form it, the obligation not only to provide help but also to reintegrate individuals into the social milieu they come from or belong to. In actual fact, however, such an objective constitutes more of a guideline than an active approach, especially in the use of an extremely general and vague expression (the territory) to designate the place which is supposed to represent the alternative to institutions. And yet this affirmation of the primacy of the territory is essential to understanding the reasons for and scope of the development of home help: the historical and political context in which it evolved and which will probably always mark it.

The transformation which occurred in the conception of help was a radical one. The traditional approach was in fact founded on the principle that it was the family's duty to provide for the various needs of its members based on a principle of natural support deeply ingrained in the institution of the family itself, without any involvement or responsibility on the part of civil society. From such a perspective, civil society was not directly involved in social policy, even though in cases of family absence or incapacity, society itself had to provide the required help. In a few cases, this role was performed by public or private institutions which took over the problem by isolating it from society and thus freeing any other resources from the need to handle it. In other cases, less structured forms of assistance furnished by lay or religious humanitarian groups sought to provide direct support to families, to help them meet their obligations and again avoid involvement by other types of resources in the problem. From this perspective, the need for assistance, arising from deviant behaviour or illness, remained a fundamentally private issue which was not supposed to impinge upon social dynamics. The institutional responses offered by society occurred in a similar perspective, in concretely providing a form of exemption from responsibility regarding exceptional occurrences and behaviour.

Again from this point of view, the situation of the elderly differs from that of other types of individuals helped: aging is an occurrence which is part of the normal course of life; the elderly are normal people living in normal families. Institutionalization of the elderly consequently involved either abnormal individuals (exhibiting severe mental or physical problems) or people lacking a family.

Institutional treatment could vary not only according to the type of occurrence which led to the need for help but also based on the degree of social legitimacy of this occurrence. For example, war orphans and victims of work accidents received a high level of help, in that their situation as individuals who were alone or disabled had resulted from occurrences seen as worthy of social recognition; on the other hand, illegitimate children (born out of wedlock or abandoned), children from poor families, and prisoners in fact received services of lesser quality, as though to thus indicate society's lack of responsibility for this type of situation. It is however true that these differences did not alter the effect of social marginalization produced by institutions, or the strictly individual, virtually private, aspect of assistance activity.

In the case of psychiatric patients, the problem occurred in a somewhat different fashion, in that "madness" often reaches beyond the confines of the family, and may represent a problem, if not a danger, to the community. This is so much a reality that society's response was not in the form of assistance as in the other cases but rather came within the sphere of public order. Asylums attempted to isolate the "mad," removing them from society and confining them in institutions providing for their custody and essential needs (and, "if" possible, improving their condition or even curing them). In any case, society did not become involved in the problem, and was not supposed to even consider it; society entrusted the problem to the institution as though it were a purely private matter.

Based on such premises, the segregation, isolation and marginalization of the individuals helped could not represent a problem for society except to a very limited extent. At most, such procedures could have affected the consciences of the families concerned by such a separation or form of isolation; but this hypothesis is fairly unlikely considering the characteristics of the persons helped and their relationships with their families.

We are now in a situation to better grasp the significance of the choice of the territory, defined as an alternative to the institution. This represented a political choice which attempted to refute any notion of help problems as "private" problems to be dealt with in closed off and segregated areas, away from society's concerns. This choice transferred help problems (the abandoned, incapacitated, dependent, mentally ill, etc.) over to the social organization as such. Through this decision, there was an attempt to assert that the emergence of a general need for help could not be seen as a private or even purely family matter. If society had contributed to the occurrence of such problems, it must become involved in their treatment, ensure that its members who had unfortunately been pushed aside be reintegrated, and prevent the emergence of new needs.

Thus the choice of the home was not to be seen as placing the responsibilities in the hands of the family, but rather as a desire to have society face its responsibilities, as specifically expressed in the notion of the territory. It was therefore a significant political and cultural choice which claimed to recognize the territory's, that is, society's, central role of involvement in social action and social policies.

## THE SIGNIFICANCE AND OBJECTIVES OF HOME CARE

In the case of Italy, as we have seen, it is important to link home care to the crisis in the institutions, precisely to avoid contenting ourselves with a virtually automatic association of home and family. In any case, when we consider the family situations of individuals lodged in asylums where the de-institutionalization movement historically originates, the call to the home would seem to have been a mere abstraction if it was an attempt to thus return these individuals to their families. If the family had in fact proved incapable of providing help to one of its members to the extent of having to resort to institutions and thus delegate this helping role to them, it would have been paradoxical to send the individuals concerned back to these same families merely to undermine the institutions. From this viewpoint, opting for the home had to mean choosing to set up a network of services at the local level to help young, mentally ill, handicapped or elderly persons, without removing them from their community, that is, their territory.

In this context, prevention assumed a specific meaning. At a time when attempts were being made to define the content of social policies so as to go beyond what we have termed a "private" or assistance-oriented approach to need, home care was simultaneously becoming the most eloquent expression of the new trend and the clearest and most concrete alternative to institutionalization. In other words, the family no longer had to feel that it alone was responsible for providing help in cases of need, in that the entire social organization could help the family itself through its basic services, or, as a last resort, partially or completely replace the family, in respecting the universal principles of equality and social justice. From then on, the territory would become the true sphere of social action, in clear opposition to the institutions; the choice of the home thus corresponded to opting for the territory, and a social service and healthcare system, and did not represent a mere transferral of responsibility back to individuals and their families.

It was in this perspective that Italy's two major political and intellectual currents, the left wing and the Catholic movement, came together, although, it is true, not always in an explicit or formal way. Although their objectives were clearly not the same, there was nonetheless acknowledgement of major areas of agreement in the name of which concrete action could often be taken and thus achieve greater force of expression.

The objective for the left represented part of an overall democratization political approach, based on the aim of greater participation by and promotion of the underprivileged classes, in opposition to the institutions which often constituted veritable power structures, with strong class characteristics. Only the impoverished mentally ill were in fact found in these institutions, since the rich could go to clinics.

Catholics, on the other hand, only recognized and agreed with some of the above objectives, while simultaneously taking the opportunity to affirm the need to rediscover and revitalize the family as a basic component of society. (It was, for example, in this context that the proposition concerning family consultation centres was formulated and the establishment of these centres sanctioned in 1975.) The service network and the entire community were supposed to support the family to satisfy the need for social belonging, which, for individuals, is also a right. Such an objective was moreover entirely compatible with the concept of the territory. In both cases, there was a strong tendency at play, to transcend both individualism and the notion of natural and spontaneous support, both being viewed as essential components of the social state, the simultaneous necessity and limits of which were acknowledged.

The closing of assistance institutions and the development of home care services then became choices so closely linked that it is difficult to speak of one without mentioning the other; together they could be seen as the most operational expression of the cited principles and objectives.

The clearest expression of these trends is undoubtedly to be found in the legislative sphere. It was during this period that the act on placement and special adoption (N. 431) was passed (1967), representing a real instrument to de-institutionalize minors. This act was subsequently incorporated into Act 184 on adoptions (1983). It took several more years for other acts to be passed, although it is not difficult to identify their origins in the historical trends of that same era: Act 180 on the mentally ill and the closing of the asylums only came into effect in 1978 after a long gestation period. The same forces were seen at the regional level, also expressed through legislative decisions which, if less central, were no less significant.

At the same time, the process of legal reform that would place the entire service system under review was unfolding. Real change could not in fact be limited to action involving one or the other category of persons helped, but rather required the creation of an integrated system of coherent services with established guidelines, particularly with respect to the involvement and responsibility of social organizations (the territory) regarding assistance problems. This issue, among others, was closely linked to that of home care, as was noted earlier.

As for the laws which were to govern the reform, it was only in 1977 and 1978 that the initial results would be known: the orders-in-council accompanying Act 382 of 1975 (orders-in-council 616 and 617 of 1977) definitively sanctioned the closing of a significant number of institutions and especially, assigned authority to the regions and municipalities concerning the organization of social services, previously entrusted to the provinces. Thus, the primordial role of the territory was recognized: it is in fact important to stress that decision-making bodies in the regions and municipalities were henceforth to be elected publicly, as opposed to the procedure whereby the prefect, chief representative of the province, is not elected but rather appointed by the Ministry of the Interior. Finally, the act establishing a national healthcare service (N. 833) was adopted in 1978. It set out the new organization of healthcare assistance, again placing the emphasis on the daily life context. Here again, the home, defined as the basic level of services, was cited as the most important aspect in healthcare policy.

## DEMOGRAPHIC CHANGE AND USE OF INSTITUTIONALIZATION

The existence of a law or number of laws to develop certain objectives regarding home help should clearly not be confused with the actual state of services provided at home. Laws must be viewed as highly effective tools to sanction one state over another, but they cannot be seen as the only instruments of a given form of change, however relevant it may be.

It could easily be said that the analysis presented up to this point is extremely general in nature and can be applied to all types of institutions. Some were clearly more concerned by the changes than others, and the results obtained consequently vary. The following tables show the evolution of the situation relative to the number of individuals institutionalized based on a national report produced by the central statistics office, referring to the main categories of persons helped. According to the official data, facilities considered as institutions are those offering actual residential services or continuing services on a daily basis throughout the year.

The first table indicates the diversified evolution of institutional usage. It highlights a decrease regarding young people, the mentally ill and the handicapped, and an increase with respect to elderly persons. This evolution clearly reflects the areas of debate we have mentioned. The forces involved in institutionalization obviously operate differently in the case of the elderly. In fact, we know that there is generally only recourse to institutionalization for the elderly in extreme circumstances, when the symptoms of dependence associated with aging become so severe that they can no longer be handled by the family.

The demographic factor, indicating a sharp increase in the number of elderly people, especially the very elderly, and an even greater decrease in the number of births, is one explanation for the phenomenon of the continually rising number of elderly persons in institutions.

An additional element explaining the situation can be found in the variations in family structure in Italy over the past forty years. Extended families have decreased, representing 22.5% of families in 1951 and 11.2% in 1981, whereas the number of single-parent families has increased, from 10.6% in 1951 to 18.3% in 1981. Since ISTAT considers extended families to be those including parents, ascendants (parents or parents-in-law) and collaterals (brothers, sisters and other related persons), it is highly probable

Table 7.1　Persons assisted in institutions, by category (1961-1986)

|  | Minors | Elderly persons | Physically and mentally handicapped persons | Mentally ill persons* |
|---|---|---|---|---|
| **1961** | 210,994 | 108,600 | 31,792 | 97,403 |
| **1971** | 154,882 | 128,008 | 36,942 | 87,778 |
| **1981** | 72,465 | 142,174 | 25,988 | 47,871 |
| **1983** | 59,341 | 143,450 | 24,943 | 42,983 |
| **1986** | 47,663 | 149,236 | 25,516 | 38,020 |
| variations (%) |  |  |  |  |
| **1961-71** | - 26.6 | + 17.9 | + 16.2 | - 9.9 |
| **1971-81** | - 53.2 | + 11.1 | - 29.6 | - 45.5 |
| **1981-83** | - 18.1 | + 1.0 | - 4.0 | - 10.2 |
| **1983-86** | - 19.7 | + 4.0 | + 2.3 | - 11.6 |
| N. indicator 1961 = 100 |  |  |  |  |
| **1986** compared to **1961** | 22.6 | 137.4 | 80.3 | 30.0 |

* For the mentally ill, the data concern the number of beds in public institutions (1985 data).

Sources:　ISTAT, *Sommario di statistiche storiche, 1926-85*, Rome, 1986 and *Annuario Statistico della Previdenza, della sanità e dell'assistenza sociale*, Rome, 1986.

Table 7.2　Aging in Italy (1961-1987)

|  | Age 65 + | Age 80 + | $\frac{80 +}{65 +}$ | Aging indicator* |
|---|---|---|---|---|
| **1961** | 9.54 | 1.5 | 14.2 | 41.79 |
| **1971** | 11.27 | 1.4 | 15.0 | 49.06 |
| **1981** | 13.23 | 3.0 | 20.4 | 61.72 |
| **1987** | 13.40 | 2.7 | 20.0 | 72.70 |

* Population aged 65 and over per 100 children aged 0-15.

Sources:　ISTAT, *Censimento generale della popolazione* and *Popolazione residente al 1 gennaio 1987*.

that the extended family groups include at least one elderly person.

On the other hand, the percentage of the elderly in single-person households is very high: in the 1981 census, it appeared that approximately three quarters of people living alone were age 65 and over, more than half of whom were widowers and more often, widows.

Table 7.3    Distribution according to sex and several age categories of single-person households (1961-1981)

| | 1961 | | | 1971 | | | 1981 | | |
| | M. | F. | Tot. | M. | F. | Tot. | M. | F. | Tot. |
|---|---|---|---|---|---|---|---|---|---|
| Age 55-65 | 18.9 | 24.9 | 22.8 | 20.4 | 25.3 | 23.7 | 14.6 | 19.5 | 18.0 |
| Age 65 + | 31.5 | 51.5 | 44.6 | 35.5 | 56.2 | 49.5 | 36.5 | 62.5 | 54.5 |
| Widowed or divorced | 27.5 | 59.4 | 48.4 | 31.2 | 63.2 | 52.9 | 31.3 | 57.0 | 55.7 |

Source:    ISTAT, *Censimento generale della popolazione.*

## HOME CARE FOR THE ELDERLY

Based on this data, we can say that the phenomenon of institutionalization of the elderly has been relatively restrained, if we place it in relation to transformations in family structures and demographic change. Between the fifties and the eighties, only some 3% of the elderly were institutionalized, throughout this period, despite the rise in their absolute number.

Such data suggest that the use of institutionalization may have been checked by home care policies. For thirty years now, the development of convalescent homes has been extremely limited to the point that today, the overall situation is being criticized for the notorious lack of available places. Legislators moreover decided in 1988 to allocate resources for the construction of 140,000 residential places for the dependent elderly.

If no specific legislation has been introduced for the elderly, in contrast to what has been done for the young and the mentally ill, various home help initiatives have nonetheless been developed, starting in the latter part of the seventies, which have helped to limit the use of institutionalization.

It should however be noted that for the elderly, the home help policy specifically developed by the regions did not follow the same theoretical and political premises as those characterizing action effected in the other areas mentioned. Four major differences can be identified: the economic aspect (the theoretically lower costs of home care services relative to institutionalization), the responsibility attributed to the family, the role of professional help, and finally, the role played by the "third sector."

## The Economic Aspect

The issues involved in providing assistance to the elderly have in fact more often appeared to be a problem of costs, as quantitative aspects have prevailed over quality considerations. Institutions for the elderly quickly proved inadequate to face growing help needs, and the costs of institutional care were and still are quite high. Elderly people were often unable to assume these costs, and thus had to resort to external help provided by either their families or the municipalities responsible for this area.

This is one of the main reasons which led those in charge of social and healthcare policies to set aside existing convalescent homes for the dependent elderly, using simple priority criteria based on severity of need and extent of help required. However, a portion of the demand for institutional assistance has not been satisfied, and home care services became in a certain sense a forced option, or a choice determined by the need to avoid the use of institutions. Home help has thus often been seen as an appropriate choice from an economic viewpoint, or as a substitute activity while awaiting a permanent solution, always in terms of an institution. Two major concerns thus come together in favour of home help: one is to allow individuals to remain in their usual environment and thus not risk being marginalized in an institution; the other is of a purely economic and practical nature. The fact that help given in the home was also an economically advantageous activity at least partially alleviated the ethical and political tension which had characterized the de-institutionalization movement in the sixties.

## The Responsibility Attributed to the Family

A second difference in implementation of policies to help the elderly compared to those targeting other categories of users involves the role of the family. If young people are often by definition "without a family," and the mentally ill very frequently have families who feel no obligation towards them, the case of the elderly is completely otherwise: the latter, in theory, not only have a family consisting of a spouse and children, but also enjoy a sort of credit status with regard to their families. Elderly persons are in fact the parents of grown children whom they have taken care of, helped with their education, etc. It is expected that this past investment will mean that they will be looked after themselves in case of need, based on a principle of recognition and reward for the care received then (and perhaps also on the basis of the implicit view that what is considered normal assistance should occur over a limited period of time). In the Catholic tradition, the outcome of attention accorded to the problems of the aged in institutions is strong criticism of the families, suspected of having abandoned their elderly parents. This abandonment is seen as symbolic of a crisis in traditional values and the consequence of an approach affirming an individualistic culture, to the detriment of a traditional culture of support.

Moreover, it must be admitted that the number of elderly people without families is not very great. To cite some statistics, in the Lombardy region in 1972, for example, the percentage of definitively single individuals (that is, the percentage of single people at age 65) was estimated to be 6.4% (source: Regione Lombardia, *Nuzialità, mortalità e fecondità della popolazione lombarda negli anni 1971-1980*). Therefore, the number of individuals without children was limited, and the vast majority of the elderly could count on help from their children or close relatives. The difference in family history and status explains why, if for the mentally ill and to a lesser degree for young people, use of help occurs on the level of the territory, the logic being to provide services in order to reduce instances of institutionalization, on the contrary, for the elderly, help is sought far more often from the family, with the goal of the services being not to reduce but rather to avoid increasing the number of institutionalized individuals.

## The Role of Professional Help

A third aspect serving to differentiate the situation of the elderly from that of other users of social policies involves the role of professional help.

The main proponents of de-institutionalization movements have been those directly concerned on a professional level: on the one hand, youth court judges, social workers and educators, and on the other, psychiatrists and psychiatric nurses. There was thus the situation of a movement supported by professionals "within" the system, who not only defended the rights of marginalized individuals but also pieced together, so to speak, through various actions and veritable struggles, a new form of professionalism. But this type of professional involvement was much less evident in the area of help for the aged. Indeed, the primary support for the development of services in the territory came from experts "outside" the service system, whereas in many cases, the "inside" specialists kept to a marginal position or remained completely on the sidelines. We have only to examine the position of geriatric physicians, who can be considered the specialists most "within" the system managing the problem of dependence among the elderly, a central issue in home help. With a few significant exceptions (Milan, Abbiategrasso and Turin), the position of geriatricians has been essentially academic and not very active. While supporting the development of home services, geriatricians have nonetheless preferred to continue working in the hospital environment and sheltered facilities, thus effectively opposing the hypothesis that the territory was perfectly capable of meeting the needs of the elderly and their dependence through the basic services, particularly home services.

## The Role Played by the "Third Sector"

The final aspect directly concerns the conditions governing the development of home help for the elderly in Italy over the past few years.

The rising number of dependent elderly with major help needs, the lack of available beds in residential facilities unable to meet the growing demand for placement and the financial crisis particularly affecting the area of hospital care are some of the factors which led to a significant increase in the demand for home care services.

Municipalities responsible for organizing these services soon found it impossible to adequately respond to the numerous demands, chiefly due to insufficient staff. It was moreover impossible to consider increasing the number of workers because of budgetary constraints, and a search for alternative solutions was therefore necessitated. Volunteer groups stepped in initially, achieving new vigour through such activity, after their eclipse during the flowering of the ideology of the welfare state. Supplementing and sometimes replacing these volunteer groups were other groups of workers, formed on a volunteer basis, such as social service or support cooperatives, which were able to provide greater stability and continuity of services.

Activity on the part of cooperative and volunteer groups was and still is effected mainly in the homes of the elderly, offering both social and healthcare assistance. In some cases, elderly persons or their families are charged for these services; but in many cases, the municipality itself provides for them out of its own resources. As can easily be observed, this solution at first glance appears satisfactory.

We must, however, emphasize the particular significance such help assumes in the overall context of the organization of services. Workers from volunteer or cooperative groups act without any connection to the service system organization, since they are accorded an official and very often real degree of independence. They thus develop a very close relationship with the elderly persons helped and their families, and yet remain marginal to and outside of the overall dynamics involving the territory as a whole. In other words, cooperative and volunteer groups tend to evolve within a helper-helpee, or at best, helper-family, relationship, unconnected to the social organization as a whole. The outcome is easy to foresee. Whereas the family is strengthened by this relationship to the extent that its role and the significance of this role are not challenged, the territory, in the sense that we represented it initially, becomes weakened, precisely due to its limited involvement. The result is that the potential development of home care services may not in fact foster a corresponding process of de-institutionalization as occurred in the sixties and seventies for young people and the mentally ill. We are thus likely to see an increase in home help as well as institutional care, along with a reduced role for the territory.

To sum up, the situation in Italy is rather confused, at least in terms of political orientations: among the various activities contributing to home care services, it is difficult to identify actions which strengthen the potential of the existing resource network, in either the public sector or that of the service cooperatives or volunteer groups.

## ACTIVITIES TARGETING THE ELDERLY

Activities intended to prevent institutionalization of the elderly can be grouped according to whether they are active support services or preventive-type services. In the first category, we can distinguish services offered to families from those linked to the territory.

## Active Support Services for Families

In this type of activity we can mention:

- Healthcare: this generally consists of simple care services (injections, catheter replacement, massage, etc.), or help in properly following pharmaceutical prescriptions. Also found in this category is a highly specialized service: home hospitalization.
- Support services centring on home help: the services provided range from help for the individual (help in getting up, personal hygiene, dressing, meal preparation) to help with housework and domestic tasks (changing sheets, laundry services, purchase of food, meal preparation) or again, accompanying the user on medical visits, or even in various activities aimed at maintaining social relationships.
- Services to reassure the elderly (telephone help services).
- Support initiatives regarding economic activities (assigning someone to accompany the person in performing economic tasks, in income management, rent payment, etc.).

Added to these are activities carried out on the level of the territory and the intermediary facilities: sheltered housing (residential facilities consisting of private apartments with organized group medical or housework services for the purpose of which architectural barriers have been eliminated); and daycare hospitals.

## Preventive-Type Services

These activities are generally primarily linked to the territory. They chiefly involve health (geriatric consultation centres) and leisure time organization (university study programs for seniors, social centres, health resorts, sports or fitness activities, etc.).

On the national level, there are a great many projects and activities. But it should be stressed that these services exist in a fairly heterogeneous fashion. Some, such as home help and social centres, are relatively widespread, whereas other types of services occur only sporadically or are at times unique (as is the case in particular with home hospitalization, which is only found in Turin, and geriatric consultation centres, which only exist in the Milan area).

Since one of the most widespread services is home help, it is interesting to take a closer look at this aspect. Let us consider, for example, the

Lombardy (Milan) region. In 1985, of the 1,546 municipalities in Lombardy, 824 (53.3%) offered some form of home help service. Of the 1,590,000 elderly persons in the region, 31,000 were able to take advantage of such services (approximately 1.8%).

Significant differences can be seen in the distribution of home help services, largely due to the size of the municipalities providing the services. There are also major differences in terms of extent of use of the services themselves by the elderly. Here, age is a determining factor: the percentage of users varies from 1.4% of the elderly between 60 and 69 years of age, to 2.3% of those aged 70-79, and 4.7% of those over 80. The relationship between age and level of service usage also parallels the link between age and severity of dependence: various exploratory studies estimate the number of the partially dependent at around 10% for those aged 60-69, 20% for those aged 70-79, and 40% for the over-80 group.

The municipality's size is also an important indicator of the variety of services offered: approximately 25% of municipalities with a population of less than 1,000 (particularly numerous in the Lombardy region) offer such services, compared to 45% of municipalities with 1,000 to 3,000 people, 70% of those with populations from 3,000 to 5,000 and finally, 90% of municipalities with over 5,000 inhabitants and indeed 100% of those with populations over 100,000. Not only are the larger municipalities those offering the greatest variety of services (providing, in addition to home help, meals-on-wheels services, laundry services, etc.), but the smaller municipalities also only supply basic services. The status of the staff employed by these services differs as well: in large centres the staff are generally stable and long-term, whereas in smaller centres, they are usually occasional workers, with a significant degree of employee turnover.

On a national scale, the heterogeneity of these various initiatives represents a limitation upon the action of social policies, rather than a sign of creativity and innovation. In other words, what is most lacking is connection and integration of the various forms of activity. Territories with a genuine network of services able to respond to the problems of the elderly in an overall fashion are extremely few and far between. This fragmented activity makes it impossible to produce any specific or overall description of the status of home help in its various forms. The studies that have been carried out look at a limited number of territories in an isolated way and employ methodologies which make any comparison problematic. These studies often focus on specific issues such as professional development, training needs, etc.; or they examine a few aspects of the elderly's lives, for example, their life experiences, relationships with their families, etc.

Moreover, the various studies generally omit one central aspect: the question of existing connections between the development of home help and the use of institutions. In other words, it is impossible to assess to what extent the development of home care services is influencing institutionalization in quantitative or qualitative terms for individuals using such resources. This aspect will obviously be one of the most important to document.

Certain activities merit more systematic analysis: for example, economic support initiatives for families, sheltered housing, daycare hospitals. Other activities are on the contrary widely and solidly documented, without contributing to an analysis of the de-institutionalization process. Most of these activities fall into the category of so-called recreational activities (fitness, health resorts, social centres, university study programs for seniors). Such services undoubtedly play a fundamental role in counteracting exclusionary and isolating mechanisms strongly linked to the emergence of pathogenic situations; but their capacity to reduce the specific demand for institutionalization appears fairly limited.

We will now examine a few cases where there has been an assessment of the impact on the territory, on the process of institutionalization or on the welfare of the elderly person, using a procedure comparing two different groups to whom various services were offered.

## EXAMINATION OF A FEW SOCIAL INITIATIVES

We will look at three types of activity: geriatric consultation centres, home help and home hospitalization. The first activity is in fact of a preventive nature, whereas the second is both preventive and curative, and the third is obviously exclusively curative. Moreover, in the first instance, the location is public, whereas in the second and third, the activity is performed in the home of the elderly person.

## Geriatric Consultation Centres

These centres operate in Milan and a few surrounding regions. They began in 1979, as an expression of openness toward the territory on the part of one of the major institutions for the elderly: Istituto Golgi de Abbiategrasso. Some 600 elderly persons are currently being followed up in this centre, with approximately 1,000 home visits occurring annually.

These services were the outcome of a profound analysis of aging. The underlying view is that aging is a process which is obviously inevitable and yet modifiable, which not only involves processes of deterioration but also positive processes of active compensation for the losses effected on the organism by aging. Old age can then be a positive experience, and can be controlled by healthier behaviour. This notion of a possible influence on the aging process results in services being oriented in a significant way towards rehabilitation, if not actual prevention. We can thus expect major achievements in terms of physical autonomy and health, justifying the extent of resources allocated. Continual evaluations are therefore necessary in addition to the establishment of verifiable objectives.

The centre provides for cooperation between medical specialists (geriatricians and geriatric nurses) and social workers.

Based on the principle that "it is not a question of fighting illness but rather of maintaining health," the key objective is to increase the number of individuals able to benefit by aging in a state of physical and mental health considered satisfactory by themselves and their families. A clinical file is kept for each patient, oriented toward evaluating their capacities. From this perspective, the diagnostic aspect, although important, is not viewed as sufficient. The process rather involves an evaluation which includes the environmental context. Preventive action is based on a healthcare education approach, to allow individuals to experience their own aging process in a better way. This education is chiefly provided on two levels: individually and in groups. Individual education is primarily based on inclusion of a third phase in the clinical visit, in addition to the two traditional phases of diagnosis and objective examination: this involves informing patients about essential data concerning their own health and highlighting the positive aspects, seen as an opportunity for growth, that illness can often have when one has reached an advanced age. Group education consists of meetings for group discussion on specific subjects (groups are formed in a homogeneous manner based on categories of symptoms) where new types of behaviour are learned.

Two indicators are used to assess the impact of this experiment: frequency of hospital stays and use of medication. Results recorded for the year preceding and the year following activities at the consultation centre are compared. In both cases, the indicators reveal a significant improvement.

## Home Help

The experiment we would like to look at is being carried out in a primarily rural area of Emilia-Romagna, in Guastalla, a small town of 10,000 people. It involves 200 elderly persons. The experiment is founded on a criticism of limitations in the previously existing services: "one cannot always speak of an assistance project; in each case, the variables considered are economic or assistance variables in the strict sense of the latter term, and psychological and existential aspects only play a minor role, the professional aspect of the services being virtually absent" (source: internal documents).

The way activities are structured is the focus of particular criticism: "In the helping activity, the emphasis is on human resources and economic factors, whereas no other resources outside the services, such as the family of origin or volunteers, are called upon" (internal documents). Distribution of services is clearly systematic but provided solely on an individual basis at home, and there is tension within the service between the desire to handle everything and the limitations in the resources required for such wide-reaching objectives. An evaluation is only performed when there is an unexpected deterioration in the client's health. In such cases, there are not a great many solutions: either the usual activities are increased, while still using the same approach, or the opportunity of placing the person in a convalescent home is discussed. The evaluation of results phase is virtually non-existent or in any case not systematic. When it does occur, it is mainly because the actual objectives of the service are not adequate.

Based on these critical observations, it was decided to set up a systematic activity project to be evaluated in various phases. Two groups of individuals were formed, of the same size and with comparable conditions and situations. For one full year, new types of activities were carried out with the first group—which we will presently describe—whereas no changes were effected in the activities targeting the control group. At the end of this period, these activities were evaluated.

The objectives were as follows:

- to monitor physical condition, with a particular focus on motor activities, sensory capacities and degenerative pathological states;
- to foster individual autonomy, especially in regard to home help needs;
- to influence the quality of social life by reducing the possibility of marginalization and isolation;
- to maintain psychological harmony by encouraging affective relationships.

The main modifications involved reducing home help activities, by trying to have the person take advantage of initiatives in this area, and also by expanding activities aimed at maintaining psycho-physical harmony in elderly persons. Ongoing evaluation of individuals at risk was stressed as well. In concrete terms, the number of activities in the areas of individual help and encouragement was increased, along with a reduction in material help services. Emphasis was placed on resources outside the service: volunteer groups, family members and other similar resources. To assess the impact of these changes, particularly significant indicators were identified in order to measure physical condition and sensory capacities as well as home help needs, while continuing to focus, as mentioned above, on attempts to encourage individuals to become more self-sufficient in terms of hygiene and nutrition. The indicators also covered the areas of social and psychological harmony, by trying to gauge the intensity of relations with the family of origin as well as the ability to maintain stable relationships on an informal level. There was particular emphasis on participant workers' involvement, including their help in determining the importance to place on the various indicators.

The main results show a significant improvement in physical condition, chiefly observable in the area of motor skills and sensory capacities. The degree of deterioration in the health of persons at risk was thus influenced, without nonetheless the ability to rehabilitate greatly deteriorated states of health. This observation is particularly true in the case of degenerative illnesses (sclerosis, diabetes, osteoarthritis, etc.). In terms of development of individual autonomy and psycho-physical harmony, the results are also positive. The initial state of well-being (seen as the ability and desire to be self-sufficient) was at a fairly low level. After the help, this level increased significantly, and the activities appeared to have positive effects on not only the individuals concerned but also their family members, especially those living with them. In this sense the situations at risk were clearly reduced, and there was particular success in rehabilitating situations of considerable deterioration, often caused by helping activities which had extensively replaced personal autonomy.

Regarding the control group, the physical condition of the majority was found to have significantly declined: reduced physical autonomy, deterioration in states of degenerative illness. The at-risk situations remained at the same level, whereas the condition of individuals with incurable illness worsened. It became clear that traditional helping activities were not very effective: there had in fact been no success in stabilizing the state of health of the individuals concerned, nor in developing some degree of autonomy. On the contrary, there was often visible deterioration in the remaining capacities of the elderly to improve on their own. The level of dependence with respect to services increased in terms of needs which could have been met without outside help. In other words, the needs kept growing. As far as psycho-physical harmony, the overall finding was of gradual deterioration toward virtually irreversible situations.

When the two groups were comparatively evaluated, it was observed that motor autonomy improved in the target group while decreasing in the control group. The finding was similar in the case of sensory capacities, although these merely stabilized in the control group, whereas the positive results obtained in the target group exceeded expectations. The same development was found in the case of autonomy with respect to individual needs or the need for home care services. In regard to psychological harmony, there were no significant positive changes, with improvement in the target group being less than expected, in terms of the work invested. The improvement in social harmony in the target group was greater than expected, a clear indication of the helpers' ability to effect change on this level.

To sum up, the activities carried out particularly affected the beneficiaries' state of well-being, whereas they were not truly successful in significantly influencing at-risk situations or those considered irremediable. From this point of view, the professionals and researchers were disappointed in their expectations. Nevertheless, based on these results, it should be stressed how easily particular states of well-being can be lost and how difficult it is to regain them. This observation shows the importance of the caring role and of preventing so-called irremediable situations.

## Home Hospitalization

Experiments with home hospitalization were begun in 1984 by geriatricians in Turin. As of 1985, the decision to open the hospital to the territory, with services oriented toward the patient's home, formed part of social and healthcare policies in the Piedmont region, with Turin as the major centre. The plan's objectives target: "rapidly reintegrating patients, especially elderly patients, into their family and social environment after a hospital stay; reducing the extent of hospitalization; improving the level of care for the chronically and terminally ill; and fostering an integrated and consistent approach to healthcare activities" (source: internal documents).

The plan is based on a number of hypotheses. Such help methods involve, aside from a process of streamlining the organization and cost reduction, "human and social benefits" ensuing from patients' integration into their family environment; "benefits in terms of the treatment's effectiveness" resulting from continuity of care between hospital and home; "benefits in terms of the organization and effectiveness of healthcare services in that hospital help at home represents a concrete method of creating openness and links between the hospital and territorial healthcare services and basic medical help in particular"; "cultural and professional benefits" in that interaction between the healthcare team and the doctor can "represent a period of mutual training and cultural enrichment, fostering an overall treatment perspective"; and "benefits in terms of healthcare education," in that the family and patient, in view of their mutual involvement, may obtain useful information (internal documents).

It should also be specified that the presence of family members in the patient's home and the existence of adequate guarantees ensuring an appropriate level of hospital care were conditions allowing for the organization of services. The activity of the healthcare professionals (hospital doctors and nurses) was organized so as to support the work of the attending physician and the nursing staff from the basic healthcare services.

The typology of patients seen as potential users of such activities includes elderly patients suffering from chronic illnesses where there is an attempt to send these patients back to their homes as quickly as possible to avoid the negative effects of a prolonged hospital stay; patients suffering from progressive illnesses requiring regular hospital stays for specialized monitoring and treatment; disabled patients who require medical, rehabilitative and psychological help to favour their reintegration on a social and family level; and terminally ill patients suffering from cancer or other serious illnesses.

Between 1985 and 1990, 632 patients, including 60 under the age of 60, were treated at home using this approach. Results indicate that the chronically ill elderly were better able to handle the acute stages of their illness, while retaining a capacity for partial autonomy. There was confirmation of the extent to which the home environment and the use of familiar household articles helped to make people feel less ill, as they were simultaneously encouraged to employ their own resources and energies to perform normal daily activities, especially in the area of social relationships, which are generally curbed in the hospital environment. Progress was thus recorded in terms of autonomy and the ability to prevent the usual types of physical and mental decline.

These aspects appear to confirm the initial hypothesis, according to which, when healthcare is organized in an adequate and specific manner, unforeseen possibilities for coping with the illness emerge, as well as ways to combat lost or diminished autonomy. This represents a net gain in the improvement of health. For such a situation to occur, the services provided must clearly be numerous, able to incorporate all the requirements, and strictly linked to the various help sectors, whether of an exclusively medical or broader socio-healthcare nature. The clinical histories presented in the documentation related to the experiment show how close the connections are between the illness situation, physical and mental suffering, and the individual's residential conditions.

## CONCERNING THE CENTRAL ROLE OF THE FAMILY AND OF WOMEN

In these various initiatives, the family plays a central role. Indeed, although home help experiments are occurring widely, those with specific reference to the territory are, on the other hand, far less frequent. Up to now, the family has been the explicit or implicit basis of almost all alternative approaches to institutionalization. However, it is difficult to see how this can continue to be the case in the decades to come. We must consider the fact that a growing number of the elderly live alone, outside any family network able to provide care on a continuing basis. And yet the existence of an active family is the presupposition underlying the possibility of a specialized and dynamic form of care.

Italy's population grew more slowly after the second world war, leading to a decrease in the number of children per couple: although for the generation of those presently over 80 the number of individuals who had at least three children was high, it is clear that this number has dropped considerably for those currently aged 60. The coming generations of the elderly will increasingly not only be situated outside the conjugal relationship but will also have less children to look after them. Again based on the Lombardy statistics, the average number of children per woman fell from 2.1 in 1972 to 1.4 in 1980. Finally, it should be stressed that in terms of marriage and birth rates, changes over the past decade are showing new decreases (also seen in the southern regions).

Such major demographic changes will clearly result in a significantly altered role for the family group and thus induce a need to find new solutions or extensively revise the entire service policy.

Providing daily support for the elderly with diminishing autonomy is in fact creating problems which have been accorded little attention up till now. This is why it is interesting to look at some results from one of our studies focussing on 144 families with dependent elderly individuals over age 75. Caring for an elderly person produces profound changes in daily activities: it is very difficult to continue seeing one's friends (stressed by 30.6% of the families studied), keep up leisure activities (34.8%), or plan for vacations (50%). Caring for the elderly person also creates stress within the family looking after the individual: family life becomes difficult, to a great extent (31.9%), or to some extent (23.6%), with this responsibility leading to psychological (36.8%) or physical (34%) fatigue. Finally, relations with the elderly persons themselves can be difficult (the person becomes extremely (19.4%) or fairly (19.4%) hostile or uncooperative).

Overestimating the capacity of the family unit to provide care (including care for long periods of time or in very difficult situations) can indeed only lead to increasing recourse to institutionalization when the situation becomes too overwhelming, or when the care provided to the elderly person conflicts with other family necessities or emergencies (caring for small children or looking after seriously ill individuals). In such situations, where too much support is required, not only regarding the actual workload but also in terms of the personal life of the individual providing the support, resorting to an alternative is often seen in terms of the guilt felt by the person who is no longer able to fulfill their "duty."

Ultimately, it should be stressed that sending the elderly individual back to their family really means sending the person back to the women of the family: we always speak of the families who provide care, when in reality it is the women who perform this role as wife or daughter of the elderly person. The vast majority of elderly men still enjoy the benefits of marriage right up to age 85, whereas conjugal life is already the case for the minority in the category of women aged 65 to 75. At this age, approximately two thirds of women are widows. This means that while men are compensated for dying at a younger age than women by the fact of being able to live in a family setting in which a woman—their wife—looks after them, women pay for their longer life expectancy by a greater probability of being widowed, and indeed for a long period of time. Elderly women very often live alone, or if they are still married, live with a husband on average three or four years older than they are, and who is very probably in a situation of asking for help rather than providing it.

The feminization of care on the part of spouses is echoed by the feminization of care provided by children: where there are several children, expectations regarding care are far more frequently directed toward daughters than sons. In the case of married sons, caring tasks are performed by the daughter-in-law rather than the son of the person involved (with all the ensuing relationship problems one can easily imagine). The rising average age of the children of the very elderly, which is often over 60, is rarely taken into account. The daughters of these very elderly individuals are thus often women of fairly advanced age themselves, whose time and energies are generally already fully taken up by their workload in their families and often as grandmothers caring for their grandchildren, or again, in many cases, by their still active status on the job market. It is thus women who accumulate a series of care tasks and for whom these tasks are concentrated in such a way as to lead to health problems and actually sap not only physical but also mental energies. The initial results of a study we are conducting on 500 Lombardy women confirm the impact of such an accumulation of tasks on every aspect of these women's health.

Finally, when families and in turn women find it impossible to adequately meet the needs of the elderly and turn to home help or some form of residential placement, caring activities will again be performed, in the vast majority of cases, by other women. It is in fact almost always women who provide home help and act as social workers, nurses, caregivers, etc.

The outlook for the situation would therefore appear to involve both a feminization of aging and also a growing feminization of care for the elderly. It thus seems important to emphasize that when we speak of family care and see families as a support for personal help and caring activities, we are in fact using a euphemism: it is in reality not so much the families we are referring to but rather a precise and specific component, women, who are proving absolutely crucial to the success of social policies.

Highlighting such an imbalance, however pronounced, does not mean that we are calling for an abstract principle of reciprocity or parity. But it does mean that in the development of social policies, the sex of the individuals referred to must explicitly be considered, whether in the case of persons in need of help or those who provide such help.

## References

Balbo, L. (1991). *Tempi di vita. Studi e proposte per cambiarli.* Feltrinelli, Milan.

Fabris, F., and L. Pergigotti (1990). *Cinque anni di ospedalizzazione a domicilio.* Rosenberg & Sellier, Turin.

Facchini, C. (1991). *Per una tipologia della condizione anziana, Anziani e società.* Milan.

Florindo, N. (1988). "La valutazione d'efficacia degli interventi : il caso dell'assistenza domiciliare agli anziani." In P.P. Donati, ed., *Salute, famigli e decentramento dei servizi.* F. Angeli, Milan.

Giorli, A. (1990). *Analisi di profili di autosufficienza/ non autosufficienza.* IRER-F. Angeli, Milan.

Guaita, A., S.F. Vitali, M. Colombo, and A. Ceretti (1991). *Gerontologia preventiva ed educazione sanitaria.* La nuova Italia Scientifica, Rome.

Maggian, R. (1990). *I servizi socio-assistenziali.* La nuova Italia Scientifica, Rome.

Scortegagna, R., ed. (1985). *Il ruolo del volontariato nell'assistenza agli anziani.* Marsilio Editori, Venice.

# eight Concluding Comments

*Frédéric Lesemann*
and
*Claude Martin*

## PROBLEMS AND LIMITATIONS IN INTERNATIONAL COMPARISONS

Attempts to draw international comparisons on a demographic, economic and social level frequently stress the risks involved in coming to conclusions too rapidly. Not only do different countries employ differing terminologies and analytical categories, but even when these categories appear to be similar, their meaning often varies from one country to the next (Prioux 1990; INSEE 1991).

Nevertheless, comparisons of national situations can be of inestimable value. They can illustrate the potential discrepancies in historically-developed cultural and social models, which seem to be increasingly intersecting with and mutually influencing one another, while retaining their specific nature. Thus, differences can no longer be grasped from an evolutionary perspective but are instead being understood in a cultural framework; multiple North-South and East-West oppositions are now manifest (Barrère-Maurisson and Marchand 1990).

However, our approach has prompted us to identify three significant limitations: the first involves the need to look at the categories or meanings of the terms used in the context being studied. The second concerns the roles of the various actors in the formal care sector and how these interrelate. The third refers to the overall orientations of research work in different countries. Varying epistemological traditions are evident, influencing both methodology and issues examined. In any one area, the elements highlighted differ considerably from country to country.

## The Terminological Issue

As an example, we have chosen to look at five key notions appearing in most of the seven national surveys: family, community, home, care and government intervention—notions that vary significantly in meaning and scope based on national usage and analytical perspectives. Their common usage would appear to demonstrate a common focus for debate. However, when we examine them more closely, we soon realize that their scope and meaning vary from one country, or rather cultural tradition, to another. Each of these notions is seen to be rooted in a national—and indeed regional and specific—history and context.

Thus, in terms of "family," the perspective is at times sociological (in viewing the family as but one type of social link, with its own particular and continually evolving configurations); whereas other approaches place greater emphasis on demographic aspects (in opting for a series of indicators and a predictive analysis), psychological references (with a particular focus on affective relationships), economic factors (where the family is primarily seen as a unit of domestic production and consumption), legal considerations (with reference to legal systems and norms of mutual obligation), administrative concerns (centring on notions such as responsibility), etc.

Depending on the analytical viewpoint, the family will be understood as a private realm for the satisfaction of essential needs, a site for domestic production and the "underground economy," a placement centre ("foster families"), a stage where exchange and support relationships are played out on the basis of interest or reciprocity, material or affective exchange, or norms of mutual obligation, or again, as a preferred arena for expressing dominance relationships between the sexes based on unequal task sharing. Other viewpoints will focus on spatial or temporal aspects or the impact of cultural or ethnic variables (such as immigration) on family structures. Depending on the perspective chosen (and many others could be highlighted), the issues examined in family support networks will vary considerably. Hence the importance of clarifying the meaning of this notion in such studies.

The notion of "community" is equally complex. First of all, we observe its prevalence in the Anglo-Saxon tradition, whether in the human sciences field or social policy sector. We see this beginning with Tönnies' fundamental distinction between *Gemeinschaft* and *Gesellschaft* right through to the longstanding tradition of "grass roots democracy" in the United States, which underlies all the so-called "community" work based on group participation and volunteer efforts (Médard 1969; Lesemann 1992). The term is however little used in France, nowadays at least. In the first half of the twentieth century, social Catholic movements did in fact make frequent reference to this notion (Astier and Laé 1991). Although we cannot truly speak of a French or Latin community tradition, this ideology has nonetheless been expressed in other forms, in highlighting the territory, the local, social interaction, etc. But can we be sure of always referring to the same reality?

In the social policy field, the "community" is currently at the centre of strategic concerns about definition and identity in most Anglo-Saxon countries. As an expression of the dynamics in civil society and a symbol of informal support practices, the community concept has been adopted by public policy-makers in developing their social action programs. All services targeting the "community," seen as a clientele, are termed "community-oriented." Some hospital services or residential resources are even included in the notion of "community care" in several Anglo-Saxon countries today. This community is integrated into the allocation of responsibilities to the point that it may even be created by government decision where it does not actually exist. It thus becomes both a stimulus and focus of state involvement, in the same way, moreover, as the "family."

For example, the reflection on "community care" for the elderly in Britain is an excellent illustration of this (Jamieson 1988). The community becomes the site where care is provided, i.e. in the home as opposed to the hospital. And by extension, the connotation of social, rather than medical, care emerges, that of non-professional care given by the family. "Community care," which implies the existence of an established form of social support or self-help activity, has at the same time essentially developed into a strategy of state devolution, where responsibility is reallocated to families with, in principle, support from various services in providing such care. The notion of community today is thus highly equivocal; its usage must be clarified since it can refer to both the dynamics of informal support as well as the limitation of public sector initiatives for groups in situations of dependency or need for care.

In France, the notion of the home, the "*domicile*," refers first of all to a legal concept, "*là où une personne est située en droit*" (the site where a person legally resides) (Encyclopedia Universalis 1990: 1043). The *"domicile"* is the place where a person establishes their activities with a certain degree of permanence (Art. 102 of the Civil Code), so that the *"domicile"* determines the exercise of most civil rights. There is no equivalent in the Anglo-American tradition, since in North America, for example, a person's civil identity is in no way connected with their address or home. Conversely, the English-language notion of "home" or the German *"Heim,"* with their affective connotations of a sense of belonging, intimacy and indeed identity, have no equivalent in French. The expression "home care" in English is clearly more affective in content, and links informal support to public services. The notions of family and community already begin to converge here. Some French authors (Clavel 1982; Bachelard 1967) have in fact made the distinction between *"habiter"* and *"habitat"*: *"habiter"* is "to invent, to create one's daily environment and become part of a vast circle of relationships" (Clavel 1982: 18). Hence the distinction, if not opposition, between *"maison"* and *"demeure,"* and *"habitation,"* *"domicile"* and *"résidence,"* with the latter being purely descriptive and functional. The animated space of the *"maison"* primarily accommodates the values of "protected intimacy" (Bachelard 1967: 23, quoted by Clavel 1982: 20), in serving as a basic refuge, a primary shelter, a place of affectivity (ibid.).

The English-language notion of "care" has no equivalent in French either, except perhaps, in a limited sense, in expressions such as *"prendre soin,"* *"s'occuper de"* or *"soigner."* But they lack all the affective content and relational closeness involved in "caring." The expression "care" is ambivalent, since one can say either "care about" or "care for," with very different connotations. The first expression clearly evokes maternal protection, tenderness and love. The second refers to the responsibility, the work involved in care and support. But "caring" most often refers to informal care, as opposed to specialized practices by care professionals, which are closer to "cure," or the activities performed by paramedical or social workers, who provide "help." Thus we see the risks of misunderstanding involved in unreflectively shifting from one notion, or one cultural tradition, to another.

Finally, the notion of "government intervention" must also be placed in its proper historical and political context. Our remarks about the notion of community have already highlighted the different types of government intervention. In some Nordic countries, for example, government involvement assumes a central role in everyday life; conversely, some governments in Britain and several American states have almost totally withdrawn from the home care services sector, in assigning communities, charitable organizations or the private service market the responsibility of caring for the elderly's needs. Other countries such as France are currently seeking to avoid the centralization of services which had long characterized their public policy approaches. The Netherlands and most Canadian provinces are themselves deeply committed to a pragmatic "welfare mix" of services of varying legal status (public, private, community, volunteer, etc.), that considerably limits the extent of state involvement, but without denying government's overall responsibilities in terms of regulation, combatting inequalities, ensuring access to services and monitoring their quality.

These few examples illustrate significant differences in government involvement, with each country, based on its political traditions and the strength of the various interest groups, developing specific arrangements between the different actors that may be called upon to meet the needs involved in home-based care for dependent individuals. If we add the fact that government intervention is tending to become increasingly diversified within countries, varying according to regions or particular population groups, it is clear that this notion comprises extremely divergent political situations and realities, which are thus very difficult to compare. Just as the notions of family or family support represented, as we saw, widely varying realities, the notion of government intervention is itself highly relative to particular national, regional or local situations.

## Roles of the Various Actors

Each of the countries examined has developed its own system of formal care through various kinds of hospitals, residential care centres and retirement homes, as well as through the work of clearly identifiable professional groups: doctors, nurses, social workers, home helps, etc. It is not enough to simply list the existence of such resources or actors in the various countries, since the relative importance of their roles and hierarchical relationships varies from one country to the next. Thus, for example, the developmental status of institutional resources and their relative influence on the political system may lead some countries to organize their public systems for caring for dependent groups around such institutions, whereas others may encourage the development of community resources under the responsibility of the municipalities, for instance.

A similar observation can be made in terms of the interaction, or lack thereof, between hospitals and various types of sheltered accommodation. In some countries these two types of institutions are relatively independent, whereas in others they are profoundly interdependent. To properly understand the situation in any given country, we must clearly take into account the relationships between such institutions.

The influence professional groups may in turn have concerning the specific healthcare aspect of care services for the dependent elderly also varies significantly from country to country. In some countries, these services are under the direct and continual authority of doctors. In others, nurses occupy strategic positions of responsibility, with varying degrees of support from social workers. In still other countries, social workers or nurses assume the role of "case managers," with primary responsibility for coordinating the various existing resources. Again, these few examples demonstrate the broad diversity of organizational models—in the context of differing traditions and extent of political influence—which will obviously vary in their sensitivity and capabilities in working with family and community resources. It is thus vital to clearly understand how, on a national level, each of these actors in the production of care is positioned relative to the others regarding relationships of power, authority and influence.

And finally, similar remarks can be made about insurance and assistance systems providing access to care. All the countries examined have developed their own forms of such systems, which determine the practices, strategies and behaviour of both institutions and professional groups as well as users and their families.

## Differences in Perspectives and Issues Examined

Aside from the terminological issue, we also seem to find, in this work of international comparison, a deep cultural division in terms of each country's approach to structuring their analysis and descriptions of existing studies, between, on the one hand, analyses emphasizing policy viewpoints and, on the other, those attempting to question policies from an external viewpoint, in this case, that of the families and informal support practices. In the first case, the contribution of family support networks is assessed in the light of institutional criteria. In the second, in opposition to this functional approach is a somewhat different analysis: that of social relationships of closeness and intimacy. This cultural division seems to be tied to differences in epistemological traditions in the social sciences and hence in the perspectives taken by researchers, which influence both the status and role of such research, especially regarding the formal organizations which generate practices, and the relationship of social practices to policies.

Some of the national analyses (particularly the Anglo-Saxon ones, it would appear) seem to be primarily concerned in this area (and probably others as well) with how organizations function: their management, efficiency, evaluation of programs, etc. They thus appear to be part of the trend toward optimizing the system, contributing to how policies are formulated, implemented and adapted. The organization seems to be a "given," the adequacy of which is gauged according to the various clienteles' needs and demands. And the various clienteles are also assessed as such, in terms of how they adapt to existing services. The organization is primarily seen as a system of tasks and objectives, around which the actors are structured and function by contributing to or opposing the objectives to be attained, thus either fostering or hindering such goals. The perspective is one of a functional and complementary hierarchical organization of tasks and task levels, based on a criterion of economic cost-effectiveness.

Other analyses from France and Italy (can we speak of a Latin influence?) seem more concerned with the meaning underlying the practices and thus appear to focus on a specific research goal: to bring to light, clarify and search for hidden relationships, and particularly to identify the origin and development of phenomena, to integrate them into a historic perspective that would in fact assign them meaning, at the risk of failing to contribute to optimizing the system being studied. From this viewpoint, the organization would seem to merely represent a temporary manifestation of the state of social relationships, which can never be subjected to direct analysis. For the formal organization is not simply the product of the actors' activity; it organizes them and influences their behaviour, situating them within a context of power relationships outside its own domain. And these relationships are characterized by constant stresses and conflicts which do not derive from the communicational aspect but rather from historic and institutional regulatory structures.

This debate on the role of research, between a social science-oriented role of development, engineering and management and a task of revelation, interpretation and comprehension, is linked to a second type of debate on the nature of the "social sphere," i.e. our conceptions of the "social relationship." Is this defined from the viewpoint of individual behaviours and their aggregation or should it be seen in terms of broader structures than those found in communicational and behavioural interactions?

Just as current theoretical debates attempt to link actor and system, determinism and freedom, individual and society, political debates on the future of social protection measures are everywhere seeking to develop new arrangements, new ways of linking policy measures and the dynamics of informal support networks (Evers and Wintersberger 1988). And this appears to be the chief concern shared by the various national contributions highlighted here. It would therefore seem advantageous in this context to note the diversity of their cultural foundations, which assign differing meanings to apparently identical notions, and thus generate dissimilar action strategies.

Neo-liberal trends, which have had growing success on an intellectual, political and economic level in North America over the past fifteen years, have centred on the individual, seen as having choices and preferences, as an interpretative vector. Thus, social research in countries under the Anglo-Saxon influence emphasizes the entry into the social system by individuals: patients, caregivers or users of services, in respect to which they must exercise their capacity to choose. Services are in turn organized on multiple levels: public, private non-profit, private profit-oriented, volunteer, etc. The state is thus viewed as a producer of services (to be supported where effective and rejected if it can be shown that other types of producers are more efficient) rather than a guarantor of social justice or universal access to measures aimed at curbing inequalities. From this perspective, families and the home are but one type of actor among many, whose beneficial role is noted, while state involvement is simultaneously downplayed in terms of economic performance and political legitimacy.

Countries with a Latin tradition have a different notion of the state, which is still viewed as one of the bodies ensuring the regulation of social inequalities. But the studies here attempt to rehabilitate the "private sector," in this case the families, seen as forming an integral part of social policies and thus countering the image of the state as having (or supposedly having) all the answers. This notion of private support does not however alter the state's regulatory function as the sole guarantor of equitable allocation and compensation in access to formal care.

In our opinion, the divergent approaches to the issue of home and family support in the various countries derive from the differing intellectual traditions. At one extreme, research is oriented from an organizational perspective, with an objective and standardized definition of services (generally categorized by type and intensity of help based on validated levels of dependency) and families (assessed according to their potential contribution to enhanced functioning of the services). At the other extreme, the studies view families as generating a complex dynamics of care, both material and affective. They then examine how public care services fit together and the strategies families use to meet the daily care needs of dependent individuals, with formal services seen as but one type of resource among many, the specific organization of which is managed by the families. Attempts are made to determine to what extent public resources enable families to successfully administrate the care commitment they have assumed in their work at home for or with the elderly person being cared for: a commitment based on their conception of aging, life and death. But this endeavour does not occur in an institutional vacuum, since the area of care is structured by legal standards, cultural traditions, community practices and formal services with varying degrees of accessibility.

## AT THE CORE OF THE DEBATE: THE INTERRELATIONSHIP OF FAMILY AND PUBLIC SUPPORT

The various contributions in this text have come out of a number of observations about the care process and the role of the home, family and informal resources, especially in relation to formal services. We will now attempt to synthesize these by listing what is known about family care and formal services and, finally, the interrelationships between the two.

### Care Provided by the Family

1. The first observation to be made with respect to the family's contribution

is that this support is being provided on a massive level. 70% to 80% of such support is provided by families in the home, based on national estimates. The family thus assumes a primary role, and family support, where existing, is clearly thriving. The family is by far the major supplier of the overall work of caring for dependent persons.

2. Family support practices involve a very limited number of individuals: most often one, or two at the most. The contrast between the central role of the extended family during active family life and its extremely limited function in caring for dependent individuals is quite striking.

This limitation generally results in the designation of a principal caregiver, in the vast majority of cases a female family member, to provide care and support based on a hierarchical model seen in most countries. This caregiver is most often the wife of the dependent person or, next in frequency, the daughter and then the daughter-in-law. Next in line are the husband (if available), the son, female friends and finally, male friends. It is estimated that 70% to 80% of care is given by women. Men are thus not totally absent. They become involved especially in cases where they are the only child or the family members are all men. Nevertheless, we can justifiably emphasize the fact that, in this context, when we speak of the *family*, we are essentially referring to women. And women are called upon to an even greater degree if they are single or childless.

3. This notion of the female caring role has been socially developed and integrated into the individual and collective consciousness of many caregivers, care receivers, their families and entire sectors of the population. This would explain why some caregivers perform their task against their own desires and interests and despite difficult and even painful relationships with their parents. We cannot therefore uncritically associate the notion of *reciprocity* with that of *altruism* or *filial love*. Care is most often associated with a more or less vague feeling or awareness of obligation. In this case, where does duty begin and love end?

However, the work of caring performed by women cannot be reduced to the notion of an exploitative relationship, except where the state bases its devolution policy on such traditionally ascribed roles in opposition to the liberal values it nonetheless proclaims. In most cases, there are powerful relationships and norms of family support, in part cultivated by women involved in active caring relationships and which in turn benefit them. Their role is not limited to this form of relationship, but rather has repercussions on the entire family network. And it is women, rather than men, who generally attempt to preserve family relationships whether or not an urgent care situation exists.

4. The history of intrafamily relationships should in fact be taken into account to properly understand the care dynamics. It would truly appear to be a situation of "descendent and ascendent transmissions based on the circulation of a debt" (Attias-Donfut 1991: 16). There is an "exchange system," centring on explicit or implicit material, symbolic and affective interaction, which must be grasped in order to understand enduring family relationships or their breakup, as well as family conflicts, mediation and strategies. Family members generally remain in close contact, which does not seem to depend on existing affinities. For most people, merely belonging to a family is apparently significant. The finding that the vast majority of children live relatively close to their parents may in fact illustrate this phenomenon. Despite growing non-cohabitation between parents and children, they seem to remain in close and frequent contact.

5. Consideration of the relational dynamics of care, its history and the family environment in which it occurs and on which it operates underscores the highly specific nature of each care situation. Family situations vary widely. Each has its own dynamics which directly affects how the dependency condition of the care receiver is perceived and assessed. Situations of relatively less medical severity may be viewed as burdensome by the caregiver and the family, or conversely.

6. Once support is undertaken, there seem to be no limits or threshold to the practice of care, except in cases of dependency associated with deteriorating mental health where the criterion of a safety threat based on aberrant behaviour seems to indicate that home care should perhaps be discontinued.

7. Caring means real work, continuous effort on a variety of levels, affective as well as physical, "a mix of work and love." It also involves the work of searching for services and initiatives, investigating numerous institutional approaches, negotiating with these institutions and coordinating the different service offerings. The home is where these service-based initiatives, which vary according to administrative, geographical and professional criteria that have little to do with the care and support needs of the dependent person or caregiver, eventually end up. Caring also implies the ability to mobilize other family members or networks, coordinate the

support they offer and mediate conflicts. Caring is long-term, permanent work, an endless task requiring flexibility, availability, versatility and adaptability to changing circumstances, i.e. managing a daily routine that is often interrupted by the unexpected. For all these reasons, the work of caring involves a high level of vulnerability, particularly where the responsibility is shouldered by a single family member. The fact that care is often provided by single, childless or unemployed individuals suggests the extent of the workload involved, which competes with parental and professional obligations.

8. Additional resources (other family members, neighbours or friends) are sometimes also asked to help. They are often described in terms of networks.

The notion of *family network* must be placed into perspective, based on the observation of a veritable hierarchy of care within families. This finding counters the generally held belief that the dependent person is cared for by a diversified family network. On the other hand, various family members, at times from different generations, may in fact represent a family network and assume the role of secondary helpers who are sometimes called upon by the principal caregiver.

In terms of neighbourhood networks, it has been found that neighbours and friends are not very likely to take on personal care or household tasks. They seem to prefer outside jobs such as running errands or lawn and garden work (Walker 1985). They are often unwilling to assume heavy tasks (Tinker 1984) or long-term commitments (Wenger 1984). They can therefore not be expected to provide regular help to family members in a caring role or even less, to actually replace them. Caregivers are reluctant to call upon neighbours except in emergency situations, and neighbours infrequently participate on any substantial level or constitute significant support networks.

9. Volunteer work plays a marginal role in home care practices. It is less often performed in the home than in the context of care support resources such as meals on wheels, respite and daycare services. However, in some countries the contribution of these volunteers is growing, thus highlighting new questions, especially the issue of paid volunteering.

10. The fact that families are carrying on effectively overall in their work of caring for dependent persons emphasizes the opposite and dramatic consequences of family absence in the case of individuals living on their

own. Family support or the fact of belonging to an active support network apparently makes all the difference. The existence or lack of such support is a major cause of *inequalities* in treatment, since these individuals are often unequally equipped in terms of support networks. Our societies today are in fact marked by situations of breakdown, whether in the context of the family, work or immigration, creating increasing vulnerability on the relational level. Cases where individuals have no families and are unable to assume the task of marshalling the various resources are those most in need of help from the public sector. We know that living alone is a major factor leading to institutionalization. For individuals who are not part of a socio-familial interactive network (Castel 1991), dependence with regard to public services is immediate and total.

11. Another aspect associated with inequality concerns social class divisions. There are inequalities in individuals' economic, social and cultural assets regarding their ability to marshal the material and symbolic resources required to obtain care (Davies 1987, 1988; Lalive d'Épinay et al. 1984), if only resulting from the fact that home care involves costs for the family that would often be assumed by the institution in cases of such care, or again, from the fact that knowledge about available services, negotiation with the professionals providing such services and understanding of how the resources operate all require a particular "cultural capital" or "security" that is generally only attainable with a high level of education.

In a descriptive focus, some researchers (Pitrou 1978; Dandurand and Ouellette 1992) note that the working classes place considerable importance on social interaction among kinship groups: frequent get-togethers and material and symbolic exchanges among family members as well as neighbours and friends. Brothers and sisters often live in the same neighbourhoods and frequently visit those whom they view as belonging to their support network. Women play a major part in maintaining kinship relationships. The aspects of home and kinship are thus closely linked. The middle classes, on the other hand, tend to view themselves as free agents in developing their networks. The importance accorded to the couple and the nuclear family seems to be associated with kinship and friendship ties that are less binding. The relationship between neighbourhood and kinship environment is less apparent. Among the wealthy, a wide variety of relationships has been observed, with an emphasis on personal affinities and more fragmentary exchange. Support networks are extensive, including kinship relationships, but seem to be more elective in nature.

The aspect of cultural class differences and inequalities would seem to be of primary importance in understanding care practices. But, paradoxically, only a very limited number of studies have as yet introduced this aspect into their approaches.

12. Family and the ideology of love may conceal something very different from support and mutual aid. It is thus not enough to have a family to in fact have support or, even less so, to be satisfied with this support. Simeone (1990) describes a study on 535 elderly persons in Geneva which indicated that "most of the elderly seem to be either very well or very poorly supported by their families" (id.: 96). The author comments that: "The family is the place where affectivity, mutual understanding and emotive aspects such as listening to the other and giving of oneself are learned, as well as their opposites: aggressivity, hatred and destructiveness.... It is difficult to statistically evaluate family harmony or psychological family violence. To distinguish conflicting realities ... filtered through words unsaid and latent actions.... For, under a beautifully mannered appearance, any family may in fact be concealing a living hell...." (id.: 97-98). As with cases of individuals on their own, such violent situations require state intervention. Finally, it is vital to consider the desires of the care receivers themselves, who, as has been noted, may prefer professional help, paid for via public funds or even by themselves, rather than being dependent on a family support network.

13. Researchers all agree on one point: we know little about family self-help strategies and how their work relates to formal care services. We also know little about the social and cultural processes involved in developing a social care structure. These research areas have primarily been examined from the perspective of the service system in terms of the "needs" of "clienteles" using or receiving such services. A number of disciplines are however interested in this area, from economists in the healthcare sector focusing on a "new" field of "domestic production," to sociologists investigating the dynamics of social, exchange- and debt-based relationships or ties of reciprocity and affectivity, political economists analyzing the utilitarian paradigm of the liberal economy and its penetration into the social sciences field, and feminist researchers seeking to highlight the social processes generating sex-based work divisions and the persistence of patriarchal relationships, to mention but a few of these research trends.

## Formal Services

14. In most countries, the care function associated with dependency is witnessing a growing distinction between *curative* and *social support*, *cure* and *care*: a technically-oriented medical practice focusing on curing patients and a maintenance-oriented form of medicine based on managing chronic situations.

A dual logic, centring on economic and insurance-related aspects, underlies this distinction. On the one hand, specialized hospitals with high operating costs are attempting to channel dependent populations toward less concentrated and less costly resources in cases where they require only routine, non-specialized care or where a strong social aspect enters into the caring process, a situation existing, for example, in the case of persons on their own, without family support. On the other hand, public health insurance systems usually only cover risks associated with illness or accident and not dependency-related risks. From this perspective, establishing a clear distinction between medical and social care is generally viewed as essential to the financial balance of existing insurance systems, at a time when the demand for social services associated with age-related dependency is continually rising.

And this is the appropriate perspective from which to assess the ongoing debates in several countries on the creation of some form of dependency insurance, as well as the various initiatives to support informal resources caring for dependent persons.

15. In most countries, formal services derive from numerous sources and are regulated by various administrative rules and standards. Because of this, such services in fact function as a non-system for the user. They are neither integrated nor coordinated. Many needs are not satisfied, whereas in other cases, a duplication of services exists. This explains the fervent call for coordination of services, as well as the rise in case management approaches, which try to help individual users choose and coordinate available services based on their specific needs. In practice, however, case management often appears to be primarily a means of managing costs, as is the case in Britain where professionals must function in the context of a very limited range of formal services.

16. Countries with a tradition of highly centralized public service systems have begun, with a certain degree of success in the view of central

authorities, to decentralize the organization and often the financing of services. In these countries, municipalities have taken on a growing role in organizing care services, although they often lack the requisite financial resources.

17. In an attempt to support caregivers and to respect the specificity of individual situations, governments in several countries have started to provide subsidies to caregivers to enable them to obtain the necessary help from either the private market or their own family circle. Experience seems to indicate that in many cases, families prefer to keep such funds themselves so as to increase their income, however modestly.

## Relationships Between Family and Formal Care

18. Informal, family care and formal care are simultaneously interdependent and separate. They do not perform the same functions. They cannot replace one another, but are instead two quite independently functioning systems.

Family care is flexible, adaptable, permanent and varied, since it responds to every kind of need except specialized care. Formal care is standardized, universal and specific, and functions from a contractual viewpoint. These two operating systems cannot be viewed in terms of theoretical continuity. The first is based on social relationships, exchange, gifts and symbolic debts. The second functions on the basis of utility and economic efficiency, although it is recognized that gifts can be included in the category of interest without being reducible to interest alone, and that families also operate according to the rules of the market.

19. Family support is predominant in relation to the formal system, in providing a far more intensive degree of support than the latter. It tends to prevent or delay the use of sheltered accommodation, and offsets and fills gaps in the public service system. It in fact regulates this system by adapting to budgetary and organizational constraints, thus enhancing institutional efficiency. It can adequately respond to "intermediate" situations—those occurring most frequently—where the care receiver is neither truly ill nor truly well and where the needs are not only medical, but social and affective as well.

20. Formal and informal care can interact effectively where a partnership approach is developed that respects the particularities of each. Such a

relationship is not linear as institutions tend to visualize it, seeing it as solely related to services and therefore masking the complexity of the caring process. It can be more appropriately defined as a "mosaic of care" (Gubrium 1991), thus highlighting both the complexity of personal experiences and their varied relationships to the care system.

The caregivers' work of caring is clearly primordial and is generally a task they willingly assume. But caregivers also need formal support to be able to continue their work. Formal care in no way reduces the amount of informal help given; it cannot replace the family, reduce the involvement of the latter or compete with its work. But, on the other hand, informal care cannot serve as an alternative to formal services nor indeed replace them.

21. The concept of substitution is continually cropping up on the agenda. From a social policy viewpoint, it is a matter of ensuring that tasks not be performed by individuals overqualified for such work. In terms of home care, this simply means determining the extent to which and conditions in which families can replace government programs. There are, however, several versions of this substitution concept, from the "hardest"—limitation or actual withdrawal of public assistance—to "softer" approaches—negotiated, complementary strategies—including various forms of professional or material help or financial compensation. Regarding this notion of substitution, the national contributions presented here and the vast majority of the literature unanimously emphasize that family care cannot substitute for government support because the two are different in nature; nor can family support be seen as a lower level of care, as suggested by how it is integrated into the service continuum by certain government services. Once again, research results underscore the inalienable specificity of family support.

22. The two systems, formal and informal, thus work best when they are interdependent and complementary, and respect the particularities of each. The formal system must therefore fully recognize the contribution of the informal system, support the latter and fill the gaps in this system.

This being said, the definition of the family as performing a subsidiary, complementary or central role varies from country to country. In our view, this is one of the most striking aspects to emerge from the comparison of the seven analyses presented here.

Although in each of the countries studied we find virtually the same trends in terms of demographic change, the shift of institutional treatment to less concentrated, locally run structures, de-professionalization of care, i.e. recognition of "lay" care, etc., the emphasis varies considerably from one country to the next regarding the specific aspect of family support and indeed the family itself.

Thus, at one national extreme, we find the American situation, with a manifest focus on evaluation, an attempt to optimize services provided to "users," centred on assessing the latter's degree of satisfaction. Although the family's contribution is very significant, family support is merely viewed as one aspect of the system which must be preserved, by preventing the caregiving burden from becoming too great (compensation measures for stresses created by such care practices, various benefits, respite, etc.) so as to avoid the social costs of discontinuing such support. From this viewpoint, cultural and ethnic variables are also recognized, which in part influence how coordination between formal and informal services is structured. Formal care tends to operate as a "non-system," whether in terms of home-based medical care or loosely coordinated and poorly qualified professional home care services.

At the opposite end of the spectrum we find the Swedish situation, which is in fact unique. In Sweden, care for the dependent elderly is almost totally ensured by government policies, with an impressive range of associated services. Here the formal system clearly outweighs the informal system in importance, in a national context where 80% of women work outside the home, professional home help is available on a massive level, intergenerational cohabitation has virtually ceased, a high percentage of broken families exists, and the preservation of women's right to work is indisputable. There is therefore far less interest in research on the family (especially families where there is a "traditional" division of sex roles) and its contribution to caring; research on informal care is, moreover, only beginning. In this situation, concerns are merely starting to be expressed about the fact that services are no longer increasing and that, with demographic pressures, families (or women, in a certain number of families) may be asked to play a larger role.

Without going into detail, we can say that the other national situations lie between these two extremes. In Britain, we find the formal "non-system," a market context, massive inequalities in terms of access to care, and the clearly predominant role of families and women in actual care, as seen in the United States. There are also, however, new concerns linked to changing family structures (an increase in one-parent or step families) and indeed changing family values (a decrease in feelings of mutual obligation between the generations). And here we are dealing with another aspect of family reality, i.e. the fact that the central element of family support is not a stable given, but is instead affected by complex regulatory dynamics at the heart of the family system itself.

23. The aspect of the economic cost-effectiveness of home care services in relation to institutional services is under debate. On the one hand, many studies emphasize that although home care is more advantageous where the amount of care is limited either due to less severe dependency or extensive family support, this advantage tends to disappear where an intensive level of services is required. Moreover, some studies note that if home care, including situations of intermediate dependency, were to be truly supported by an optimal level of resources, its costs would probably match those of institutional care (see, for example, Weissert 1985, 1989). Once again, the importance of the family's contribution becomes apparent, as does, on a related level, the inadequacy of the support provided by formal resources when home care is solely favoured as a means of curbing care expenses.

## THE IMPORTANCE OF ENHANCING OUR KNOWLEDGE OF FAMILY FUNCTIONING AND DOMESTIC PRODUCTION

In concluding this reflection, we cannot underscore too strongly the profound lack of understanding of the specific processes involved in family functioning and domestic production (Corbin and Strauss 1988), and hence the need for more investigation into these areas so as to clarify their interrelationship with public support. Approaches to the relationships between family and public support too often consist in assessing the first solely in light of the second, thus emphasizing a functional and evaluative perspective, without acknowledging the potential specificities in the exchanges operating within modern families. In her contribution here, Martine Bungener expresses this peculiarity in showing that public policy-makers do not understand the economic contribution of families: "For when the poorly-acknowledged work done by families fails, the patient is often sent to a hospital or institutional care facility. Family activity thus, by default, assumes a great deal of economic and financial visibility which, moreover, helps to mask its real nature by leading decision-makers and public opinion to solely emphasize its shortcomings...." Or, in the words of Attias-Donfut (1991), for whom the use of services and particularly sheltered accommodation represent "forms of compromise" between the needs of the individual and the inevitably limited capacities of family support, "these different forms of compromise appear to create the context for the intervention of social policies that are now seen as having to integrate the reality of family support in interrelation with institutional support" (id.: 17).

In failing to grasp that this private sphere cannot be reduced to the rules of exchange seen in the public services (Godbout 1990), we risk totally misapprehending the costs involved in what is often viewed as a way to save money.

It would appear that there is a long way to go before overcoming the still dominant tendency to limit an examination of family support to a social policy viewpoint stressing a functional and even utilitarian approach to issues, and in order to clarify the complex mechanisms of an exchange which inevitably combines public, private (market-driven) and private (in the sense of intimacy) resources. The need for further research to integrate such complex and interacting perspectives is clearly evident.

## References

Astier, Isabelle, and Jean-François Laé (1991). "La notion de communauté dans les enquêtes sociales sur l'habitat en France : Le groupe d'Économie et Humanisme, 1940-1955." *Genèses*, No. 5 (September): 81-106.

Attias-Donfut, Claudine (1991). "Dépendance des personnes âgées : pourvoyance familiale et pourvoyance sociale." Ronéo. Unpublished.

Bachelard, Gaston (1967). *Poétique de l'espace*. Paris: PUF.

Barrère-Maurisson, Marie-Agnès, and Olivier Marchand (1990). "Structures familiales et marché du travail dans les pays développés." *Économie et Statistique*, No. 235: 19-30.

Castel, Robert (1991). "De l'indigence à l'exclusion, la désaffiliation. Précarité du travail et vulnérabilité relationnelle." In J. Donzelot, ed., *Face à l'exclusion. Le modèle français*, 137-168. Paris: Édition Esprit.

Clavel, Maïté (1982). "Éléments pour une nouvelle réflexion sur l'habiter." *Cahiers internationaux de sociologie*, Vol. LXXII: 17-82.

Corbin, Juliet M., and Anselm Strauss (1988). *Unending Work and Care. Managing Chronic Illness at Home*. San Francisco: Jossey-Bass.

Dandurand, R.B., and F.R. Ouellette (1992). *Entre autonomie et solidarité, parenté et soutien dans la vie de jeunes familles montréalaises.* Quebec City: IQRC. Research report. Mimeo.

Davies, B.P. (1987). "Equity and efficiency in community care." *Ageing and Society* 7: 161-174.

Davies, B.P. (1988). "Financing long term social care: challenges for the nineties." *Social Policy Administration* 22 (2): 97-114.

Evers, A., and H. Wintersberger, eds. (1988). *Shifts in the Welfare Mix.* European Centre for Social Welfare Policy and Research. Vienna.

Godbout, Jacques (1990). "L'État, un ami de la famille ?" In D. Lemieux, ed., *Familles d'aujourd'hui,* 173-185. Montreal: Institut Québécois de la Recherche sur la Culture.

Gubrium, Jabert F. (1991). *The Mosaic of Care, Frail Elderly and Their Families in the Real World.* New York: Springer.

INSEE (1991) Institut National de la Statistique et des Études Économiques. *Actes du colloque* "Beyond national statistics: household and family patterns in comparative perspective." Centre for Economic Policy Research. London, INSEE collection "Méthodes," No. 8.

Jamieson, Anne (1988). "Politiques pour les personnes âgées en Europe." *Gérontologie et société* 47.

Lalive d'Épinay, Christian et al. (1984). *Vieillesses.* Saint-Saphorin, Éd. Georgi.

Lesemann, Frédéric (1992). "Community Development." In György Széll (Ed.), *Concise Encyclopedia of Participation and Co-Management.* Berlin, New York: De Gruyter.

Médard, Jean-François (1969). *L'organisation communautaire aux États-Unis.* Paris: A. Colin.

Pitrou, Agnès (1978). *Vivre sans famille ? Les solidarités familiales dans le monde d'aujourd'hui.* Toulouse: Privat.

Prioux, France, ed. (1990). *La famille dans les pays développés : Permanences et changements.* INED, UIESP, CNAF, CNRS. Collection "Congrès et colloques."

Simeone, Italo (1990). "Les affects de la famille : entre l'amour et la haine." *Gérontologie et société* 48: 96-98.

Tinker, A. (1984). *Staying at home.* London: HMSO.

Walker, Alan (1985). "From Welfare State to Caring Society? The Promise of Informal Support Networks." In J.A. Yoder, ed., *Support Networks in a Caring Community,* 41-58. Dordrecht: Martinus Nijhoff Publishers.

Weissert, W.G. (1985). "Seven reasons why it is so difficult to make Community-based long-term care cost effective." *Health Services Research* 20 (4): 423-433.

Weissert, W.G., C.C. Matthews, and J.E. Pawelack (1989). "Home and community care: three decades of findings." In M.D. Peterson and D.L. White, eds., *Health Care of The Elderly: An Information Sourcebook,* 39-126. Newbury Park: Sage.

Wenger, C. (1984). *The Supportive Networks.* London: Allen & Unwin.

# ABOUT THE CONTRIBUTORS

**John BALDOCK** is Senior Lecturer in Social Policy at the University of Kent at Canterbury. He has conducted research and published mainly in the area of care for frail old people. He is currently engaged in a major empirical study of the care and assistance received by people who have suffered a stroke.

**Martine BUNGENER** is a Health Economist and Researcher at the Institute for Research on Health and Medicine (INSERM) in Paris. She has published extensively on families caring for dependent frail elderly persons and is now working on AIDS and informal support.

**Carole COX** is Associate Professor of Social Work at the National Catholic School of Social Service, Catholic University of America, Washington, D.C. In addition to her work on home care, her research and publications have focused on health care issues regarding the elderly, older persons' use of community services and the special needs of minority populations.

**Carla FACCHINI** is Professor of Sociology at the University of Milan. She has conducted research on the life conditions of elderly women, changes in welfare policy and families caring for elderly people in Northern Italy.

**Lennarth JOHANSSON**, Psychologist, Dr. Med. Sci., is Senior Research Officer at the Swedish Planning and Rationalization Institute for Health and Social Services in Stockholm. He is affiliated with the Department of Social Medicine at the University of Uppsala; his research mainly involves care for the elderly.

**Frédéric LESEMANN** is Professor of Social Policy at the University of Montreal. His research relates to the evolution of welfare policy, poverty, the family and care for the elderly. He has published numerous books and articles on these topics and is the editor of the International Review of Community Development.

**Claude MARTIN** is Professor of Sociology of Health and Social Policy at the National School for Public Health in Rennes. His research mainly concerns family policy, relationships and support among family members.

**Abraham MONK** is Professor of Social Work and Gerontology at the Columbia University School of Social Work in New York City. He is the author of several books and numerous publications. He has conducted research on intergenerational relations, housing and sheltered environments, long-term care, retirement adjustment and elderly policy formulation.

**Daphne NAHMIASH** teaches Social Gerontology at McGill University, Montreal. She has conducted several research studies on home care for the frail elderly, privatization of services and abuse of the dependent elderly.

**Marja PIJL** is Coordinator, International Relations, at the Netherlands' Institute for Social Work Research, The Hague. Her recent publications deal with elderly women, shifts in the welfare mix, payment for care, caregiving in the Netherlands and policy for the elderly.

**Renzo SCORTEGAGNA** is Professor of Sociology of Organization at the University of Padua. His field of research relates to the organization of public and private services with particular attention to health and the welfare state.

**Mats THORSLUND** is Associate Professor at the Department of Social Medicine, University of Uppsala and Senior Researcher with the Swedish Medical Research Council's Health Services Research Division. He is the author of numerous articles, including topics on policy for the elderly.

# Subject index

Printed by
Ateliers Graphiques Marc Veilleux Inc.
Cap-Saint-Ignace (Quebec)
in July 1993